Understanding Investments

An Australian Investor's Guide to Stock Market, Property and Cash-Based Investments

5TH EDITION

CHARLES BEELAERTS
WITH KEVIN FORDE

Wrightbooks

First published 2010 by Wrightbooks
an imprint of John Wiley & Sons Australia, Ltd
42 McDougall Street, Milton Qld 4064

Office also in Melbourne

Typeset in 11.5/13.8 pt Garamond

© Charles Beelaerts and Kevin Forde 2010
The moral rights of the authors have been asserted

National Library of Australia Cataloguing-in-Publication data:

Author:	Beelaerts, Charles.
Title:	Understanding investments: an Australian investor's guide to stock market, property and cash-based investments / Charles Beelaerts; Kevin Forde.
Edition:	5th ed.
ISBN:	9781742469508 (pbk.)
Notes:	Includes index.
Subjects:	Stocks — Australia.
	Investments — Australia.
Other Authors/Contributors:	Forde, Kevin, 1949–
Dewey Number:	332.678

Tax rate table (used in chapters 2 and 7): From ATO web page 'Individual income tax rates' 2009, copyright Commonwealth of Australia, reproduced by permission.

Cover images: © iStockphoto/pamspix; © iStockphoto/DSGpro; © wrangler, 2010, used under license from Shutterstock.com; © max blain, 2010, used under license from Shutterstock.com; © Beluza Ludmila, 2010, used under license from Shutterstock.com.

Extracts from *The Weekend Australian* (chapter 8): AAP content is owned by or licensed to Australian Associated Press Pty Limited and is copyright protected. AAP content is published on an 'as is' basis for personal use only and must not be copied, republished, rewritten, resold or redistributed, whether by caching, framing or similar means, without AAP's prior written permission. AAP and its licensors are not liable for any loss, through negligence or otherwise, resulting from errors or omissions in or reliance on AAP content. The globe symbol and 'AAP' are registered trademarks.

Extracts from the Parliamentary Joint Committee on Corporations and Financial Services — Terms of Reference and Conclusion (chapter 5): from Inquiry into financial products and services in Australia, Parliamentary Joint Committee on Corporations and Financial Services, November 2009, copyright Commonwealth of Australia, reproduced by permission.

Printed in Australia by McPherson's Printing Group

10 9 8 7 6 5 4 3 2 1

Disclaimer

The material in this publication is of the nature of general comment only, and does not represent professional advice. It is not intended to provide specific guidance for particular circumstances and it should not be relied on as the basis for any decision to take action or not take action on any matter which it covers. Readers should obtain professional advice where appropriate, before making any such decision. To the maximum extent permitted by law, the authors and publisher disclaim all responsibility and liability to any person, arising directly or indirectly from any person taking or not taking action based upon the information in this publication.

Contents

Dedication

We would like to dedicate this book to our mothers for the encouragement and support they gave us.

About the authors

Charles Beelaerts is an economics graduate of the University of Sydney and a graduate of Harvard Business School. He is a financial consultant and author who has previously worked as an analyst for banks and finance companies.

Kevin Forde holds a Master of Economics degree from the University of NSW, where he has lectured for 10 years. He has worked as an industrial analyst and as a funds manager.

What you need to know

Part I outlines the knowledge you need to have to make sound investment decisions. It begins by looking at investing today, including a discussion of the global financial crisis. Chapter 2 then introduces fundamental investment terms such as simple and compound interest and how, by saving a small amount regularly, you can accumulate a large sum over a long period. More complex investment terms such as negative gearing, derivatives, diversification and dividend imputation are also explained. The factors you need to consider when structuring an investment portfolio are examined, as are the records you need to maintain to track your investments for tax purposes and to measure the return from your investment portfolio.

The important issue of obtaining sound financial advice is considered with a review of the questions you need answered to ensure you get appropriate guidance. The potential disadvantages of paying financial advisers via commission are considered and the findings of a government inquiry on this issue are summarised. Most investors will want to know how to make best use of the internet in trading and researching investments. This is outlined in chapter 6. The final chapter in part I summarises the main sections of the Australian tax system that apply to investors and provides you with an understanding of what you need to know to legally minimise your income tax liability.

Investing today

Why learn about investing?

In the 1960s and 1970s only about 10 per cent of Australians owned shares directly. In the 1980s and 1990s this changed dramatically following major privatisations, including Qantas, Telstra, the Commonwealth Bank and AMP. Currently around 50 per cent of Australians own shares directly or through managed funds. This puts Australia in equal first place with the US in share ownership per head of population. Unfortunately, most of the privatisations took place in a bull market. As a result, many investors did not really understand the risks they were taking by investing in shares. When world sharemarkets turned down in 2000, these new sharemarket investors were taken by surprise by the severity and suddenness of the decline. Since then worse has happened with the global financial crisis (GFC), when share prices declined by much more. These events highlight that there are numerous traps for the unwary in financial markets.

As there are now more investment products from which to choose, investing wisely has become more important than ever. The government has made it clear that everyone should be more financially responsible for their retirement. So if you do not save and invest successfully during your working life you may suffer a major decline in your standard of living when you retire.

Remember that the average life expectancy in Australia is around 80 years. So if you retire when you are 60 the savings you accumulated during the approximately 40 years of your working life will have to last you around 20 years.

Interest rates and the Australian dollar are now determined more by market forces than government decree. Again this can provide profitable opportunities for anyone who understands the implications of this. Or it can simply be another trap for the unwary investor.

It is essential to educate yourself about investing, as there are many people who make a living by selling investment products. There are over 16000 licensed investment advisers in Australia and not all of them are competent. If you decide to seek guidance from an investment adviser, it is still a good idea for you to have some basic understanding of how financial markets work so you do not put your hard-earned money into the hands of a less-than-professional financial adviser.

Most daily papers contain numerous advertisements extolling the virtues of one investment product or another. How can you tell whether a particular investment product is right for you? The only sure way is to become familiar with the language used in the financial industry.

The long-term benefits of becoming more financially wise are enormous—as are the costs of allowing yourself to remain financially illiterate. These days we are all bombarded by people trying to sell financial products such as life insurance, managed funds, superannuation, home loans, margin lending schemes, exchange-traded funds, contracts for difference, hedge funds, warrants and personal loans. Unless you know how these products work you could end up paying too much, losing your money or buying something you don't really need.

The chance of losing money through unwise investments seems to have increased. In recent years in Australia there have been several spectacular corporate crashes, such as Timbercorp, Opes Prime and Storm Financial. These resulted in investors losing thousands and sometimes tens of thousands of dollars. In addition, the Australian Securities & Investments Commission estimates that more than 100000 Australians have lost money in fraudulent or illegal investment schemes in the last 15 years, and many of these were intelligent people. In the US, Bernie Madoff 'lost' US$50 billion of investors' money.

Does this mean you should play it safe by keeping your money in the bank or under your bed? Generally the answer is no—but there certainly is a need to understand the types of risks you are taking when you invest.

With this changed investment environment has come a need for investors to know more than they have ever known before.

Financial information

These days everyone is an investor. Investing is not difficult, but to be a competent investor you need to understand what you are doing. There are many traps for the unwary. Knowing how to use financial information is crucial for making sound investment decisions. Establishing what information you need and where to obtain it is another essential part of this book. Clearly, not all areas regarding the provision and use of financial information can be covered at the same time. The foundations for effectively using financial information are twofold. Part I of the book deals with what you need to know. Part II looks at investment options.

Financial information is published constantly in numerous forms that are often not comprehensible to the layperson. Many investors, financial advisers and stockbroker analysts are expert in using financial information and already know where to obtain it. This book is written for non-experts who are interested in deriving a working knowledge of financial information and its sources.

Ground rules for successful investing

Before examining different financial investments in detail there are some ground rules for successful investing that have stood the test of time. With time, patience and effort you can be a successful investor in all of the arenas that are open to you. This will not come overnight and you will have to confront the risk of losing some of your money. But, if you persevere, you will be a successful investor. The road is not always easy, but nothing worthwhile is.

My ground rules for successful investing have not changed from previous editions of this book, and they are:

1 *Be your own investment manager.* No 'adviser' or stockbroker should do it for you. Only you know what your real needs and temperament are and only you are motivated by your own best interests — not by the chance of earning a sales commission. It is also more fun to do it yourself.

2 *Confront risk and then reduce it through spreading your investments.* This is referred to as 'diversification', 'asset allocation' or 'portfolio balance'.

3 *Take a 'contrarian' stance in investment markets.* That is, look for opportunities to watch what the 'herd' is doing and then do the opposite.

4 *Do not be put off by investment jargon.* After reading this book you will be on top of it.

5 *It's always a good time to start.* Do not wait for markets, such as the sharemarket or the property market, to get better. If the sharemarket is filled with gloom, it may be the time to buy bargains.

6 *Make good-quality shares the core of your investment strategy.* Then you can rest easy when you invest in more speculative areas.

7 *Always consider the tax implications of making investments, but never let tax minimisation be your main objective.* The fundamental rule is to think in terms of after-tax returns.

8 *Keep up to date through reading the financial pages of a major daily newspaper.* Later you can extend this to include more specialised publications such as *AFR Smart Investor, BRW* magazine and others.

9 *Discussing investment is stimulating.* Condition your mind to talking to others about it, especially those more knowledgeable than you are.

10 *Do not be greedy.* Discipline yourself to cut your losses with a bad investment and to cash-in when you have made a reasonable profit.

11 *Be patient.* You probably will not become a millionaire overnight through investing, but you can expect to make money over time.

12 *Never invest in anything you do not understand.* If a particular investment sounds too good to be true it probably is.

13 *Pay yourself first.* Many people put off learning about investing because they claim they do not have any money to invest. The solution is to set aside a portion of your income each month —say 5 or 10 per cent—to build up your initial investing capital. By doing this you will force yourself to become an investor and the longer term benefits will be enormous.

If you can master these 13 ground rules you will be a successful investor. You will rival so-called professionals and you will sleep easily at night knowing that money is the least of your worries.

The aim of this book is to inform you so that you can make better investment decisions. Alternatively, if you wish to entrust your money to a professional investment adviser, you will be better able to assess how well he or she is doing with your money. This book focuses on the relevance, use and acquisition of information relating to investment. It explicitly recognises that many investors are new and unfamiliar with the sources of financial information that are available, and their use.

This book gives you an introduction to the main types of investments available to individual investors in Australia. Before focusing on specific investment choices there is some discussion of basic investment terms as well as the very important matter of risk and return. This will show that risk and return go hand in hand and that the best way to hedge against risk is to spread your investments across different areas. The tax implications of various investments are discussed, as is the importance of keeping track of your investments.

Reading this book will empower you with financial knowledge. Hopefully you will never be 'sold' a financial product ever again.

The global financial crisis

The global financial crisis threatened to undermine the very foundations of the world financial system and provided a much needed reality check for individual investors. There are many lessons to be learned from this experience—primarily that investing involves both risk and return. Leading up to the GFC, most investors became too focused on returns, ignoring the risks they were taking to achieve these returns.

The 1980s saw the deregulation of both local and overseas financial markets, bringing an array of new financial products. With the arrival of the GFC, the situation has changed and there are calls for more government regulation of financial markets. Thirty years ago investing was relatively easy, mainly because there were only a few places you could put your money. Today investing is more complex than it has ever been. Not only have many new investment products been launched, but there have also been changes to income tax rates, numerous alterations to the superannuation system, the introduction of capital gains tax, and on top of this it has to be accepted that there will be more government regulation of financial markets.

Causes of the GFC

The causes of the GFC had been building up for years, but the trigger was the collapse of the sub-prime market in the US. Banks in the US had embarked on a course of action whereby they made increasing numbers of risky loans available to home buyers, many of whom had little prospect of repaying them. These loans were then packaged into securities (a process called 'securitisation') which could be bought and sold like any other securities. Financial institutions in the US—for example, investment banks —pushed turnover of these packaged securities to enormous levels, which boosted the demand for more securitisation. Short-term profit was being placed ahead of risk management. Then home loan borrowers began to default as the US economy became overheated. The trend worsened and the sub-prime market eventually collapsed completely. Holders of the packaged securities were left with worthless paper, and financial institutions faced bankruptcy across the board, as did home loan borrowers.

The US Government bailed out many of the banks and financial institutions, but this merely enabled those institutions to stay afloat and lose more money. One investment bank that the US Government did not save was Lehman Brothers, one of Wall Street's most prominent. Meanwhile the tidal wave of financial disaster had spread to world sharemarkets, which declined by 30 to 40 per cent in 2008 and early 2009, wiping off over US$14 trillion in the value of companies. Governments around the world introduced measures to stimulate economic activity involving a combination of increased government spending and tax cuts. In addition, central banks around the world reduced interest rates to historically low levels.

The main losers from the GFC

Individual investors were losers from the GFC because world sharemarkets dropped quickly and significantly and a great deal of wealth was wiped out. The average Australian superannuation or pension fund lost 30 to 40 per cent over 18 months from 2008 to early 2009. As a result many retirees saw their living standard eroded, and some were even forced to apply for the aged pension. People who did not understand risk and return before the GFC are certainly more familiar with these terms today. Many investors took out loans to invest and saw the value of their investments collapse, but the value of their loans remained. In many cases they lost their jobs as well so they had no means of servicing their debt. Between March and December 2009 the sharemarket rose by around 50 per cent in Australia, but many investors no longer had money to invest or feared the repercussions of re-entering the sharemarket. They are the main losers from the GFC. The other losers were investors who panicked and sold their shares at relatively low prices, and therefore missed the significant rebound in share prices.

At least in the short term, people are wary of high-risk products or any products that they do not really understand. This includes hedge funds and sub-prime mortgages. In such circumstances, investors resort to traditional products, which are basically property, shares, fixed interest and cash. Unfortunately, history shows that investors have short memories. After the sharemarket crash in 1987 and the 'dotcom' bust in early 2000, investors also shunned high-risk investment products. But in the subsequent sharemarket booms the lessons of the previous crashes were soon erased from their memories.

The main winners from the GFC

Not everyone was a loser from the GFC. Winners include companies that engage in the infrastructure projects financed by the bailout packages of major countries. The G8 group of countries—which is made up of Canada, France, Germany, Italy, Japan, Russia, the UK and US—individually introduced bailout packages running into the billions of dollars.

The history of sharemarket collapses shows that share prices eventually begin to rise, and the most significant gains are usually in the first 12 months of the recovery phase. However, some companies will rebound faster than others. For example, any companies in industries that were going to benefit from the stimulus packages are likely to recover more quickly. In Australia, the four major banks were also significant beneficiaries of government bailout policies as well as receiving a government guarantee on their deposits of up to $1 million per depositor. Unless you think that the world economy is going to collapse and never recover, you need to continue to look for profitable investment opportunities.

Lessons learned from the GFC

The saying, 'History repeats itself and those who forget it are condemned to repeat it' applies to investors as much as anyone else. In the last 25 years, the GFC was not the first time that the sharemarket had crashed. In October 1987 the Australian sharemarket fell about 25 per cent in a matter of hours, and it crashed again in the dotcom bust in 2000. Circumstances were repeated during the GFC.

There are several notable lessons to be learned.

The GFC highlighted the dangers of negatively gearing share portfolios. (Negative gearing is a concept explained in chapters 7 and 20.) In the period leading up to the GFC, many investors borrowed money against the value of their share portfolios to such an extent that the interest payments on the loans exceeded the dividend income from their portfolios. While the losses they were making as a result could be offset against other income and were therefore tax deductions, they found that the value of their portfolios dropped 30 to 40 per cent. This is the opposite of what you would hope would happen with the value of a negatively geared share portfolio. Consequently, many investors were faced with both losses from having to pay interest and a capital loss.

Many investors mortgaged their homes to either buy shares or invest in superannuation. In the latter case, the Australian Government was encouraging the public to invest in superannuation through the tax system. However, when sharemarkets fell dramatically, those who had done what the government had been encouraging found that the value of their superannuation had dropped alarmingly, and they were left with hefty mortgages as well. In the case of investors who mortgaged their homes to buy shares, many lost their homes. The lesson to be learned is: never invest more than you can afford to lose.

At the peak of a bull (rising) market investors tend to ignore risk and chase high returns instead. The lead up to the crash that accompanied the GFC was no different, with investors taking unprecedented risks with their money. This meant that investors bought financial products they did not understand, such as hedge funds (see chapter 14), in the hope of making quick profits. The lesson to be learned is: if a return seems too good to be true, it probably is.

The ultimate responsibility for your investments lies with you. With one or two isolated exceptions, no one saw the GFC coming. So-called 'experts' were caught up in the mania as much as lay investors. The lesson to be learned is: do not rely on your investment adviser to monitor your investments.

As people retire or approach retirement, they should rebalance their superannuation and other investments so as to have more interest-bearing and less risky investments in their portfolios. In the lead up to the GFC such people were active participants in the sharemarket and paid a huge price for shunning less risky investments which promised lower returns. Some investors, who relied heavily on dividend income for their retirement income, were badly affected by the GFC when companies cut dividends or did not pay them at all. The lesson to be learned is: if you are in or near retirement, have a spread of fixed-interest, rental property and dividend-paying investments, so if one source dries up you still have others.

The GFC demonstrated the dangers of buying at the top of the sharemarket and selling out at the bottom. Many investors were affected because they thought that worse was to come. The lesson to be learned is: do not panic—for longer term investors the rebound in the sharemarket was almost as quick as the fall.

The GFC also demonstrated the dangers of being fully invested in the sharemarket. If you do that you risk not having sufficient funds for when other profitable opportunities arise. Always have some money available to take advantage of cheap shares such as Australia's major banks in late 2008 and early 2009.

Another lesson to be learned from the GFC is that you should separate your share buying and selling decisions (see Charles Beelaerts and Kevin Forde, *You Only Make a Profit When You Sell*, Wrightbooks 2001, chapter 16). If you were fortunate or astute enough to sell shares in 2007, it would have been wise not to have used this money to buy other shares. As a general rule, if you sell shares because they are overpriced, it is highly likely that at the same time the share prices of most other companies are also relatively expensive.

The GFC highlighted the importance of diversifying outside of the sharemarket. As you will see in later chapters, most investment risks can be mitigated through having a diversified portfolio of investments. Although market risk, which is the risk that the whole sharemarket declines, cannot be reduced through diversification, other risks can be. It is a case of not 'having all your eggs in one basket'.

Share prices sometimes go up 1 or 2 per cent in a day and down by the same amount the next. Something that differentiated the GFC from many previous sharemarket crashes is that it brought with it extremely volatile share price movements. The lesson to be learned is: do not try to pick the sharemarket, but rather, take a long-term view and invest in shares you think are undervalued and sell expensive ones.

As stated above, these phenomena are generally not new. Think about what you will do the next time there is a bull market followed by a bear market (falling prices) or indeed another crash, because it will happen again. Hopefully you will be well prepared to negotiate the difficult investment landscape.

Key points

o   The global financial crisis is over but its impact will continue to be felt for many years.

o   Through good fortune and good management, Australia fared well during the global financial crisis and the prospect of strong economic growth is good.

- o Note the lessons to be learned from the crisis and consider how well placed you are for next time.

- o Investing is more complex than it has ever been, and you need to be aware of the vast number of investment opportunities as well as the pitfalls and traps.

- o The sooner you get your finances into order the better. Remember it's never too early to start.

- o Financial deregulation since 1980 has meant a huge increase in the number of financial products in the marketplace. To keep pace with this increase, investors need to know more than they have ever known before.

- o Because of the global financial crisis it is likely that there will be greater government regulation of financial markets in the future.

- o Read the 13 ground rules in this chapter. How do you see yourself in terms of each of them?

- o Resolve to begin your savings and investing plans today by setting aside some income each month.

- o It's *your* responsibility to take control of your finances—do not rely on others to do it for you.

Investment terms

2

Many novice investors are discouraged from attempting to devise their own financial plan because they are overwhelmed by the number of financial products on the market and they are bamboozled by the jargon used in the finance industry. As a result they often hand over responsibility for their investment strategy to a financial adviser. Unfortunately this frequently means that investors are 'sold' financial products which make a lot of money in commissions for the adviser but cause financial misery for the investor. This has been highlighted by events stemming from the fallout from the GFC, where many investors were sent bankrupt even though they followed the advice of licensed financial advisers.

For individual investors the lessons from the GFC are clear: you need to educate yourself about the workings of financial markets, and it is essential that you take responsibility for devising your own investment plans rather than delegating this to a financial adviser. This does not mean that you should never seek advice from a financial adviser. Certainly with superannuation, where the rules are complex and government policy is constantly changing, it is wise to get opinions from experts in this field. But unless you have some basic understanding of fundamental investment terms and concepts you will not be able to evaluate whether the advice you are given is competent and right for your situation. For example, similar-sounding investment products can involve substantially different risks and returns. If you do not understand the potential risks you are taking you could end up losing a lot of your hard-earned money.

So in this chapter you will be introduced to some important financial terms which will enable you to assess whether a particular investment product should be included in your financial plans. This will also help you understand and evaluate any advice you are given by finance professionals.

What is a financial institution?

Twenty years ago there were major differences between banks, building societies, credit unions and insurance companies, and professional fund managers virtually did not exist. These days banks sell insurance and offer general financial advice, building societies and credit unions offer cheque accounts and issue credit cards, and many insurance companies have extended their activities by becoming professional fund managers. Therefore, it seems to make sense to lump them all together and call them 'financial institutions'.

Very simply, financial institutions are go-betweens. They act as a pipeline between people who have money to save and invest and those who need to borrow money. The primary function of a financial institution is to lend out money invested by depositors. By doing this it makes a profit as it lends money out at a higher rate than it pays its depositors. For example, a bank might pay its depositors an interest rate of 4 per cent and lend this money out at 8 per cent. But what happens if some people who take out these loans cannot repay them? Well, the bank will make less profit than it thought. If a lot of loans go bad at the same time, as happened during the GFC, it may not have enough money to repay its depositors. This is precisely what happened to many banks throughout the world during the GFC, and was the prime reason why governments implemented substantial 'bail outs' in order to stop some banks from collapsing. Australian banks were generally in much better financial shape than banks in other parts of the world. Nevertheless, the federal government saw the need to guarantee bank deposits in order to restore investor faith in the local banking system.

So here is lesson number one for beginner investors: be sceptical. Never assume that a financial institution will automatically repay the money you have invested. If the financial institution lends money to people who don't pay it back, you could be the one to suffer.

Although financial institutions have become more and more like each other over the past few years, there are still many real differences in their financial strengths, their size and the types of services they offer. So before you make any investment decisions it is important to become aware of some basic investment terms.

Basic investment terms

Unless you understand some fundamental investment terms you will have little chance of developing a sound investment plan.

Principal and interest

Principal refers to the size of your investment or loan. Thus, if you invest $500 in a savings account this is referred to as a principal amount. Further deposits also are called principal. If you borrow $20 000 this would be referred to as principal.

Interest is simply the price of money. If you decide to lend money to a financial institution, the interest you receive is your reward for not spending. Or another way of looking at it is that it is the price the financial institution has to pay to encourage you to save.

If you borrow money, the interest you pay reflects the cost of using someone else's money. You could think of this as being similar to hiring a car or a DVD. In these cases you have the use of the car or DVD for a limited period of time and pay the car owner or DVD owner for letting you use it. With a loan you are borrowing money for a limited period of time and therefore have to pay interest to the owner of that money.

The miracle of compound interest

The earlier you start investing sensibly, the more benefit you get from compound interest.

For example, if you invested $1000 each year, or $20 a week, for 40 years and received an average return of 15 per cent per annum, this would accumulate to around $1.8 million. Getting rich slowly might not have as much appeal as getting rich quickly, but it is within the reach of ordinary investors — not just high-flying risk-takers.

Table 2.1 (overleaf) shows how just one dollar a year grows at various interest rates compounded over 5 to 35 years. Note how the rate at which your money grows accelerates as time goes by — see how the really big gains come towards the end.

Imagine what the total would be if you were investing not just one dollar a year but many hundreds or thousands. And if the interest is compounded more frequently than once a year, your savings will grow even faster.

Table 2.1: investing one dollar a year, interest compounded annually

Rate	Years						
	5	10	15	20	25	30	35
8%	6.34	15.65	29.32	49.42	78.95	122.35	186.10
10%	6.72	17.53	34.95	63.00	108.18	180.94	298.13
14%	7.54	22.04	49.98	103.77	207.33	406.74	790.67
16%	7.98	24.73	59.93	133.84	289.09	615.16	1300.03

Income and capital growth

The return you get from any investment can be divided into either income or capital growth. Income is the regular return you get through interest payments from interest-bearing deposits, dividends from shares or rent from property investments. It can be paid weekly, monthly, quarterly, six-monthly or annually.

Capital growth is the difference between what you paid for an investment and what you eventually sell it for. For example, if you bought a share for $1.00 and sold it for $1.50 you would have received 50¢ in capital growth. However, not all investments increase in value. If you bought a share for $1.00 and sold it for 80¢, you would have suffered a capital loss of 20¢.

Some investments only pay an income return, others only give capital growth and others give a combination of the two. So what you get back from an investment can take two forms: income, such as interest, rent or dividends; and capital growth, where you can sell your investment for a higher price than you bought it for.

You should not get the impression that all investments are successful. Anyone who buys shares knows only too well that share prices go down as well as up.

The total return you get on an investment is the sum of the income you receive and any capital gain or loss. All investments fall into three categories:

- Those offering income with no capital growth, such as bank deposits.

- Those offering no income but with the prospect of capital growth, such as shares which are not paying any dividends.

- Those offering a combination of income and the prospect of capital growth, such as property investments and shares paying dividends.

Table 2.2 classifies some common investments according to whether they give income, capital growth or a combination of the two.

Table 2.2: returns from different investments

Income only	Capital gain/loss only	Both income and capital gain/loss
• Bank, credit union accounts • Short-term bank deposits • Cash management trusts • Mortgage trusts • Bank bills	• Options • Futures • Shares not paying dividends • Some warrants • Gold, commodities • Collectables: antiques, paintings, stamps	• Dividend-paying shares, convertible notes • Rental property • Government bonds • Property trusts • Sharemarket trusts • Bond trusts, some warrants

Yield on investment

The first thing that most people look at is what yield, or rate of return, a particular investment offers.

In some cases, the investment yield will be worked out for you. For example, if you put money into a bank fixed-term deposit paying an interest rate of 5 per cent per annum, the yield or return on this investment is 5 per cent. Thus, in everyday terms, a yield measures how much you get back as a percentage of how much you have invested.

If you buy shares you can receive dividends, not interest. To work out what yield you are receiving—usually referred to as dividend yield—you use the following formula:

Dividend yield = Dividend per share ÷ Share price × 100

For example, if you bought a share for $1.00 and it paid you an annual dividend of 5¢ per share, your dividend yield would be 5 per cent (5¢ ÷ $1.00 × 100). Your total investment return on shares is a combination of this dividend yield and any profit or loss you make on buying and selling the shares. If you bought these shares for $1.00 and sold them a year later for $1.20 you have made a capital gain of 20 per cent. Your total investment return would then be 25 per cent. If you sold these shares for 50¢, you would have made a capital loss of 50 per cent (50¢ ÷ $1.00 × 100), offset by the dividends you have received. Therefore, your overall return would be minus 45 per cent.

Similarly, if you purchased a house or unit to rent out, the return on this investment would be the rent you received during the year, minus your costs such as council rates and interest payments on any borrowed money, divided by the price of the house or unit.

Thus, if you bought a unit for $300000 and received rent of $30000 per year and had costs of $7000, the yield or return on this investment would be 7 per cent ($30000 – $7000 ÷ $300000 × 100). As in the case of shares, your total yield would depend on whether you eventually sold this unit for more than, or less than, the price you paid for it.

How good is this yield?

After you have established what rate of return you are likely to get from an investment, you then have to ask yourself three things:

- Does it keep pace with inflation? That is, what is the 'real' rate of return?

- Are there any risks that I will lose money?

- What rate of tax will I have to pay?

These three issues are looked at in this chapter.

Real rate of return

The 'real' rate of return is the difference between the return you are getting on your investments and the rate of inflation. What is so special about the 'real' rate of return? Basically, it shows whether the purchasing power of your money is being maintained or increased, or whether you are going backwards.

Inflation measures the overall increase of prices in the economy. It can also indicate what is happening to the purchasing power of your money and hence your standard of living. In 2009 inflation was around 3 per cent per annum. Essentially, this means that prices were 3 per cent higher in 2009 than they were in 2008. Therefore, if you received an investment return of less than 3 per cent in 2009 the purchasing power of your money was being eroded.

A simple example can illustrate why this is so. Suppose that a second-hand car currently costs $6000 and that in 12 months' time its price will rise by 3 per cent—the rate of inflation—to $6180. Suppose that you have saved $6000 and could either buy the car today or invest your money at a rate of 6 per cent per annum. If you decide to invest rather than buy, your $6000 will increase by 6 per cent to $6360 in 12 months' time, which means you would be better off delaying your purchase of the car.

Clearly, it is most important that your investment return is at least as great as the rate of inflation—otherwise you are better off spending rather than saving. For example, if inflation is 3 per cent and you are investing in an old-style bank account paying interest of less than 1 per cent after tax, your real rate of return is negative. If your real investment return is negative it is time to completely rethink where you are investing your money.

Risk and return

Risk and return go hand in hand. Generally speaking, the higher the potential returns from an investment the higher the risk associated with it. Today there are more Australians confronting risk than there ever have been before. Take retirement as an example. People commencing retirement realise they have a choice between shares and less volatile fixed-interest investments. Shares offer potentially superior returns, tax advantages and high growth, but are riskier investments than money in a bank account. Indeed, many retirees found this out the hard way during the GFC. After reaching a historic high of 6854 on 1 November 2007, the Australian All Ordinaries index fell by 55 per cent to its lowest point of 3112 on 6 March 2009, thereby significantly eroding the investment nestegg of many retirees.

Risk is often measured by the volatility of investment returns. For example, if you invest in a bank term deposit for one year at 5 per cent you can be reasonably confident that you will get a 5 per cent return on your money. But if you invest in the sharemarket you cannot be certain what your investment return will be. In some years your investments could grow by 30 per cent; in other years you could incur losses of 25 per cent.

Sometimes investments such as term deposits with banks are classed as 'risk free' because there is basically no risk associated with payments of interest or the repayment of capital. Yet many so-called risk-free investments may not be that way because their returns do not keep pace with inflation.

All investments involve taking some risk. The important question for most investors is how much risk does a particular investment involve and do the potential returns justify those risks?

The riskiness of different investments

Basically, investment risk refers to the chances of losing money on a particular investment. When assessing the risk of an investment there are several factors to consider, including:

- How sure are you that you will receive the interest, dividends or rent which were paid in the previous year?

- Is the income you will receive likely to be stable or fluctuate from month to month, or year to year?

- Is the price of the investment stable, or can it go up and down?

The riskiness of investing in different financial products varies widely. At one end of the spectrum are highly secure investments such as bank deposits and government bonds, while at the other end are high-risk investments such as options and futures. As you would expect, the higher the risk, the higher the potential return, but also the higher the potential loss. Shares, for example, are relatively risky investments compared with bank deposits.

Although bank deposits are very secure they are not entirely free of risk. The Reserve Bank of Australia regulates the financial position of all banks, and if a bank gets into difficulties it will step in to manage its affairs in the interests of depositors. But it does not usually guarantee that depositors would get all their money back if a bank gets into financial difficulties. However, from 28 November 2008, under the Australian Government's Financial Claims Scheme, total deposit balances up to and including $1 million per customer held in eligible authorised deposit-taking institutions (ADIs)—including banks, building societies and credit unions—are guaranteed by the government without charge. This Australian Government deposit guarantee is effective until 12 October 2011, and the government will review the guarantee during this three-year period.

The risks involved with investing in any financial institution depend on where your money is ultimately invested. A finance company that lends money (that is, your money) to people to buy houses and cars is less risky than one which lends money to people to buy shares.

Higher return is closely linked to higher risk. But this does not mean that a higher risk automatically ensures a higher return—it can mean a greater chance of a significant loss. Even in a rising sharemarket you might pick the wrong shares and lose money. The art and science of successful investing involves the use of techniques for minimising risk while maximising return.

Different types of risk

To this point risk has been used to refer to the extent to which there is a chance of loss from an investment. In the world of investing, especially in the sharemarket, however, it has another meaning. It refers to the deviation from your expected return. If you expect a return of 20 per cent and actually get only 15 per cent, the difference between the two reflects risk.

The total risk associated with an investment is made up of systematic risk and unsystematic risk. Systematic risk emanates from common factors that affect all investments. It affects all shares in the same manner; for example, changing economic or political circumstances. The sharemarket crash resulting from the GFC is a good example of systematic risk as nearly all share prices fell. Investing in a range of different shares, called diversification, will not usually protect against this as in dire circumstances most share prices fall at the same time.

Unsystematic risk is due to unique factors affecting a particular company; for example, a specific event that affects an individual company such as a strike, fire or flood. It affects one company only, and diversification will reduce the overall risk of your share portfolio. For example, if you had all your money invested in one company and it went bankrupt you would lose all your money. If instead your money was equally invested in 10 different companies, the profits you made on the other nine companies would partly or fully offset the loss you made on the company which went bankrupt.

The sources of risk underlying systematic and unsystematic risk are:

- interest rate risk

- purchasing power risk

- business or financial risk

- political or social risk

- currency risk.

Interest rate risk is the risk that the value of a fixed-income investment such as a government bond will decrease because of an increase in interest rates.

Another name for purchasing power risk is inflation, which decreases the buying power of your capital or interest income.

Business or financial risk is the chance that an individual firm may fail due to bad management or changes in consumer demand or market share.

Political or social risk is the chance that changes in government policy may adversely affect your investment or, in the case of an overseas investment, the chance of a political upheaval such as a revolution.

Currency risk is the chance that changes in relative values of currencies will affect import- or export-driven companies, or that you may be faced with an unfavourable rate of exchange when you wish to sell a foreign investment.

Table 2.3 gives a snapshot of the risk profile of popular forms of investment. It should be recognised that within many categories there are lower and higher quality alternatives that may justify a slightly better or lesser ranking.

Balancing income and capital gains

Some investments only give you income, but no capital gains. Others, such as speculative mining shares, give no income, but do give the potential for capital gains or losses. Dividend-paying shares give both income and the chance of capital gains. So what type of investment is best for you?

As has been seen, risk and return are two important concepts for investing. An important consideration in your ability to take investment risks is whether you need to receive secure and regular income from the investment.

Most investment decisions involve a trade-off between capital gains on the one hand and maximising income while preserving capital on the other. These two elements act like a seesaw. If you are nearing retirement you will favour income and capital preservation, while if you are younger and have good prospects for high income in the years ahead, you will be aiming for maximum capital gain.

Your preference for the different types of investment will be affected by your attitude to risk. Aiming for maximum capital gain is riskier than aiming to maximise income while preserving capital.

Diversification

Diversification, sometimes referred to as portfolio balance or asset allocation, is a way of hedging against risk. It is fundamental to a sound investment strategy. Basically, the concept tells you to 'not put all your eggs in one basket'. The underlying objective is to spread risk by investing in different areas. For example, you may choose to put some money into a term deposit with a bank which is highly secure, while investing other money in the sharemarket, which is less secure but which offers a potentially higher return.

To diversify a portfolio of shares, you could invest in different sectors such as mining, manufacturing, retailing, banks, media and property.

Table 2.3: risk rating of investments

Negligible	Bank deposits Bank bills Government bonds Semi-government bonds
Very low	Credit union deposits Building society deposits Cash management trusts
Low	Capital-guaranteed insurance bonds Capital-guaranteed friendly society bonds Bank-backed finance company debentures First mortgages over residential property Mortgage trusts Prime real estate (not borrowed)
Medium	Commercial and industrial property Unlisted property trusts Second-ranking residential property Unit-linked insurance bonds Unit-linked friendly society bonds Broadly based equity trusts Bond trusts Non-bank finance company debentures
Medium/high	Blue-chip shares Reset preference shares Specialist property trusts Convertible notes Specialist share trusts Unsecured notes Overseas share trusts Vacant land Second mortgages
High	Warrants Options Contracts for difference Currency futures Commodity futures Films Agricultural investment schemes Commodities Gold Collectables: antiques, paintings, stamps Speculative shares

You could diversify geographically by investing in the Pacific, the UK, the US and Europe. Or you can combine these by putting your money into different sectors in different parts of the world. Also you need to diversify into asset categories which move in different cycles. Be careful not to diversify just for the sake of diversification. For example, it does not make sense to diversify into the sharemarket when prices are generally overvalued.

It is also possible to over-diversify. This occurs when you have too many different securities for the total amount you have invested. As a result each holding of shares becomes insignificant. Say you have $20 000 to invest in shares and you put $500 in the shares of 40 different companies. If one share doubles, the effect on your total portfolio is negligible and is offset by the others which did not do as well. An overly large number of shareholdings also increases dealing costs and makes it difficult to follow their progress.

You can also have under-diversification, which occurs when you hold too few investments. It can happen when you have too much money invested in the shares of just one company or sector or industry.

In some respects, investments of the same kind carry the same degree of risk. For example, bank deposits have similar degrees of risk. On the other hand, not all types of shares carry the same degree of risk. Shares in solid, established companies are relatively safe and it is highly unlikely that you would lose all your money with them. In the jargon of the sharemarket these companies are referred to as 'blue-chip' companies. On the other hand, there are substantial risks involved in investing in speculative mining and oil companies.

While diversifying is undoubtedly sensible, there is often a lot of nonsense talked about the need for, and benefits of, diversification. Just because you do not have shares or property among your investments does not mean you should have money invested in them. If you thought that the sharemarket was about to fall it would make no sense to diversify your investments by buying shares. All you would be doing is increasing your risk and lowering your potential return — the very opposite of what a smart investor wants. In addition, you are not diversifying your share portfolio by having shares in all the major banks — ANZ, Westpac, National Australia and Commonwealth — rather than having all your money invested in one of these. Share prices of banks tend to move in the same direction at the same time because they are all influenced by similar economic factors.

What you need to aim for is a balance between risk and return. This balance will vary from person to person. Some people are born risk-takers while others are much more conservative and want iron-clad money-back guarantees on their investments. Also your ability to take risks will change at different stages of your life. If you are unmarried with a high income you are much more capable of taking risks with your money than a married person with a mortgage and several children to bring up. What this emphasises is that financial planning is an individual affair. There is no such thing as a model investment portfolio that everyone should adopt. Instead, you must work out an investment plan with which you feel comfortable. There is no point borrowing heavily or wheeling and dealing on the sharemarket simply because your friends are doing it. Rather your investment plan should be tailor-made to suit you.

Although you must be aware of the risks involved in different investments, you should not attempt to eliminate risk entirely. Low risk and low returns usually go hand in hand. By playing it too safe you might not keep pace with inflation and your investment plan will be a flop.

Tax

The person who said that there are only two things certain in life—death and taxes—must have been an investor. Table 2.4 sets out income tax scales in Australia as at 1 July 2009. In fact the actual tax you pay is slightly higher than this as you might have to add on an additional 1.5 per cent for the Medicare levy.

Table 2.4: personal income tax scale 2009–10*

Taxable income	Tax on this income
$1–$6000	Nil
$6001–$35000	15¢ for each $1 over $6000
$35001–$80000	$4350 plus 30¢ for each $1 over $35000
$80001–$180000	$17850 plus 38¢ for each $1 over $80000
$180001 and over	$55850 plus 45¢ for each $1 over $180000

* Does not include the Medicare levy of 1.5 per cent, or the Medicare surcharge of 1.0 per cent. The low-income tax offset gives an effective tax-free threshold for those taxpayers eligible for the full LITO of $15000.

What table 2.4 shows is that if you earn less than $6000 per year you do not pay any income tax. But if you are eligible for the low-income tax offset (LITO) your effective tax-free threshold is $15000. For every dollar you earn above $35000, you pay 30¢ in tax. This is called your marginal rate of tax. Clearly this can put a big hole in your investment return.

Suppose you are earning $35 100 and invest $1000 in a bank deposit paying 5 per cent per annum. The bank pays you $50 in interest, but then you must pay 30 per cent (30¢ in every dollar) of this, or $15, in income tax. Therefore, your after-tax return is $35, or 3.5 per cent.

As well as income tax, you might have to pay capital gains tax (CGT) on your investments. For example, if you bought shares for $1000 and sold them 12 months later for $1500 you have made a capital gain of $500, and this must be included in your income for the year. Generally, you pay CGT at half your marginal income tax rate. So if you earn more than $80 000 a year your marginal rate of income tax would be 39.5 per cent (including the Medicare levy) so you would pay 19.75 per cent of any capital gain in tax. In the above example you would be liable to pay $98.75 in CGT (19.75 per cent of $500). If you hold investments for less than 12 months you pay CGT at your full marginal income tax rate of 39.5 per cent.

The house you occupy is excluded from CGT, which is one reason why buying your own home is so attractive.

Your marginal tax rate

When you receive a pay rise or are considering a particular investment you must calculate what you will receive after paying tax. To do this you need to know your marginal tax rate. This is the tax you must pay on each additional dollar you earn — whether by salary or investment returns.

For example, suppose you earn just over $80 000 per year and you are given a pay rise of $5000. Because your marginal tax rate is 39.5 per cent you will pay an extra $1975 to the taxman, leaving you with $3025. Similarly, if your salary is just over $80 000 and you receive an additional $1000 per year in investment income, you will lose $395 of this in tax.

Perhaps even more important is when you move from one tax bracket to another. If your salary doubled from $30 000 to $60 000 you have moved out of the 16.5 per cent bracket into the 31.5 per cent bracket. This means that you will now be taxed at this higher rate on all your investment income. You should then completely review your investment strategy, as investments that were suitable when you were on the lower tax rate might now not be as attractive in after-tax terms.

The importance of after-tax returns

Basically, there are two types of investments: one where you have to pay tax on the income or capital gain you receive, and the other where tax has already been paid on your behalf by the business or financial institution. Depending on the amount of tax paid on your behalf you will have either little or no more tax to pay.

Smart investors always think in terms of after-tax returns, as this is the only way of comparing different investments and not making the wrong choice.

Suppose you are earning $50 000, have $1000 to invest and are considering the following investments, which have the same degree of risk. One offers a taxable return of 14 per cent. The other offers a 10 per cent tax-free (more accurately described as tax-paid) return. Which one should you take? The answer is the one offering 10 per cent tax-free. If you invest at 14 per cent and then have to pay 30¢ in the dollar tax (ignoring the Medicare levy), your after-tax return is 9.8 per cent. If you invest tax-free at 10 per cent your after-tax return also is 10 per cent.

The moral is that you must not be mesmerised by the seemingly higher return—it's what is left in your pocket after paying tax that is important.

Liquidity

The liquidity of an investment refers to how easily and quickly you can get your money back. The most liquid investments are 'at-call' deposits with banks and other financial institutions such as credit unions. This means you do not have to give any advance notice of your intention to withdraw some, or all, of your money. (This assumes that your money has 'cleared'. If you deposit a cheque, these funds are not available to be withdrawn for several days until the bank is satisfied that the person who wrote the cheque has sufficient funds in the account to cover the cheque.)

Most shares are highly liquid as they are traded every day, although you may have to sell at a lower price than your original buying price. In contrast it usually takes several months to sell land or property. Thus these types of investments are considered to be illiquid.

Credits and debits

These are fundamental investment terms and it is crucial not to confuse them. When you make a deposit in a savings account your account is being credited with that amount. If you make a withdrawal, your account is being debited. A credit balance means you have money in your account. If you become overdrawn on your cheque account you have a debit balance.

Secured and unsecured

If you borrow or lend money you can either do it on a secured or unsecured basis. For example, if you borrow money to buy a car, the lender might require that the loan is 'secured' by the car. Then, if you have trouble meeting the repayments on the loan the lender can, under certain circumstances, repossess the car, sell it and use the proceeds to repay your outstanding debt. The most common form of security underlying a loan is a house or property.

On the other hand, if you borrow money on an unsecured basis and you have trouble repaying the loan, your lender does not have any specific claim on your assets; for instance, they cannot force you to sell your car or big-screen TV to repay the loan. Nor can they repossess any of your assets. The only way a lender can recover an unsecured debt from you is by taking you to court. Examples of unsecured debts are credit cards (such as Visa and Mastercard), store credit accounts and some personal loans.

Dividend imputation

Although dividend imputation was introduced on 1 July 1987, many people still do not understand what it is and how it works. Before the introduction of dividend imputation, dividends were taxed twice. Firstly, companies paid tax on their profits before paying out dividends, and then these dividends were taxed again when they were received by shareholders. All this changed in 1987, with the tax paid by the companies being 'imputed' or allocated to individual shareholders. In other words, the company has paid tax on your behalf.

Any dividends paid from profits on which the company has paid the current company tax rate of 30 per cent are called 'fully franked dividends'. If a lower rate of tax has been paid, the dividends are called 'partly franked'. Whether you still have to pay tax on the dividends you receive depends on whether the dividends are fully or partly franked and your marginal tax rate.

If you are on the top personal tax rate of 46.5 per cent, the company has only paid tax on your behalf at 30 per cent with fully franked dividends. Therefore, you will have to pay a small amount of extra tax. On the other hand, if your tax rate is 15 per cent the company would have overpaid tax on your behalf and you will get a tax credit. You can use this credit to reduce the amount of tax you have to pay on your other sources of income, such as your salary, or get a cash refund from the Tax Office for the overpayment of tax.

When a company pays out a dividend it must tell you how much of it is franked. Since you might be able to claim a tax credit or cash refund as part of the dividend imputation system, it is essential to keep this information for inclusion in your tax return.

Negative gearing

Gearing is just another word for debt or borrowing. A highly geared company is one which has borrowed heavily. If you are negatively geared it means you have borrowed to buy an asset and that the income this asset generates is less than your interest payments and other costs. For example, if you borrowed $200 000 to buy a house at an interest rate of 8 per cent, you would be up for $16 000 in interest each year, plus council and water rates and minor repairs, which might come to $5000. Suppose you rent this house out for $300 per week, or about $15 000 per year. Overall, you are making a loss of $6000. This means that the property is negatively geared. Why would any sensible investor want to do this? The answer revolves around the tax system. This $6000 loss is allowable as a tax deduction. Thus, if you are paying a marginal rate of 46.5 per cent, the government picks up nearly half of your loss. But you are still making a loss.

What you are hoping for is that you will sell this property for much more than you bought it for, thereby making a capital gain. Effectively what you have done is use someone else's money to get access to capital gains. In the meantime your losses can be written off against your tax.

This is the positive side of negative gearing and it undoubtedly can give exceptional investment returns. But there are substantial risks, such as:

- the value of the asset drops rather than rises

- the interest rate on your loan goes up

- your income from other sources goes down so you have trouble making up the shortfall between the income you receive and your interest payments.

Consequently, you should do your sums carefully before negatively gearing any investment.

Derivatives

A derivative is a financial product that owes its existence to, or is 'derived' from, another financial product. Examples of derivatives are options, futures and warrants. For instance, an option over BHP Billiton shares is derived from BHP Billiton shares themselves; that is, the options could not exist if there were no BHP Billiton shares. The main advantage of derivatives—which is also one of their dangers—is that you can get higher 'leverage' from each investment dollar. Derivatives are usually priced at a fraction of the cost of the underlying investment. If BHP Billiton shares are selling for $40 you might be able to buy an option over these shares for $2. So instead of using $40 to buy one BHP Billiton share you could buy 20 options. By doing this you have 20 times the exposure to movements in BHP Billiton's share price with the same $40. Derivatives are explained in more detail in chapter 17, and are not recommended for novice investors.

Key points

○ Before you invest any money it is essential that you understand the potential risks and returns you are likely to receive and whether you will have to pay tax on any income or capital gains. This involves spending some time learning the peculiar language used in finance markets.

○ One of the lessons of the GFC is that you need to take greater responsibility for your financial future—do not leave it solely in the hands of investment advisers.

○ Although many financial institutions offer similar products, the riskiness of investing in them is not the same, nor is the rate of return they offer. It is essential to understand the risks you are taking before deciding to invest.

○ A sensible rule is that you should never invest in anything that you do not understand.

○ If you have some general knowledge of the meaning of typical financial market language you are less likely to invest in products that are not suitable for your financial situation and your ability to take risks.

○ Ask yourself this question before investing in any financial product: if things go wrong with this investment, how much could I lose?

3

Structuring your investment portfolio

Investments can be divided into four main categories: shares, property, interest-bearing securities and cash. These markets usually move in different economic cycles. Therefore, it is unlikely that all four investment categories would boom or bust at the same time. So by having your money spread among these four areas you are diversifying your investment risk. The percentage of your investment portfolio you have in each of these categories is referred to as asset allocation.

As a general rule you should aim to have at least half of your investment portfolio in growth-oriented assets such as shares and property. Certainly these assets carry with them the possibility of capital losses as well as capital gains. Furthermore, you do not want to be investing in shares or property near the top of a booming market as this can adversely affect your investment returns. There are times when it is better to have a considerable amount of your money in cash while you wait for share and property prices to fall so that you can buy in when prices have bottomed out. However, unless interest rates are historically high—as they were in the early 1990s—the longer term danger of having too much of your money tied up in cash is that inflation and taxes will erode your capital.

In this chapter we examine the returns you could achieve through different asset allocation strategies. Past performance may not be a good indicator of future performance, but these figures show how you could have increased your investment return by several percentage points per year.

Now you may think that it does not matter much whether you get an overall return of 8 per cent per annum or 10 per cent per annum from your investments. Yet over the long term a small increase in your investment return each year can make a substantial difference.

For example, suppose you start with an initial investment of $10 000 and add $5000 to it each year for 30 years. If your investment return averaged 8 per cent over this period you would end up with $667 043. This figure does not take taxes into account. If instead you were able to get an average 10 per cent return over this period you would accumulate $996 964. If you achieved a 12 per cent average return you would end up with $1 506 262.

The differences are even more dramatic if you look at a 40-year investment period. Achieving a 12 per cent annual return on the above figures would give you a nestegg of $4 765 966—compared with $1 512 527 if your investment return averaged 8 per cent over this period.

As the following sections will show, altering your asset allocation can significantly increase your average investment returns without unduly raising your investment risks. In the long term this can make a huge difference to your financial position.

Asset allocation and your circumstances

Asset allocation involves dividing an investment portfolio among different asset categories, such as shares, property, interest-bearing securities and cash. Determining what mix of assets to hold in your portfolio is a personal one. The asset allocation that works best for you at any given point in your life will depend largely on your age, your investment goals and your ability to tolerate risk.

Your age

Generally speaking, your attitude to investing and taking risks changes when you are approaching or in retirement. As the experience of the global financial crisis highlighted, many retirees have too much of their portfolio invested in shares and therefore saw the value of their portfolio drop dramatically in less than two years. With the benefit of hindsight, many retirees wished that they had more of their money invested in relatively low risk interest-bearing investments. When you are young your ability to take risks is greater because you have income from your job to cover any losses you might have with your investments.

Your investments also have more time to recover from a downturn. In contrast, when you retire preservation of your capital becomes the number one priority and you would probably adopt a more conservative approach to investing.

Your investment goals

Your investment goals relate to the expected number of months, years or decades you will be investing to achieve a particular financial goal. For example, those in their late 20s who are planning for their retirement will usually feel more comfortable having a high proportion of riskier investments in their portfolio because they are not as affected by the short-term ups and downs of financial markets. In contrast, for people who are the same age but are saving for their children's education it would be more sensible to take on less risk because they have a shorter investing horizon and the money is needed at a specific time.

Your risk tolerance

Risk tolerance is your ability and willingness to risk losing some or all of your original investment in exchange for greater potential returns. An investor with a high risk tolerance is more likely to risk losing money in order to get better results. A conservative investor, or one with a low risk tolerance, tends to favour investments where the potential for losing money is lower—as are the potential returns.

There are two overriding rules which you should use in determining the asset allocation that is right for you:

- For a given level of risk you should aim to obtain the highest return possible.

- For a given level of return you should aim to achieve the lowest risk possible.

Your goal is to achieve the highest return on your investments that you can, within your comfort risk level. So it is essential for you to try to establish what type of investor you are, to gauge your risk tolerance, and then tailor a portfolio to suit your risk profile. Most importantly, it is essential that you feel comfortable with your investment strategy. If you are losing sleep worrying about whether the value of your investments is falling it is a definite sign that you are not in the right investments.

What type of investor are you?

Developing an investment plan is a very personal exercise. There is no such thing as 'one size fits all' when it comes to investing your money. One of the crucial first steps is to determine what type of investor you are, and in particular what risks you are willing and able to take with your money. Here is a short quiz that will help you learn how tolerant of risk you are, with a few comments after each question.

Such insights can help you choose a mix of investments suitable for both your financial goals and your temperament. However, it should be emphasised that this is a guide only—you should make a more comprehensive assessment of your financial position and objectives before you make any investment decisions.

Question 1

How long until you will need at least some of the money from your investments?

a) One to five years

b) Five to ten years

c) More than ten years

The length of time you can hold an investment largely determines how much risk you should tolerate. Shares may be risky for periods of less than two years because the sharemarket might not have enough time to recover from a downturn.

Question 2

Imagine that you buy shares, and three months later, the share price jumps up 20 per cent. What would you do?

a) Sell the shares and lock in your profit

b) Hold on

c) Buy more shares

Those who chose to take the profit after three months are probably less risk tolerant, while the more aggressive investors would hold on for further gains or even add to their holdings.

Question 3

Say you buy shares and instead of the price rising it drops 30 per cent after three months. What would you do?

a)   Sell to avoid further losses

b)   Hold on and hope for a rebound

c)   Buy more shares at the new lower price

If you opted to sell at a loss, explore your risk aversion further, and don't buy shares you won't be able to hold through volatile times.

Question 4

Take the same situation as in the previous question, but this time the shares are part of a portfolio you won't need until retirement in 15 years. What would you do?

a)   Sell

b)   Hold on

c)   Buy more shares

A longer time frame and a more diversified portfolio make many investors more comfortable during downturns. If you still choose to sell here, consider learning more about all types of risk and how you can manage it more comfortably. By holding on, you are hoping that the market will rebound and place your investments in a better position over the long term.

Question 5

What best describes your approach to long-term investing? Do you aim to:

a)   Minimise losses

b)   Maximise returns with the possibility of short-term losses

c)   A balance between these two

Diversifying—that is, spreading your money among a number of different types of investments—lessens your risk because even if some of your investments go down, others go up, or vice versa.

Question 6

When it comes to investing, do you generally:

a)   Develop your own investment strategy

b)   Invest with a professional fund manager

c)   Have trouble making a decision and just leave your money in the bank because it's safe

One of the greatest investment risks is the risk of doing nothing—and missing out on the chance to increase your wealth.

*   *   *   *   *

Your answers to these questions may help you determine which of the following categories best describes the type of investor you are.

Conservative investor

Conservative investors typically select investments with little or no risks associated with capital loss. They are willing to accept other risks to avoid capital loss, such as a rate of return that does not keep pace with inflation.

Moderately conservative investor

Moderately conservative investors are willing to accept slightly more chance of capital loss than a conservative investor, but still focus on avoiding potential capital losses and volatility. Typically, these investors are most comfortable with investments that normally have less severe and less frequent changes in their value.

Moderate investor

Moderate investors are willing to tolerate more possibilities of suffering capital losses. Typically, these investors are 'in the middle of the road' in regard to both potential risks and rewards. They do not mind some fluctuations but will stay away from investments that have more dramatic or frequent changes. A moderate investor's portfolio will often have some investments that fluctuate in value balanced with investments subject to less frequent fluctuation.

Aggressive investor

Aggressive investors are willing and usually eager to accept a greater chance of capital loss. They sometimes focus on short-term market timing as opposed to long-term investing. They are comfortable accepting a high level of risk in the hope of greater opportunity for returns. Typically, aggressive investors are less concerned with the rate of inflation and their ability to reinvest earnings at the same rate. They also tend to put a lot of their investment eggs in one basket rather than having a diversified portfolio.

How to get started

Establishing the asset allocation that best suits your financial situation is a complicated task. Basically, you're trying to pick a mix of assets that has the highest probability of meeting your investment goals at a level of risk you can live with. In addition, you need to be able to adjust the mix of assets to suit your changing financial circumstances.

Research indicates that determining your asset allocation is the most important investment decision that you'll make—it is even more important than the individual investments you buy.

Returns from an investment portfolio are generally determined by three factors:

- market timing
- individual investment selection
- allocation between different asset categories.

Market timing (when you decide to buy or sell a particular investment) or individual asset selection (whether you buy Australian bank shares or mining shares), while important, are not the most significant factors in determining your overall investment return. Asset allocation itself is by far the most important determinant of your overall investment return.

During times of sharemarket uncertainty, many investors panic and sell their shares at depressed prices with the intention of buying back when share prices fall further. This strategy is known as 'market timing'. However, just as significant declines in sharemarkets tend to be concentrated in short periods of time, the best gains similarly occur over a three- to four-month period. This means that an investor who tries to time the entry and exit into and from the sharemarket is highly likely to miss the best gains. Indeed, this often results in an unintended strategy of selling when the main fall in share prices has occurred and buying back in after the major rise in share prices has finished.

Missing just a few days of performance can significantly impact your longer term investment return. Making decisions based on short-term performance, or attempting to 'time the market', can lead to poor investment decisions. For example, one of the worst one-day returns on the Australian sharemarket in the last 15 years happened on 10 October 2008, when the market dropped 8.3 per cent. The very next business day, the market rose 5.6 per cent—one of the best increases in share prices in the last 15 years!

Risk and diversification

It is an almost universally accepted principle that any investment portfolio should include a mix of investments. These investments could include a combination of shares, interest-bearing securities, property and cash. A portfolio should also be balanced. That is, the portfolio should contain investments with varying levels of risk to help minimise exposure if one of the portfolio holdings declines significantly. Another consideration is how much income is generated. Some investors want a high current income return while other investors prefer a portfolio with more emphasis on assets with capital growth and less current income.

A diversified portfolio should be diversified at two levels: *between* asset categories and *within* asset categories. So in addition to allocating your investments among shares, interest-bearing securities, property and cash, you will also need to spread out your investments within each asset category. For example, if you have 25 per cent of your portfolio in shares, but all of this money is invested in one company, then this is not a diversified portfolio.

The underlying principle is that different classes of investments have shown different rates of return and levels of volatility over time. Also, since different asset classes respond differently to the same news, your shares may go down while your interest-bearing securities and property go up, or vice versa. Diversifying your investments over different asset classes helps you minimise volatility while maximising potential returns.

It should be emphasised that diversification does not eliminate all risk from your portfolio. Assets in the same market are typically affected by some risk factors in the same way; for example, share prices of most companies fell because of the global financial crisis. It is useful to draw a distinction between systematic risk and unsystematic risk, which together comprise total investment risk. Systematic risk results from risk factors that affect all assets in the market in the same way, such as the global financial crisis. Unsystematic risk results from risk factors that affect individual companies in isolation, such as a company discovering a new oil deposit or losing a major contract. Systematic risk is also referred to as market risk, because it is inherent in all assets in the market. It is also undiversifiable risk, as it cannot be diversified away by holding different assets in your portfolio. The only way of reducing market risk with shares is not to hold any shares. In contrast, unsystematic risk can be reduced or eliminated by holding a diversified portfolio of assets.

Risk versus reward

The reward for taking on risk is the potential for a greater investment return. If you have a financial goal with a long time horizon, you are likely to make more money by carefully investing in asset categories with greater risk, such as shares or property, rather than restricting your investments to assets with less risk, such as cash and fixed-interest investments. On the other hand, investing solely in cash may be appropriate for your short-term financial goals.

You should not aim to eliminate risk entirely from your investment portfolio. If you don't include enough risk in your portfolio, your investments may not earn a sufficient return to meet your financial goals or even keep pace with inflation. For example, if you are saving for a long-term goal, such as retirement, you will be better served by including at least some shares in your portfolio. On the other hand, if you include too much risk in your portfolio, the money for your goal may not be there when you need it. A portfolio heavily weighted in shares would be inappropriate for a short-term goal, such as saving for a family's summer holiday.

Achieving good diversification

One way of diversifying your share investments is to identify and invest in a wide range of companies and industry sectors. You'll need at least a dozen carefully selected individual shares from different areas of the economy to be truly diversified. So your share portfolio would not be diversified if you only held bank shares. You need to include shares from different sectors such as retailing, property, health, telecommunications, transport, building materials and mining.

To achieve a well-diversified portfolio you need a minimum investment of between $50000 and $100000. Some investors who do not have this amount of funds to invest find it easier to diversify by using managed funds rather than buying shares or property directly. A managed fund, or managed investment, is where a professional fund manager pools money from many investors and invests in shares, bonds and other financial instruments. So for a relatively small investment you get access to a diversified portfolio.

Be aware, however, that a managed fund doesn't necessarily provide instant diversification, especially if the fund focuses on only one particular industry sector. If you invest in narrowly focused managed funds—for example, gold—you may need to invest in more than one fund to get the diversification you seek. This means you may have to consider investing in a range of managed funds, such as large company share funds, small company share funds and international share funds. Of course, as you add more investments to your portfolio, you'll pay additional fees and commissions, which will, in turn, lower your investment returns. So you'll need to consider these costs when deciding the best way to diversify your portfolio.

Changing your asset allocation

The most common reason for changing your asset allocation is your age. As you get closer to your investment goal, it is advisable to reassess your asset allocation. For example, most people investing for retirement hold fewer shares and more bonds and cash equivalents as they get closer to retirement age. You may also need to change your asset allocation if there is a change in your risk tolerance, financial situation or the financial goal itself.

Savvy investors typically do not change their asset allocation based on the relative performance of asset categories; for example, increasing the proportion of shares in their portfolio when the sharemarket is booming. Instead, that's when they 'rebalance' their portfolios.

Rebalancing

Rebalancing is bringing your portfolio back to your original asset allocation mix. This is necessary because over time some of your investments may become out of alignment with your investment goals. Some of your investments will grow faster than others. By rebalancing, you'll ensure that your portfolio does not rely too heavily on one or more asset categories, and you'll return your portfolio to a comfortable level of risk.

For example, let's say you determined that share investments should represent 60 per cent of your portfolio. But after a recent sharemarket increase, share investments represent 80 per cent of your portfolio. You'll need to either sell some of your shares or purchase investments from an under-weighted asset category to re-establish your original asset allocation mix.

When you rebalance, you'll also need to review the investments within each asset allocation category. If any of these investments have moved out of alignment with your investment goals, you'll need to make changes to bring them back to their original allocation within the asset category.

There are basically three different ways you can rebalance your portfolio:

- You can sell off investments from over-weighted asset categories and use the proceeds to purchase investments for under-weighted asset categories. However, be aware that this could result in capital gains tax being payable.

- You can purchase new investments for under-weighted asset categories.

- If you are making continuous contributions to the portfolio, you can alter your contributions so that more funds go to under-weighted asset categories until your portfolio is back in balance.

What sort of returns can you expect?

By including asset categories with investment returns that move up and down under different market conditions within a portfolio, you can usually protect your investment portfolio against significant losses. Historically, the returns of the four major asset categories—shares, property, interest-bearing securities and cash—have not moved up and down at the same time. Market conditions that cause one asset category to do well often cause another asset category to have average or poor returns. By investing in more than one asset category, you'll reduce the risk that you'll lose money and your portfolio's overall investment returns will be less volatile. If one asset category's investment return falls, you'll be in a position to counteract your losses in that asset category with better investment returns in another asset category.

Table 3.1 shows the performance of the major investment categories from one year to ten years to 30 June 2009. These figures do not take tax into account, and returns from property are measured by the performance of listed property trusts, which would not reflect the returns if you invested in property directly. As you can see, there are significant differences in the rate of return you can expect to get from different types of investments. Also keep in mind that you are taking different levels of risk to achieve these returns.

Table 3.1: investment returns by market sector to 30 June 2009

	Total returns over (% p.a.)			Range of returns over last
Investment	1 year	3 years	10 years	20 years (p.a.)
Australian shares	−20.14	−3.82	7.40	−20.14 to 28.66
Australian listed property	−42.27	−22.66	2.61	−42.27 to 29.29
Australian residential property	−1.39	5.43	8.77	−1.39 to 33.11
International shares (unhedged)	−16.25	−10.77	−3.00	−23.60 to 42.16
Australian fixed interest	10.82	6.36	6.20	−1.13 to 22.33
Australian cash	5.48	6.41	5.72	4.66 to 18.43

Source: Pitcher Partners.

The figures in table 3.1 might surprise you as they show that investing in Australian fixed interest over this 10-year period returned only 1.2 percentage points less per year than investing in Australian shares. But remember that even a one percentage point per year difference in your investment return can make a significant difference over a 40- or 50-year time period.

However, these figures would have been vastly different if they had been taken over the 10 years to June 2007. In the four years to June 2007, Australian shares averaged an annual return of 25.14 per cent compared with 4.48 per cent per annum for Australian fixed interest. The years to June 2008 (−13.4 per cent) and June 2009 (−20.14 per cent) were two of the worst years on record for Australian shares as a result of the global financial crisis. In the second half of 2009, Australian share prices rebounded strongly—up by nearly 40 per cent between March 2009 and December 2009.

Similarly, the investment returns for unhedged international shares would have been considerably improved if the figures were taken over the 10 years to June 2007. In the year to June 2008 international shares fell 21.26 per cent, and in the year to June 2009 they fell 16.25 per cent. Like Australian shares, international shares also rose strongly in the second half of 2009.

This highlights two important investing lessons:

• Trying to predict significant turning points in the sharemarket is an impossible dream and is very costly if you get it wrong.

• In the short term sharemarkets can be extremely volatile and you need to keep a calm head and not panic if share prices fall suddenly —as they often rebound just as quickly.

Table 3.1 also highlights the volatility in annual returns from sharemarket and property investments. For example, the best return over this period for shares was +28.66 per cent, while the worst was −20.14 per cent. In contrast, the return from investing in cash was never negative and reached 18.43 per cent in the year to June 1990 when interest rates were at historical highs.

Table 3.1 does not take tax into account. Dividend income from Australian shares is often fully franked. This means that dividend income may be partly or wholly tax-free in the hands of shareholders. Secondly, capital gains on the buying and selling of shares and property are taxed at half your marginal income tax rate if you hold the investments for at least 12 months. In contrast, income from fixed-interest investments is taxable at your full marginal income tax rate. Savvy investors realise that it is after-tax, not before-tax, returns that are important—it is what the taxman allows you to keep from your investments that is important, not what you earned from them. This is why holding investments within a superannuation fund can be so attractive for many investors as the tax rate on super funds is generally much lower than holding these assets as an individual.

Using the information from table 3.1 it is possible to develop hypo-thetical investment strategies involving different degrees of risk, return and diversification using investment returns achieved over the 10 years to June 2009. To begin with, say you had invested 50 per cent of your portfolio in Australian shares, 10 per cent in property, 20 per cent in international shares and 20 per cent in fixed interest. Then your investor profile would look like table 3.2 (investor profile A).

Table 3.2: investor profile A

Sector	Return (%)	% of portfolio	Weighted return (%)
Australian shares	7.40	50	3.70
International shares	–3.00	20	–0.60
Residential property	8.77	10	0.88
Fixed interest	6.20	20	1.24
Weighted average return		100	5.22

The weighted return is the overall sector return times the percentage of the portfolio invested in that sector. Hence the weighted return from Australian shares is the sector return of 7.40 per cent times 0.5 (the percentage of the portfolio invested in Australian shares). This equals 3.7 per cent. The weighted return for international shares is –3.00 per cent times 0.2, or –0.6 per cent, and so on. The weighted average return, of 5.22 per cent, is the total of all the weighted returns and represents the return you could expect from this particular diversification strategy. Note that the figures have been rounded.

Investor profile A indicates a relatively risky portfolio because 70 per cent of it is tied up in shares. A major sharemarket downturn in the short term would see you losing money. But it does illustrate the importance of diversification—even though you would have lost money on international shares over this period your overall investment return was still positive.

Now say you adopted a more conservative diversification strategy and invested 10 per cent of your portfolio in Australian shares, nothing in international shares, 20 per cent in property and 70 per cent in fixed interest. You would now be investing only 10 per cent in shares. Your new investor profile would look like table 3.3 (investor profile B).

Table 3.3: investor profile B

Sector	Return (%)	% of portfolio	Weighted return (%)
Australian shares	7.40	10	0.74
International shares	–3.00	0	0.00
Residential property	8.77	20	1.75
Fixed interest	6.20	70	4.34
Weighted average return		100	6.83

Profile B is a less risky portfolio because there is a higher percentage of the portfolio invested in fixed interest compared with Australian and overseas shares. Surprisingly, this return is actually higher than for the more risky portfolio A. But this is mainly because the years to June 2008 and June 2009 were particularly poor years for sharemarkets around the world.

As a final example, say that you adopted a balanced diversification strategy and invested 25 per cent of your portfolio in each of the sectors: Australian shares, international shares, property and fixed interest. Your investor profile would look like table 3.4 (investor profile C).

Table 3.4: investor profile C

Sector	Return (%)	% of portfolio	Weighted return (%)
Australian shares	7.40	25	1.85
International shares	−3.00	25	−0.75
Residential property	8.77	25	2.19
Fixed interest	6.20	25	1.55
Weighted average return		100	4.84

This return is less than that for investor profile A in table 3.2, but is less risky as it has a lower percentage of the portfolio in shares and a higher percentage in fixed interest and residential property.

These examples illustrate how asset allocation can make a significant difference to your investment returns. Generally speaking, the higher the risk you are prepared to take—for example, the higher the percentage of shares in your portfolio—the higher your potential profits and losses. However, you should not aim to eliminate risk entirely from your portfolio—the main risk associated with doing this is that your investment returns will not keep pace with inflation.

Key points

o   Risk and return are closely linked. Ordinarily, the higher the potential return from an investment, the higher the risk.

o   In the long term you are best served by investments with capital growth potential.

o   The best way to hedge against risk in investing is through diversification—but there is some risk that cannot be reduced through diversification.

o   Evaluate where you stand in terms of your investment goals. Are you primarily interested in income and security, or are you looking for capital gain with less security? How much security are you prepared to give up for the potential for capital gain?

o   Asset allocation is the most important investment decision you will make regarding your investments—it is more important than market timing or what individual investments you buy.

o   Asset allocation is a very personal decision and can alter over your lifetime. It is essential that you rebalance the asset allocation in your portfolio if your financial circumstances or goals change.

Keeping track of
your investments

The extent to which you will need to keep records of your investments will partly depend upon how active you are as an investor. Obviously, if you only make a few investments during a year, you will usually not need to keep elaborate records. For tax and certain other legal purposes, as well as to measure how well your investments have performed, it is essential to keep good records, even if your transactions are few in number.

Because of capital gains tax (CGT) legislation you need to distinguish between three types of assets:

- those bought before 20 September 1985

- those bought between 20 September 1985 and 30 September 1999

- those bought after 30 September 1999.

Assets purchased before 20 September 1985 are free of CGT. Assets purchased between 20 September 1985 and 30 September 1999 are subject to CGT with the cost base adjusted for increases in the Consumer Price Index. This concept is referred to as 'indexation'. For assets purchased after 30 September 1999 you have a choice. Providing the asset has been held for 12 months or more a discount of 50 per cent applies to any capital gain, or alternatively, you can use the indexation method but with indexation frozen at 30 September 1999. If an asset is held for less than 12 months, no discount applies. In any event, CGT is levied at your marginal rate of tax on applicable capital gains.

Legal requirements

In some cases the law requires that you keep detailed investment records and that these must be kept for a specific number of years. If you do not, you may be heavily fined. Unfortunately, income tax legislation does not specify the type of records that should be kept or the means by which they should be presented.

In other cases, such as for CGT, it is also important to keep records to help determine your tax liability when you buy and sell assets. For tax purposes, any books of account, records or documents relating to the preparation of your income tax return must be retained for a period of at least five years. In relation to CGT matters, the five-year period begins when you sell the asset, not when you buy it. Other legislation, such as that relating to fringe benefits tax, requires that records be kept for seven years.

The Corporations Law requires that—with regard to companies —accounting records must be kept for seven years from the end of the accounting period in which a transaction took place. For non-accounting records, the requirement is that records be kept for five years.

Tax records must explain all transactions and must be kept in English. The records must include any documents that are relevant for the purpose of ascertaining income and expenditure. If you or your company are selected for a tax audit, business records will be required. This may include detailed records such as accounting journals, ledgers and invoices.

Separate rules apply for CGT. Records must be kept from the date of acquisition until at least five years after the disposal of the asset. You need to record the following information:

- the date the asset was acquired
- the amounts of expenditure for purchase and capital improvements
- when you sold it
- how much you sold it for.

Self-assessment

Self-assessment is where individuals or companies prepare their own tax returns, which in turn are accepted at face value by the Australian Taxation Office. The Tax Office then issues a notice of assessment. Before self-assessment was introduced the Tax Office would carefully scrutinise each return. Although this is no longer done, an individual's or company's tax return can be subjected to a tax audit.

Audits

With self-assessment you stand a much higher chance of being audited by the Tax Office. And there are substantial penalties if you are guilty of submitting false or misleading information in your tax returns, or if you cannot substantiate your claims for tax deductions.

In fact, a common area for individuals to be 'caught out' is where they have not kept receipts for the deductions they claim. Notwithstanding that this may be an innocent mistake the Tax Office will generally penalise you if you are audited and you do not have all of the required receipts.

Investment registers

A good way to keep track of your investments is through an investment register. You can design one yourself or ask for help from your accountant or financial adviser. An example of what an investment register could look like is shown in table 4.1 (overleaf).

The register may be kept on anything from paper to a computer, depending on the volume of transactions you have and your requirements for information.

Naturally, the more investments you have the more you will need to keep track of them. Table 4.1 is an example of what an investment register could look like when recording share transactions. The same principle could apply to any investments from fixed-interest securities to property. In the latter cases the information to be recorded would be set out differently. For example, the item 'average price', which appears in that part of the register set aside for shares, would ordinarily not apply to property or fixed-interest investments.

How an investment register works

Table 4.1 relates to a hypothetical company, XYZ Limited, which is listed on the stock exchange. It is assumed that the record for these shares is kept on a computer with separate pages for 'Acquisitions', 'Sales' and 'Other information'.

Initially your holding of XYZ shares was nil. You then purchase 10 000 shares on 2/5/08 at a price of $1.00 each. Brokerage is $20, making a total outlay of $10 020. The next transaction occurs on 30/11/09 when you sell 5000 XYZ shares for $1.30 each. After deducting brokerage of $40 on buying and selling you make a profit of $1460.

It is worthwhile pointing out that, although you made a profit, on relatively small transactions the brokerage you pay can severely affect your overall profit. Here it is assumed that you are using an online broker. Some 'full-service' brokers have a minimum charge of around $100, which makes them unsuitable for many small investors.

Table 4.1: investment register—XYZ Limited (shares)

Acquisitions

Date acquired	2/5/08
Opening balance	Nil
Quantity acquired	10 000
How acquired	Market purchase
Balance	10 000
Average price	$1.00
Cost	$10 000
Brokerage	$20
Total consideration	$10 020
Closing balance in units	10 000
Market price (31/12/09)	$1.35
Comments	Purchase price was near a low for the year
Unrealised profit (loss) (excludes brokerage)	–

Sales

Date sold	30/11/09
Opening balance (units)	10 000
Opening balance ($)	10 000
Quantity sold	5 000
Price	$1.30
Amount	$6 500
Less brokerage	$20
Total consideration	$6 480
Balance of units held	5 000
Cost (excludes brokerage)	$6 500
Comments	Realised profit of $1 460 ($1 500 – $20 – $20)

Dividends

Date rec'd	# of shares	Interim (¢ per share)	Final (¢ per share)	Amount	Franking status	Imputation credit
30/9/08	10 000	3	–	$300	Unfranked	–
31/3/09	10 000	–	5	$500	Fully franked	$214.29*

* Assumes a corporate tax rate of 30 per cent.

Capital gains

In this example you made a profit of $1460, which is subject to CGT at your marginal rate of tax. Because you held the shares for more than 12 months (from 2/5/08 to 30/11/09) you are entitled to a 50 per cent discount. Assuming you are on the highest marginal tax rate, CGT on the above transaction would be: $1460 × 50% × 0.45 = $328.50. So your after-tax profit is $1131.50, which represents a return on investment (ROI) of 22.63 per cent ($1131.50 ÷ $5000 × 100), excluding dividend income. If you had held the shares for less than 12 months you would not be entitled to any discount when calculating your CGT liability. The above ROI is based on a period of approximately 19 months so on an annualised basis ROI is: 22.63% ÷ 19 × 12 = 14.29% p.a.

Dividends

With an investment register it is also possible to have an additional section or page to record dividends—whether they are interim or final—and what franking credits you received (see chapter 7). Also you can record details of any bonus or rights issues that XYZ Limited has made (see chapter 8). The result is a synopsis of your investment in XYZ. In this example, the company paid an interim dividend on 30/9/08 of 3¢ per share and a final dividend on 31/3/09 of 5¢ per share. Total dividends from 2/5/08 to 30/11/09 were therefore 8¢ per share or $800. The shares cost $10 000 so over the 19-month period the ROI from dividends was: $800 ÷ $10 000 × 100 = 8.00%. On an annualised basis this is 5.05 per cent per annum (8.00% ÷ 19 × 12). In chapter 8 we will see that what really matters is current dividend yield, which relates dividend income to the current price of the shares. On 30/11/09 the price of the shares was $1.30 so current dividend yield was: 8¢ ÷ $1.30 × 100 = 6.15% p.a.

It is important to keep a record of the dividends you receive from share investments. You will need this information for your income tax return as well as a means of determining how well you are doing with your investments. It is particularly important to distinguish between dividends which are partly or wholly franked and those which are unfranked. The significance of this and the dividend imputation system are explained in chapter 7.

The information you need will be sent in the form of an advice by the company when it pays a dividend. If you receive a cheque, this advice accompanies the dividend cheque. If you have a dividend paid directly into an account with a financial institution, you will just receive advice detailing the amount of the dividend and any franking credits. You should keep all of these advices in one place. When it comes time to prepare your tax return you can refer to them for the information needed. One problem associated with doing this is that you do not have a running record, at your fingertips, of how much in the way of dividends is being paid on your investments, and their franking status. If you have 'excess' franking credits — that is, the amount of tax paid on your behalf is greater than the amount of tax you need to pay on your taxable income — you will receive a cash refund when you lodge your tax return. So it is more important than ever to keep an accurate record of the dividends you receive and their accompanying franking credits.

An alternative is to keep a record of dividends paid to you in your investment register. This can be in a different part of the Acquisition/Sale section, or on a separate page. Some companies also have dividend reinvestment plans whereby you can elect to have a dividend reinvested in the company's shares instead of receiving it in cash. If you take advantage of a dividend reinvestment plan, you can usually acquire the shares at a slight discount to market price. In recent times these schemes have lost a lot of their appeal to companies because they do not need cash to the extent they did a few years ago, and they are happy to pay dividends in cash. Consequently, some companies that previously offered dividend reinvestment schemes have ceased to do so. If you take advantage of a dividend reinvestment plan you will need to record the acquisition in your investment register. The dividend is subject to the same amount of tax as if it was paid in cash.

For CGT purposes you will need to record the price at which you acquired the shares and the number purchased.

Other aspects of an investment register

As noted above the intention with an investment register is to have different pages for each investment. The example here is for shares, but all investments can be incorporated into the one register. However, the content of the register will differ according to the investment type. For income-producing property, for example, it is prudent to keep a careful watch on outgoings associated with the property. The fact that you are making a loss on a property is not necessarily a bad thing because these losses can be offset against other income while, hopefully, the value of the property increases (see chapter 20).

There is software available that will enable you to keep track of your investments efficiently. Unless you are a large investor with many investments you can design your own investment register to suit your needs, or even record the progress of your investments manually.

Share registries, such as Link Market Services and Computershare, also have websites where you can get information on your share investments. So if you do lose information about dividends and their franking credits you can download the information from these websites. However, different companies use different share registries, which means that it is unlikely that you will be able to obtain all the information on your share portfolio from the one website.

Expenses versus capital expenditure

The income tax law requires you to distinguish between running expenses on the one hand and expenditure of a capital nature on the other. Running expenses, such as interest on loans to purchase investments, are fully allowable tax deductions in the financial year in which they are incurred. Capital expenditures may not be allowable tax deductions at all, or may only be written off over a period of time, or may reduce the 'cost base' of your investments for CGT purposes. It is therefore necessary to have a recording system that distinguishes between running expenses and capital expenditure.

Similarly, with regard to property expenditure it is necessary to differ-entiate between 'repairs', which are classed as expenses, and 'renovations', which are classed as capital expenditure. Repairs can be fully written-off against assessable income in the year in which they are incurred, whereas renovations can only be written-off over a number of years. As to what constitutes a repair and what renovations, a hallmark case was decided more than 40 years ago in the High Court. The management of a cinema installed a new ceiling and claimed the cost of doing this as a tax deduction in the year in which the expenditure took place. The court disallowed the claim on the grounds that the expenditure was, in effect, a replacement of the ceiling, not repairs, and was therefore expenditure of a capital nature. This meant that the ceiling should be depreciated over the life of the ceiling.

Generally speaking, capital expenditure includes spending on:

* plant and equipment

* goodwill

* buildings

* patents

- business names

- copyrights.

Even where capital expenditure is incurred in the course of producing assessable income it may not be allowed as a tax deduction. Some such expenditure may be an allowable deduction under specific provisions of the Tax Act.

It is essential that you maintain separate records of running expenses and capital expenditure. One way of doing this is by having a capital register in which you keep a record of all capital expenditure, including the date of the expenditure, the nature of the expenditure and the basis upon which it is to be written-off, if at all.

Although expenditure of a capital nature is not usually a tax deduction, it may be allowed as an addition to the cost base when calculating CGT. For example, the costs incurred in improving an asset may be added to its cost base. Other costs that may be added to the cost base and which you should keep a record of include:

- incidental costs associated with acquiring or disposing of the asset; for example, fees, commission or remuneration for the professional services of a surveyor, valuer, auctioneer, accountant, broker, agent, consultant or legal adviser

- costs of transferring the asset, including stamp duty or similar

- any capital costs incurred in maintaining a right over or a title to the asset.

The above list is not exhaustive and you should consult an accountant to establish what other costs may be allowable for CGT purposes.

Share watchlists

It is wise to create a watchlist of shares in your portfolio because this provides an accurate record of their progress over time. Watchlists can usually be created with your stockbroker, or you can create them on the Australian Securities Exchange (ASX) website: <www.asx.com.au>. They enable you to monitor the performance of shares that you currently hold or are interested in buying in the future. Watchlists are straightforward to set up and they enable you to receive price and other information on your securities quickly and conveniently. To create a watchlist with the ASX you will first need to complete the free registration by visiting the 'My ASX' section of the ASX website. Once you have completed the registration you can subscribe to newsletters, access online classes, create watchlists, join a sharemarket game and more.

The advantages of creating watchlists with the ASX include:

- The portfolio of shares you are interested in can be stored in one place, making it convenient to check them regularly.

- You can create up to 15 watchlists, each with 20 shares.

- You can also monitor interest rate securities, options, warrants, futures and indices.

- There is a portfolio function which enables you to continuously compare the original value of your securities with their current value.

- It is easy to update or change a watchlist quickly.

- An individual watchlist or all of your watchlists can be conveniently downloaded for further analysis.

You will need to know the ASX code of each security you wish to add to your watchlist. If you do not know the code, you can use the code lookup feature, which requires that you type in the beginning of a company or index name.

As well as being a useful tool for following the performance of your portfolio, you can create watchlists for the securities you are interested in buying. You can then follow the progress of these hypothetical portfolios and compare their performance against the All Ordinaries index. You can also identify particular securities and, over time, assess whether you should buy them or delete them from your watchlist. Another possibility is to compile a watchlist of stockbroker tips and see how they perform. This is helpful in evaluating a broker's recommendations.

To read more information about creating watchlists with the ASX go to: <www.asx.com.au/resources/myasx/watchlists/help.htm>.

As stated above, the use of ASX watchlists is free. Many stockbrokers also have this facility but you may need to be a client to use it.

Measuring investment performance

From using an investment register and watchlist you can calculate the increase (or decrease) in the value of your investments over time. Let's be positive and say that your portfolio is trending upwards. Although the value of the sharemarket fell by 40 per cent during the global financial crisis, it recovered in 2009 to post an increase of 33 per cent. The first step in evaluating the performance of your portfolio is to ask: what does it mean to say that the sharemarket increased by 33 per cent in 2009? In Australia, what it means is that the value of the S&P/ASX All Ordinaries index (All Ords) increased by that amount.

There is more about the All Ords in chapter 8, but for present purposes suffice it to say that the All Ords comprises the 500 largest companies in Australia listed on the ASX based on market capitalisation. The market capitalisation of a company is simply the number of shares a company has issued multiplied by its current share price. So if a company has issued 10 million shares and they are selling for $50 per share, its market capitalisation is $500 million (10 million shares × $50). As there are over 2100 companies listed on the ASX a lot miss out on being included in the All Ords. However, it is a good broad measure of sharemarket performance, and changes in the value of the All Ords are quoted throughout a trading day in real time; that is, as they happen.

Now comes the tricky part. The All Ords increased by 33 per cent in 2009, but it is an index of a basket of shares and its performance reflects the net result of changes in all the shares that make up the index. Some shares increased by 33 per cent, some by more and some by less. And some will have fallen in value. The important question is: which shares were you holding? For a start, you may not have held any shares that were in the All Ords. Or you may have held some which were in the index and some which were not. Furthermore, the All Ords ignores dividends and the effect of income tax and CGT, which an astute investor never does. In addition, you most probably bought and sold some shares during the year, while using the All Ords as a benchmark assumes that you just held your shares without trading them. The upshot is that if you had a portfolio of shares during 2009 your investment return may have been vastly different from 33 per cent.

Keeping a watchlist will tell you what the value of your portfolio is at any point in time. It will also tell you the unrealised profit you are making on securities purchased during the year. However, it will not tell you what profit you have made on the shares you have sold and it does not provide a record of dividends received or the tax consequences of investing. For this you need to maintain a good investment register. Your sources of income from investing in a year can be broken up into the following categories:

- capital appreciation or losses at year end on securities purchased during the year and those held from the beginning of the year

- dividends, interest, property income and so on

- profits or losses from trading securities, property and so on.

Having recorded the above, you can calculate income tax in terms of the level of franking of dividends, and calculate CGT in terms of realised capital gains. Bear in mind that any capital losses can only be offset against capital gains and that you cannot claim a CGT discount on assets held for 12 months or less.

Inflation

One benchmark you will always want to keep ahead of is the rate of inflation as measured by increases in the Consumer Price Index (CPI). As noted elsewhere in this book, if your investment return after tax is not at least as good as the rate of inflation the purchasing power of your money is being eroded. However, CPI figures only come out quarterly so you will not know how you have done with this measure for a few months at a time. When the All Ords is going down 40 per cent in one year and up 33 per cent the next a few percentage points in inflation may not matter much. However, in less volatile times it should be closely monitored. Over a period of 100 years the historical real return from investing in the sharemarket—that is, adjusted for inflation—is likely to be around 5 per cent per annum (see Charles Beelaerts and Kevin Forde, *You Only Make a Profit When You Sell*, Wrightbooks, 2001, pages 147 to 150). Although the sharemarket fell dramatically during the GFC and rebounded in 2009, bringing with it unprecedented volatility, in more 'normal' times if inflation is running at 3 per cent you need to be earning 8 per cent per annum if you are to keep pace with a realistic historical return.

Property

As explained in chapter 18, investing in property is very different to investing in shares and interest-bearing securities. For example, when buying a property in which you are going to live, emotion often comes into play whereas investing in shares requires a clinical mind. When buying property for investment, one consideration is that you generally cannot buy or sell a part of a property (it's either all or nothing), whereas you can sell a part of a share portfolio quite easily.

Like shares, it is possible to compare the performance of a property investment with an index. Various real estate investment organisations publish indices of property prices against which you can evaluate the performance of your property investments; for example, have a look at <www.rpdata.com>. The value of properties can vary markedly in different parts of Australia so you will need to make sure that you are comparing like with like. This is unlike shares in a company, for example, which have the same value on the ASX at any given time.

Portfolio balance

An investment portfolio is normally made up of shares (domestic and international), property, fixed-interest securities and cash, although a particular portfolio may not include all four. All categories have their own risk and return characteristics, and individual investors have different requirements with regard to such things as investment goals, their requirements for liquidity, their attitude to risk, their age, marginal rate of tax and so on. If you have all your money tied up in property, your portfolio will lack diversification and its performance is tied exclusively to property prices. The same applies to the other investment categories. However, because of the risk of loss there are distinct advantages emanating from diversification. As was seen in chapter 3, you can have a diversified portfolio which performs better than a high risk–high reward one. Hence it is important that you monitor the balance of your investment portfolio over time and make adjustments if it becomes too heavily weighted towards one category.

Balance is not only important between asset categories, it is also important within categories. So if you have a high percentage of your share portfolio allocated to one or two shares, it is time to review the situation and perhaps sell off some of those shares and buy others. Whenever assessing whether your overall portfolio or one of the categories within it is in balance, it is essential that you use current market prices, not what you paid for the investments. You may have purchased some shares that took off, and on a cost basis they may not represent a significant percentage of your share portfolio. However, the important measure is what they can be sold for now at market prices. Rebalancing should take place at least semi-annually, and more often if there have been substantial changes in values.

Key points

o   You need to keep records for tax purposes and to measure your investment performance.

- o It is relatively easy to construct your own investment monitoring system; alternatively, you could consult your accountant or other financial adviser to design an appropriate recordkeeping system.

- o Without comprehensive records you could end up paying more tax than legally necessary.

- o For income tax purposes you need to keep records for five years. You may be fined heavily if you are audited and have not kept adequate records.

- o The extent to which you will need to keep records for evaluating investment performance will depend on how active an investor you are.

- o Watchlists are a useful tool for keeping track of your share investments and when considering shares you might buy in the future.

- o The All Ords is a useful index for measuring the broad sharemarket performance of the 500 largest companies listed on the ASX, but it has limitations if you own shares that are not included in the index.

- o Other useful benchmarks include the CPI and property price indices.

- o If you wish to maintain your desired asset allocation, it is essential that you rebalance your investment portfolio from time to time between different asset categories and within categories, and sell-off assets in which you are too heavily invested.

5

Finding an adviser

This chapter is for those of you who wish to enlist the services of a professional financial adviser in making your investment decisions. There is always the option of being a do-it-yourself (DIY) investor, which simply means that you make investment decisions without taking advice from a third party. If you are knowledgeable about all kinds of investments you can effectively be a DIY investor if you are able to:

- objectively assess your current and future financial position

- prepare a balanced portfolio

- regularly put in the hours of research necessary to manage your investments

- let your head rule your heart when it comes to investing.

For many people it is unrealistic to expect that the above is possible, in which case you need to find an investment adviser who theoretically will help you make better investment decisions or, indeed, make investment decisions for you. As will be seen, this is no easy task as you need to find a financial adviser who is highly competent and with whom you feel comfortable and can build a rapport. This includes being aware of potential conflicts of interest between your financial adviser and yourself. For these types of reasons, many people rely on 'qualified' friends and colleagues for investment advice.

As a result of a string of corporate collapses during the financial crisis, including Storm Financial and Opes Prime, the Parliamentary Joint

Committee on Corporations and Financial Services (PJCCFS) resolved on 25 February 2009 to enquire into, among other things, the role of financial advisers. The committee reported back on 23 November 2009 with a comprehensive report and a list of 11 recommendations (for the full report go to: <www.aph.gov.au/senate/committee/corporations_ctte/fps/report>). The committee did not have judicial authority so no legislation is pending, but the report is indicative of the direction in which the federal government may be heading. The PJCCFS report is considered further below. What immediately follows is a general guide to what you need to do to find a good financial adviser.

Where do you start?

Despite all the publicity and soul searching in the finance industry over the past 15 years, the sad truth is that choosing an investment adviser is a tricky business. You can start by searching the internet or looking in the *Yellow Pages* under 'investment services' and 'financial planning', where you will see the names of insurance companies, fund managers, investment banks, retail banks, stockbrokers, venture capital companies, accountants, superannuation fund advisers and so on. Many of the companies in the listings do not provide the kind of financial advice that you need. Also many of the organisations listed are affiliated with other organisations and you need to be aware of this. You particularly need to be careful when dealing with investment advisers associated with a bank or insurance company. They tend to recommend investing in products offered by that bank or insurance company. Consequently, they are not 'independent' advisers in the true sense of the word.

Other companies that started out as independent advisers have become wholly or partly owned by other financial institutions. They should also be approached with some caution. Still others may have all the right traits and qualifications but turn out to be incompetent in determining your investment needs.

The websites of the Association of Financial Advisers, <www.afa.asn.au>, and the Financial Planning Association of Australia, <www.fpa.asn.au>, contain information and resources useful to help you find the names of financial planners in your area. But then it is your responsibility to determine whether a particular financial planner is likely to give you advice that is appropriate for your financial situation and investment goals and objectives.

The first step for anyone looking for an investment adviser is to talk to your friends and colleagues and see if they have used a financial adviser who they would recommend. Make a shortlist of two or three advisers and talk to each of them before committing yourself.

A difficulty you will find is that many professional advisers are simply not much good at what they do. The problem is not new. A study conducted by *Choice* magazine in October 1998 assessed 100 investment advisers across Australia. Six were rated as very good, 28 were good and 48 'acceptable'. But 18 failed—10 because their advice was inappropriate and eight because their financial planning advice broke the law! This was a slight improvement on the previous time *Choice* surveyed financial planners in 1995—when a quarter were found to be substandard. The 1998 survey also found that the more you had to invest the better the service tended to be. Investors with less than $500 000 to invest received poorer advice than those with over $500 000 to invest. More recently, in September 2005 *Choice* found that finding a good planner was a bit like a lottery. Stockbrokers had significantly lower scores than other types of financial advisers. A whopping 69 per cent of their plans were graded 'borderline', mainly because they tended to over-emphasise investing in shares to the detriment of other considerations. In June 2009 *Choice* wrote that there were 16 000 financial advisers in Australia, and while many were good, consumers should not be expected to play 'Russian roulette' with their life savings.

The Australian Securities & Investments Commission

The Australian Securities & Investments Commission (ASIC) administers the *Corporations Act 2001* as well as various other Acts (for a full list go to <www.asic.gov.au>). It also has a consumer website, <www.fido.gov.au>, which contains information on personal finance and on finding a financial adviser. For example, you can download booklets such as *Getting Advice* and *Your Money* which contain helpful information for individual investors. Alternatively you can ring ASIC on 1300 300 630 and the information will be posted out to you.

ASIC estimates that thousands of Australians lose money through fraudulent and illegal investment schemes each year. Also, one issue of concern is that many financial advisers recommend investments marketed by their shareholders that are mainly financial institutions, such as banks and insurance companies. So the chances of you getting truly 'independent' advice are often slim. In addition, many advisers are paid on a commission basis. These commissions come straight out of investors' capital—and go straight into advisers' pockets. This means that the more financial products that an adviser recommends, the higher the amount of commission he or she is paid. Furthermore, some products involve higher adviser commissions than others, so unscrupulous advisers are likely to recommend investment products that give them the highest commissions—rather than products that best suit your financial needs.

A licence is required

Under the Corporations Law, any person or business that offers you financial products or advises you about them must be one of the following:

- an Australian Financial Services (AFS) licence holder

- a director or employee of an AFS licence holder

- an authorised representative of an AFS licence holder.

'Financial products' include debentures, shares, government bonds and managed funds. But they exclude insurance company products such as annuities, superannuation, life insurance and insurance bonds. Thus, some insurance agents may be licensed to give advice only on insurance products. Always check what products your adviser is legally able to give advice on. You can check whether a particular adviser or business is licensed by searching the ASIC registers at <www.fido.asic.gov.au>.

Authorised representatives

AFS authorised representatives may be individuals or businesses. If an authorised representative is a business, each director or employee of that business who offers or advises you about financial products must hold a separate authorisation to represent the licence holder. Most licences are held in the name of a company. Therefore, most advisers are likely to be 'authorised representatives'. Authorised representatives are not examined by ASIC. They are selected and trained by the licence holder. It's a good idea to ask to see a copy of the licence. If your adviser is an authorised representative, he or she must have a 'proper authority' to act for the licensee. Ask to see the proper authority during your first interview with your adviser.

Investment advisers licensed by ASIC have to meet certain conditions. The main ones are that they must know their clients and understand their financial situation, and they must have good reasons for making specific recommendations. An AFS licence provides you with various legal protections if something goes wrong. If someone you are dealing with does not have a licence, you do not have protection so you should not seek financial advice from them.

The costs

It is essential that you find out how much the advice is going to cost before you deal with any financial adviser. Fortunately, it is now necessary for licensed advisers to disclose fully all fees and commissions received, and you can demand this information. A good adviser will provide it voluntarily.

Basically, you can pay fees to a financial adviser in one of four ways:

- as commission on the investments you make

- as a percentage of the funds you have invested

- as a flat fee based on a fixed hourly rate

- as a combination of the above.

A fundamental problem that arises from charging commissions is that it leads to potential conflicts of interest between your financial adviser and you. For example, if a financial adviser receives commissions from fund managers on the investments you make, the temptation may be too great for the adviser to recommend investments which return him or her high commissions. While an adviser still has to justify the recommendations and disclose commissions, there is certainly a potential conflict of interest.

Consequently, in its submission to the PJCCFS, *Choice* magazine recommended that fees be charged on the basis of a fixed hourly rate in the same way that you pay an accountant or doctor. The Financial Planning Association (FPA) and others responded by saying that if commissions were eliminated, it would make financial advice too expensive for many investors.

The main problem with charging fees on the basis of the funds you have invested is that financial advisers are inclined to devote more time to large investors and smaller investors lose out.

It is important to appreciate that the fees that a financial adviser charges you are not always set in concrete. While many financial advisers have a set policy, it is often possible to negotiate fees with them. Many financial advisers will rebate the commissions they receive if you pay them on an hourly rate basis. Indeed, if you are paying your adviser on an hourly rate basis you should insist that any commissions received from recommending financial products are rebated to you. Whatever approach you take, it is essential that you negotiate fees at the initial meeting.

In past years, the prevalence of undisclosed commissions led to unrealistic expectations about the costs involved in financial planning. First-class professional financial planning will cost you money, just like accounting or medical services.

Historically, most advisers in Australia have charged on a commission basis. This meant that they would charge you for the initial meeting in one of two ways. Most would give you an initial consultation for 'free' in the hope that they would pick up commissions if you accepted their recommendations. For example, when you invest in managed funds, insurance bonds or friendly society bonds there are upfront management fees ranging between 3 and 6 per cent of your initial investment. This fee is paid to the fund manager concerned, who then pays some of it to the investment adviser as a commission. Around 50 per cent of this upfront fee finds its way to your adviser. There are also ongoing or 'trailing' commissions that are paid to the adviser.

Other advisers charge for this initial consultation (usually around $150) and rebate this fee against commissions if you accept their recommendations. Either way, at an initial meeting you should get a good opportunity to see how a financial adviser works, and more importantly, how well he or she understands your needs.

What you should tell your adviser

Competent advisers should devise a financial plan for you. A good financial plan will be specific about its recommendations. It will look at the five main components of financial planning—investment, insurance, retirement, tax and estate planning—and will coordinate strategies for each of these areas.

To assist your adviser in devising a suitable financial plan, you will need to tell him or her about such things as:

• your investment objectives

- any health problems you may have

- what type of risks you are prepared to take with your money

- your present and likely future income

- your age and number of dependents

- your current level of insurance cover and superannuation arrangements.

You will also need to provide:

- a detailed budget of your income and expenses

- an up-to-date list of your assets and liabilities.

You can expect to spend several hours with your adviser on the initial review of your financial position. This means going over your bank statements, tax returns, current investment portfolio, insurance policies and will.

You need to determine long-term and short-term goals, and if your finances are complicated you might have several meetings before your investment plan is drawn up. Then you will meet again, review the portfolio structure, make sure you understand it and confirm that this is what you want to do.

If you do not give a full and frank disclosure of your current financial situation and your investment objectives, it will be extremely difficult for your adviser to help devise a portfolio of investment products to suit your needs. In addition, your financial adviser should be prepared to work with your existing accountant, stockbroker and lawyer, rather than trying to divert your business to his or her colleagues. As investment conditions or tax laws change, your adviser should update the plan. Even without major changes, it should be reviewed at least every six months.

The important thing is that you understand the rationale for all aspects of your financial plan. If this happens your financial adviser is doing the job properly.

What your adviser should tell you

A financial adviser will generally explain advice face to face and then hand over various documents. The documents must include:

- A statement of advice, which explains what the financial adviser is recommending and why he or she thinks it is suitable for you. This need only be a 'record of advice' if no product recommendations are made or if the adviser is not receiving any remuneration for giving you the advice. Also it need only be a record of advice if the amount to which it relates is not substantial.

- Product disclosure statements (PDSs), which describe each product that is recommended by the adviser.

Licensed advisers are required to have an in-house complaints-handling procedure, as well as being members of an approved industry complaints scheme. ASIC has a free booklet titled *You Can Complain*. This is available from ASIC by telephoning 1300 300 630 or from the ASIC consumer website.

Examine the recommendations

If they are worth their salt, advisers will recommend a range of investments across each of the four main investment categories: shares, property, fixed interest and cash. The actual weightings of these in your overall portfolio—whether shares make up 50 per cent or 15 per cent of your total investments—are determined by the level of risk you are prepared to take, not by your adviser's preferences.

It is important when looking at this plan to make sure the adviser justifies why he or she has made each recommendation, and why that recommendation is right for you. Simply saying 'X is a good fund manager' is not an adequate reason for including a particular investment in your portfolio.

It's also important to look at your adviser's research and administrative back up. Some advisers buy in research from independent research organisations, while others have a full team in-house. Ask to see recent reports and in-house research material.

Ongoing support is also critical. Make sure the advisers you are looking at have a formal monitoring service and institute regular portfolio reviews. This can help distinguish real long-term financial planners from salespeople who are simply after upfront commissions.

Pay particular attention to the control procedures used to ensure that advice is always consistent and of a high standard. A clear, comprehensive and objective research process is needed, one which can be clearly explained to clients.

All portfolios should be centrally checked to ensure compliance, and the systems for handling client monies should be clear and open to scrutiny. Regular, ongoing training of advisers is a must and proper professional indemnity insurance should be in place.

Is the adviser independent?

An adviser must make any ownership links or other possible conflicts of interest known to you at your initial meeting. While bank advisers and similar agents may claim to give independent advice, it is usually better to stick with someone who is truly independent. There is also the issue of independence when making recommendations. It must be established whether the organisation runs its own funds and, if so, what percentage is used in client portfolios. If more than 20 per cent of the portfolio is going to one manager, ask why. Determining whether an adviser is independent is not always easy—the name of an investment is not always an adequate guide, as an organisation can manage funds under several different titles.

You may, of course, be happy to have one manager control your funds but you do need to know if this is the case. The virtues of reducing investment risk through using a variety of carefully selected managers are well established. In particular, some investment styles are better suited to certain market conditions than others.

Advisers should also tell you of their fees at the first meeting. One of the problems with the commission system is that it provides an almost irresistible temptation for advisers to recommend high-commission products to boost their own income. Thus, a product might be recommended because it pays the adviser 60 per cent of the upfront fee while a superior product is not recommended because it only pays 25 per cent of its upfront fee to the adviser. This type of problem is particularly relevant to hedge funds, which traditionally have paid advisers higher fees than competing products.

Some managed funds, such as cash management trusts, have no fee, and as such pay no commission to advisers. If your adviser truly has your interests at heart, he or she will try to keep your upfront costs as low as possible while maintaining a good spread of products.

If none of these appeal, there are many reputable fixed fee-based advisers around, and several of the big accounting firms have moved into this area.

Do not make cheques out to the adviser

If you are investing in a managed fund it is advisable to make out a 'not negotiable' cheque to the trustee of the fund, the responsible entity or whoever the prospectus instructs you to make out the cheque to. Do not make it out to your adviser (except for a cheque for the adviser's fee). There have been cases where advisers kept the money for themselves.

Qualifications

Does the adviser hold relevant tertiary or industry qualifications such as a degree in economics or accounting, a Securities Institute diploma or a diploma in financial planning? Ask your adviser whether he or she has studied these or similar courses. Experience can be established, not just by the number of years in the industry, but also by looking at references from clients.

The credentials of the organisation to which the adviser belongs should then be checked. Who owns the company and what is its financial backing? Is the company an active member of industry bodies, and does the firm have a stated code of ethics and a good reputation?

Ongoing service

One significant issue in considering costs is whether you will need ongoing advice. Every financial plan needs fine-tuning from time to time to adjust investment strategies because of changes in legislation, tax, the economic environment and the outlook for particular products. Changes in individual circumstances, such as retirement, reaching age 65 or marrying, also call for adjustments to the plan.

Retaining an adviser by paying a tax-deductible fee for ongoing service ensures you are kept fully informed. Make sure your adviser is part of an organisation committed to continuing to provide quality service.

Matters of opinion

The foregoing are all matters of fact, but matters of opinion are also important. In the final analysis, you must be able to trust your adviser. A positive recommendation from a friend or colleague can be helpful but you must be personally convinced of the adviser's integrity and competence before agreeing to do business. Take time to visit two or three recommended advisers and check them out thoroughly but, having made your decision, stick to it and build up a personal rapport with your adviser. Sticking to one trusted and competent adviser will pay long-term dividends as he or she becomes familiar with your investment aims and objectives. It makes it easier to devise a portfolio of investments which best suit your needs and financial situation.

Questions to ask an adviser

Following are some important questions you should ask an adviser before hiring him or her:

- Do you hold an AFS licence or are you a director, employee or authorised representative of an AFS licence holder?

- What does your licence allow you to advise on?

- What are your specific areas of expertise in the financial services industry?

- What are your fees and/or commissions?

- Do you have any professional qualifications?

- How long have you been an adviser?

- Do you have professional indemnity insurance? What is the name of the insurance company and how much is the insurance for?

- Are you or your firm associated with a fund manager, bank, insurance company or other finance organisation?

- Do you do your own research? If not, whose research do you use?

- Are you a member of the Financial Planning Association of Australia (FPA) and/or any other industry association?

Remember, ultimately it is your money which is at risk, not your adviser's. Do not rely on your adviser to regularly monitor the progress of your investments. You should review all your investments at least every six months to see whether they are still appropriate for your investment needs.

Parliamentary Joint Committee on Corporations and Financial Services

As stated previously, the PJCCFS was asked to report on the issues associated with recent collapses of financial product and service providers. The particular terms of reference of the committee were to look at:

- the role of financial advisers

- the general regulatory environment for those financial products and services which were at the heart of the collapses

- the role played by commission arrangements relating to product sales and advice, including the potential for conflicts of interest, the need for appropriate disclosure and remuneration models for financial advisers

- the role played by marketing and advertising campaigns in the collapses

- the adequacy of licensing arrangements for those who sold the products and services

- the appropriateness of information and advice provided to consumers considering investing in those products and services and how the interests of consumers can be best served

- consumer education and understanding of the financial products and services

- the adequacy of professional indemnity insurance for those concerned and the impact on consumers

- the need for legislative or regulatory change

- the involvement of the banking and finance industries in providing finance to investors who invested through Storm Financial, Opes Prime and similar businesses, and the practice of margin lending associated with these businesses.

See <www.aph.gov.au> for more details.

The committee took submissions from a broad range of sources, including investors (clients of financial advisers), banks and other financiers, individual advisers, advisory groups, product providers, industry bodies, consumer action groups, legal firms, regulatory bodies and government departments. The committee acknowledged that it was not necessarily appropriate to recommend reforms in response to particular events; however, it concluded that over the course of the inquiry it collected sufficiently broad and consistent evidence to justify making the following recommendations:

- that the Corporations Act be amended to include a fiduciary duty for advisers with an AFS licence to place their clients' interests ahead of their own

- that the government ensure that ASIC is adequately resourced to perform risk-based surveillance of the advice provided by AFS licensees and their authorised representatives

- that the Corporations Act be amended to require advisers to more prominently disclose in marketing material the restrictions on advice they are able to provide and potential conflicts of interest

- that the government consult with the industry and support it in developing the most appropriate mechanism by which to stop payments from product manufacturers such as fund managers to financial advisers; that is, to eliminate commissions

- that the government consider the implications of making the cost of financial advice tax deductible

- that ASIC be given extended powers to ban individuals from the financial services industry

- that ASIC require agribusiness MIS (managed investment schemes) licensees to demonstrate they have sufficient working capital to meet current commitments

- that ASIC be allowed to deny or suspend a licence where there is a reasonable belief that the licensee may not comply with their obligations under the licence

- that ASIC commence consultation immediately with the financial services industry on the establishment of an independent, industry-based professional standards board

- that the government investigate the costs and benefits of last-resort compensation funds for investors

- that ASIC provide better education facilities to groups in the community that are likely to be seeking financial advice for the first time.

The committee consisted of Labor, Liberal and National Party parliamentarians, and it is clearly their intention that there be a major shake-up in the financial services industry. However, whether this will happen — and, if so, how and when — is yet to be seen.

Discount funds brokers

So what happens if you wish to be a DIY investor and don't wish to use an adviser and invest directly with managed fund managers or superannuation funds instead? Unfortunately, fund managers won't refund any of the upfront fees. However, you can get most of it back if you invest through a discount funds broker.

Discount funds brokers don't give advice and share their commissions with their clients. They can do this because without the researchers, special equipment, required professional indemnity insurance and time necessary to provide initial and ongoing advice they have few overheads. They attract new clients through word of mouth and advertisements in investment magazines and newspapers.

Once you've decided to invest, you contact a discount funds broker and request prospectuses for the specific investments that interest you. Each prospectus carries the discounter's stamp and comes with a notice-of-investment form to be returned to that discounter. You then send a cheque directly to the manager of the fund of your choice, and notify the discounter of your investment. For your own safety you should never make out a cheque to the broker. In around four to six weeks the discounter will forward your rebate.

The prospectus will tell you how much of your investment will be deducted as an entry fee, and how much of that can be considered commission. An investment with a 6 per cent upfront fee, for example, might charge 1 per cent for management services and allocate 5 per cent to the investment adviser or broker as commission, or brokerage. However, the prospectus will tell you only the maximum possible brokerage. Fund managers do not pay the same commission to every adviser or broker and so it is up to you to enquire about the commission received by your broker or adviser.

Rebates also vary, depending on the discounter, the size of your investment and whether you put a large sum into a single fund. Most discounters have two or more rebate tiers, with an additional 10 to 20 per cent rebate on that part of the investment over a set margin. Margins are based on either annual or cumulative investment totals. In some cases by investing a large amount in a single fund your rebate may be as much as 90 per cent of the commission on that part of the investment over a specified level, usually $50 000.

In recent times the trend has been to rebate 100 per cent of the upfront fee. The discount funds broker then relies on a 'trailing' commission to generate revenue. A trailing commission is where your investment adviser or discount funds broker is paid a commission for every year you maintain your investment in a particular managed fund.

Some discounters will arrange for your rebate to be issued as additional 'units' of the investment instead of cash. Notify the broker in advance if you'd prefer extra units. If the fund manager permits rebate investment, the discounter will place a stamp on the investment application in your prospectus, directing the manager to invest your share of the commission. This allows you to invest a bit of money for 'free', as further fees are not charged for extra units.

Discount funds brokers' services

Discounters offer around 1000 different products from as many as 130 fund managers. The type of investments offered include unlisted property trusts, mortgage trusts, sharemarket trusts (both local and overseas), insurance bonds, debentures, friendly society bonds and hedge funds. Most discounters handle investments from $1000 to $500 000 or more. Discount funds brokers disclaim responsibility for their services, but their selection of products to sell and promote in brochures, advertisements and newsletters could be construed as de facto advice. Whether discount funds brokers are liable to be sued for providing prospectuses for managed funds or superannuation funds that prove to be poor investments has not been tested in the courts.

When should you use a discount funds broker?

It is crucial to understand the limits of discounters' services. Discounters provide only 'a price', without ongoing service, and are probably not liable for investment advice. An adviser, on the other hand, will review your portfolio every three to six months, if this is required, and you may be able to take legal action if the adviser is negligent when giving investment advice.

Some Australian discount funds brokers

The following companies provide discount funds broking services for managed funds and superannuation investments:

* InvestSMART, <www.investsmart.com.au>, telephone 1300 880 160

* CommSec Direct Funds, <www.funds.commsec.com.au>, telephone 13 15 20

* 2020 DIRECTINVEST, <www.2020directinvest.com.au>, telephone (02) 9493 6555 or outside Sydney 1800 352 021.

There are other discount funds brokers in existence but they are usually owned by one of the above three.

Key points

o   There is no rule that says you must seek financial advice. If you are knowledgeable about investment and have the right temperament, you can do it yourself.

o   Before taking advice from any financial adviser, make sure that the adviser holds an appropriate licence. Also, enquire about his or her qualifications and background, and, most importantly, discuss the fee structure. In short, do not be reluctant to ask questions!

o   When you are looking for a financial adviser, shop around and make sure you see a shortlist of at least three before making your final decision.

o   The findings of the Parliamentary Joint Committee on Corporations and Financial Services may cause a significant shake up in the financial services industry.

o   If you are confident about being a DIY investor, discount funds brokers can save you hundreds of dollars in commissions.

6

Trading and researching over the internet

Easy access to investing information and the availability of online trading have made life much more enjoyable and less costly for serious do-it-yourself investors. The internet has brought the trading floor of the sharemarket into the homes of individual investors, so now it is possible to buy and sell shares, options, warrants, interest rate securities and managed funds with the click of your mouse. In addition, you can do your own research on a particular company or fund manager, as well as find out what some stockbrokers are recommending to their clients. More importantly, much of this information is free or available for a reasonable fee.

You can save yourself hundreds—or even thousands—of dollars in commissions and fees per year if you invest via the internet rather than go through a full-service stockbroker or investment adviser. But there are some traps for the unwary. For example, many unsuspecting small investors bought shares in BrisConnections, the builder of Brisbane's Airport Link toll road, when the value of its shares fell to less than 1¢. What most of these investors did not understand was that these shares were 'partly paid' and there were two more instalments of $1 to be paid to the company. As a result, many small shareholders were faced with the prospect of having to pay hundreds of thousands of dollars—and in some cases millions of dollars—to the company when these instalments fell due. This clearly shows that there are traps for the unwary and for the poorly informed if you invest over the net.

There can be other disadvantages to investing via the internet. For a start, trading can become addictive or too accessible. This can result in 'over-trading' as you react to every piece of good or bad news that is released to the market. You may become 'too connected' to short-term swings in the market and lose sight of the bigger and longer term picture.

Another concern is that there is actually too much information available on the internet—much of it contradictory in its advice. Consequently, new investors often suffer from two conditions. The first is 'paralysis of analysis'. Too much information causes investors to seize up and be paralysed into inactivity, waiting for that final piece of information that will tell them definitely that a particular share is worth buying. Unfortunately, this type of information is never available—if it was everyone would be rich.

The second problem with information overload is more important. People have some unique idiosyncrasies when it comes to processing information. The first is related to our confidence in our decision-making ability. Let's assume that you are thinking of investing in News Corporation, and you receive a single piece of information and are asked to rate how confident you feel about any outcome based upon that limited information. Let's say that with one piece of information you are 10 per cent confident of your decision to buy News Corporation shares. If you get another piece of information your confidence may go to 20 per cent. This is reasonable; you have doubled the information you have received so your confidence level doubles. However, if you get a third source of information your confidence level, instead of going to 30 per cent, will suddenly rocket to 90 per cent. Investors seem to become disproportionately more confident with a slight increase in information.

Also, the more information investors get the more they tend to focus on the superfluous and the irrelevant. In fact, it has been found that investors become less accurate the more information they receive. There is overwhelming evidence that you will not get rich listening to the advice of others. Investors need raw information, not recommendations.

Despite these limitations, there is little doubt that the internet has made investing much cheaper and more accessible for small investors. So long as you use it wisely it can be an important tool in developing and implementing your investment strategy. The net has empowered thousands of people to take control of their financial futures. No longer do investment ideas have to come from the golf course, someone at work or your stockbroker.

How to research a company

There are over 2000 companies listed on the ASX. Yet both the media and stockbroker analysts focus most of their attention on the largest 50 to 100 companies. This is hardly surprising as these companies are household names such as Telstra, Woolworths, Harvey Norman and Westpac. Also from a stockbroker's point of view there is more investing in larger companies and therefore the brokers are able to earn more commission.

Because of all this attention, investors are generally well informed about the current financial position and future prospects of the sharemarket's largest and best-known companies. As a result it is unusual to find outstanding bargains among the ASX's biggest companies. The same is not true of the 1500 or so smaller companies listed on the ASX.

But you wouldn't choose a car by merely looking at it, and you shouldn't spend $10 000 buying a company's shares just because you've heard of it. There's no point in trying to take control of your finances if you're going to rely solely on a tip from a newspaper or a broker or an internet chat room. It's true someone may know more about a company than you do but they've probably got as much talent for crystal ball gazing as you have. They could easily be wrong—so you might as well check out what's being said yourself.

You need to be certain that your reasons for investing in a particular company are sound. Does the company have an instantly recognisable name? Do you understand what the company does? Do the products or services stand a good chance of being in high demand in 10, 20 or 30 years' time? Does it have a management team that moves with the times, is innovative, and yet keeps a firm grip on the company's finances? Who is the competition and how serious a threat are they to the future growth of your chosen company?

You can find out a lot of this information from the company's annual report. Make sure you read it with a degree of scepticism, as the annual report is one of the ways a company promotes itself. But it will give you an idea of how the company sees its past successes and future prospects. The important thing to look at in a company annual report is the financial statements: the balance sheet, profit and loss statement and cash flow statement. They are important because they will help you assess whether the company is providing value for money. You're going to be buying shares at a certain price and you will want to make sure you're not paying too much for them. The financial numbers will give you a snapshot of the financial structure, strength and growth rate of the company.

Here's a simple example. Suppose that you and your family spend a considerable amount of money buying computer games and software at Harvey Norman. So you decide to research the company as every time you go to your local Harvey Norman store it is always very busy.

Your first stop should be the ASX website: <www.asx.com.au>. Under 'Company research' you should click on 'Company information'. This will prompt you to either enter the company's ASX code—which for Harvey Norman is HVN—or the company's name or principal activities. This will then give you:

- the share price for HVN for that day

- recent company announcements to the ASX

- a price history chart

- details of the company's address, phone number and internet site (if there is one)

- recent dividends

- whether there are exchange-traded options and warrants over the company's shares.

Harvey Norman's corporate web address is <www.harveynormanholdings. com.au>. Here you can get access to a wide range of information, such as HVN's annual reports, including its balance sheets, profit and loss statements and cash flow statements for the last 10 years. This information can be downloaded so you can digest it at your leisure. In addition, you can read background information about the company's history and main activities.

Other sites

Naturally, the information provided by HVN will attempt to portray the company in a positive light. Depending on how serious you want to be about investing, it could be worthwhile to read or subscribe to an investment newsletter or to a number of sites dedicated to analysing financial information for individual investors.

Sites that you might find useful to visit include:

- <www.irate.vaneyk.com.au>: This site has information and its own ranking system for the largest 300 companies listed on the ASX plus ratings of fund managers. There is often an offer of a free trial period but after that you need to pay to access this information.

- <www.openbriefing.com.au>: This site has transcribed interviews with many listed companies' management covering such issues as their latest profit results and future directions. This site is free.

- <www.egoli.com.au>: The 'News and views' section of this site has commentary on announcements made by companies to the ASX. You can also get access to other research and a monthly research report. This site is free.

- <www.morningstar.com.au>: This is another site with comprehensive data on Australian listed companies. You can view profiles on all companies listed on the ASX. Each profile has up to 10 years of history, data and industry-relevant ratios.

- <www.intelligentinvestor.com.au>: This is the site of the *Intelligent Investor* newsletter and has a considerable amount of free information plus links to other websites in the 'About us' section of the site.

- <www.incomeinvestor.com.au>: This site offers information on both upcoming and historical ex-dividend dates, including dividend amounts and franking.

- <www.fido.asic.gov.au>: This is a site developed by the Australian Securities & Investments Commission (ASIC) which provides general tips on investing, warnings about current investment scams, information about financial services businesses and various tools and other investment resources.

Companies without a website

Not all listed companies have websites. But you can still get the company's address and phone number from the ASX site. Where there is no website you need to ring the company—try asking for the company secretary—and ask to be sent the latest annual and half-yearly reports. Companies generally are keen to encourage people to buy their shares so they normally are cooperative in sending out this material. It is also useful to ask whether they know of any stockbrokers' reports that have been written on the company. Remember that these are likely to be positive about the company—so take them with a handful of salt—but they often give a useful introduction to the company's history and recent financial performance. Try to get the name of someone in the company who is willing to answer some of your questions—either now or in the future. With smaller companies it is often relatively easy to get access to senior management—so long as you do not make a nuisance of yourself.

It can be extremely revealing to visit some of the company's operations—either its factories or offices. Published reports always paint a rosy picture of the company's activities. But if you visit their showroom or offices and they look disorganised or empty of customers you will get a more realistic view of the company's profit potential and efficiency.

Beware of hype and fraud

Beware of hype and even fraud when surfing internet sites. Check all suspicious claims through the company's investor-relations staff or its annual reports. You will undoubtedly come across internet sites and chat rooms that give investment advice or tips for investment. Some of these tips are made by people who are not licensed investment advisers and are not qualified to give advice. The information you find on the internet may be wrong or misleading and some web pages repeat incorrect rumours.

Only deal with Australian licensed advisers and their authorised representatives. You can check if an adviser is licensed—or authorised—by going to ASIC's website, <www.fido.asic.gov.au>, and clicking on the 'Licensed financial services businesses'. This service is free of charge. You can check on a business or adviser by searching ASIC's registers, even if you haven't made contact with them yet, and the site also has a list of people banned from practising as investment advisers.

Overseas websites

Be particularly wary of overseas websites. If an adviser is not from Australia, you may not get protection under Australian law. There are many investing scams operating on the net so it is generally wise to avoid any offers to invest that you see on the internet. You may come across advertisements saying something like, 'Please invest in my company. I've got this great business but I need extra capital to expand'.

Some companies are now publishing their prospectuses electronically on the net. Most investments are required by law to give you an Australian prospectus to examine before you buy. The prospectus must set out all the information that you and your professional advisers would need to make an informed assessment about the investment. You can check if a prospectus is current by looking at the expiry date. This is usually on the first page or on the front cover of the prospectus.

Here are a few examples of investments that must have a prospectus:

- shares

- property trusts

- equity (share) trusts

- cash management trusts

- agricultural investment schemes (for example, pine trees, ostriches, flowers, fish farming)

- film schemes (where you invest in the making of a movie)

- timeshares.

Generally it's illegal to offer investments without a prospectus that has been approved by ASIC. A website advertising an investment should give you details of the prospectus and the date it was lodged with ASIC. It should also tell you how to get a copy.

Trading over the internet

There are numerous Australian stockbrokers that offer online trading facilities. The Infochoice website, at <www.infochoice.com.au>, has a comparison of their fees and the services they offer. This site also compares home loans, bank accounts, margin loans, personal loans and credit cards.

Before you begin trading you must open an account with a broker —this can usually be done online. You must also either open a cash management account with the broker or give permission for an existing bank account to be used to provide funds to buy shares and transfer money into when you sell shares. To open up a cash management account with a broker you will need to provide proof of identification under the '100 point' system, as you would when opening a normal bank account.

Your broker will also want the shares that you buy to be CHESS sponsored with them, so it is easy to sell your shares through them. CHESS is short for Clearing House Electronic Sub-register System and allows the electronic transfer and settlement of securities bought and sold on the ASX. The benefits of electronic transfer and settlement include faster processing time and reduced risk of incomplete or incorrect settlements. CHESS has also assisted in the development of T+3 settlement, under which the settlement of share transactions occurs on the third business day after the day of the transaction. With CHESS you do not receive share certificates. Instead, you receive a statement similar to a bank statement.

You do not have to use the same broker for buying and selling. However, if you buy through one broker you need to arrange for the shares to be transferred to your selling broker via the CHESS system before you can place a sell order.

Your online broker will give you a brochure explaining how trading is done through their system. Read this carefully and seek clarification of any issues before you begin trading—any mistakes you make could be costly. Generally speaking, most online trading systems will ask you for the following information:

- Are you buying or selling?

- What is the ASX code for the company? For example, the Woolworths code is WOW. If you are unsure of the code you can usually find this out from another section of the broker's website or via the ASX website: <www.asx.com.au>.

- Are you buying or selling 'at market' or at a price limit? When buying, 'at market' means you are prepared to accept the current lowest price being offered by sellers. When selling, it means you are prepared to accept the highest price being offered by buyers. For example, suppose the last sale price for a company's shares is $5.20 and there are sellers at $5.25 and the highest bid from buyers is $5.15. If you buy the shares 'at market' you are instructing your broker to buy at $5.25. If you are selling 'at market' you are instructing your broker to sell at $5.15. Be aware that there is a time lag between when you place the order and when it is carried out. In the above example, the sellers at $5.25 might be bought out before your order enters the market and the next lowest seller might be at $5.30. If this occurs, your 'at market' order would be executed at $5.30. In contrast, a price limit means that you want to buy at a particular price—for example, $5.20—or you want to sell at a particular price—for example, $5.40. Note that you cannot enter an 'at market' order outside ASX trading hours.

  Most brokers have a 'market depth' facility that allows you to see the number of buyers and sellers and the prices they are bidding and offering for these shares. You can use this to determine what price you should be bidding or offering. For example, if there are numerous buyers at $5.20 and some sellers at $5.25, you might put in a bid at $5.22.

- How long do you want the order to be active? Usually you can choose from one day to several weeks. If your order is not completed during your specified time period it will be cancelled and you would need to place the same order again to reactivate it. Normally you are not charged for orders where no shares are actually bought or sold. However, you will be charged brokerage for partly completed orders.

If you are selling shares that are CHESS sponsored with this broker there is no further paperwork. If the shares are issuer-sponsored by the company you need to supply the security reference number for these shares. It is common to be charged an extra fee for selling issuer-sponsored shares.

Once you have completed this information you will be asked to review and confirm your order and give your trading password. Make sure you check this information carefully, as mistakes can be costly. For example, if you wanted to buy 1000 shares but typed in 10000 then your broker will buy 10000 shares (as long as there is enough money in your account to pay for them). When a broker offers 'straight-through processing' this means trades are fully automated — you're trading directly into the market yourself. Once you submit a buy or sell order, that's it, it can't be cancelled and the trade will be automatically executed. Manual processing sees trades go to a person in a broker's office first before being submitted to the market.

You can later check whether your order has been executed by looking up your 'order history' or 'outstanding orders' or something similar on your account. You will also usually receive an email to confirm that your order has been executed.

Costs of internet trading

Some online brokers offer significant discounts for frequent traders, and others have a monthly fee whether you trade or not. Others will give you a discount on brokerage if you use one of the broker's cash management accounts rather than effect settlements through an external bank account. Before opening an account, check what you get for your money and whether it suits your likely trading pattern. You can also buy and sell options and warrants online — but make sure you are clear about the costs involved. Some online brokers offer margin trading — again, do some comparison shopping before signing on. When comparing fees among brokers, you need to consider the likely size (dollar value) of your trades. Fee scales can vary considerably, so a broker who is cheap for smaller trades may not be at higher levels.

Before you sign up, check the account opening requirements of the brokers. These may involve initial deposits of up to $5000. Check whether you can monitor your balance in this account online and if you can withdraw money from this account. You also should investigate whether interest will be paid on the balance in your account. While some online brokers pay you a competitive interest rate, others do not.

Other services

Apart from online trading, brokers generally offer a range of other services such as research (you need to check what organisation provides it), watchlists, charting tools and company announcements to the ASX. The quality of these services varies from broker to broker so make sure these other services suit your needs. In particular there is no point paying for a service that you do not use. Another issue that can be important is: how timely is the broker's price data? 'Real time' market price data offered via a website is not always instant—it can be delayed by minutes. Even when it is not delayed, you often have to refresh the page in your browser to see the latest prices. If you really want to be sure you are seeing up-to-the-second prices, get 'dynamic' data, which updates on the page before your eyes without you having to refresh the page. This is usually a more expensive option.

Low-cost access to managed funds

Just as online brokers have made buying shares more accessible and attractive with lower brokerage fees, there are also a number of companies allowing discounted entry into managed funds (as discussed in chapter 5). You pay entry fees of up to 6 per cent when investing in managed funds via a financial planner, but discount brokers often cut that fee to zero by rebating this upfront fee, or allowing you to purchase extra units in the fund with it. These organisations make money because they are paid a 'trailing' fee by the fund manager on your investment.

As with online sharebrokers, these discount brokers do not give you advice on whether the specific managed fund is suitable as part of your financial plan. But they do give you tools, information and research to make your own decision.

Discount brokers

The following organisations offer discounted entry into managed funds over the internet:

- Commsec Direct Funds, <www.commsec.com.au>, has online research tools to compare and research funds, track fund performance and find a fund that matches your investor profile.

- E*Trade, <www.etrade.com.au>, gives you access to a comprehensive selection of over 500 retail and wholesale managed funds. There are also tools to help you select the right one for you.

- InvestSMART, <www.investsmart.com.au>, rebates 100 per cent of entry fees and contribution fees on over 4000 managed funds.

Not all managed funds are available through each of these sites. As with online stockbrokers these sites have a variety of research and other tools that will help you evaluate whether a particular managed fund is right for you. If you are confident about investing in managed funds yourself, it is well worth the effort to spend some time examining the above websites to see which one you find to be the most user-friendly.

Key points

- Trading in shares and managed funds over the internet can save you thousands of dollars per year in fees and commissions, but you need to take care as mistakes—such as the case of people who bought shares in BrisConnections —can be costly.

- Today there is often too much information—that is why it is essential for you to develop a system to help separate information that is useful and relevant from that which is not.

- Identify two or three websites that you feel are reliable and visit them at least once a week, or more regularly if you can.

- Doing your own research into both shares and managed funds these days is much easier, quicker and cheaper because of the internet.

- Do not believe all you read on the net—there are many scams. Certainly do not reply to any unsolicited emails that you receive inviting you to invest or buy shares.

- o   Be particularly wary of overseas websites.

- o   Many stockbrokers have their reports and recommendations
   on buying and selling for specific listed companies available
   free from their websites. You can also receive newsletters from
   these firms. Remember that you might be a better analyst of the
   company's future prospects than the people who write these
   reports.

Tax considerations

7

The global financial crisis had an effect on most areas of the financial world, and this includes the Australian Taxation Office. Greater numbers of people could not pay their tax liabilities or were late in submitting tax returns. Some people who had their income garnisheed by the Tax Office found it difficult to make repayments while others went bankrupt or risked doing so. Many Australians lost their jobs, or took on second jobs in order to pay the bills. Still other people found that their investment funds had been frozen, which was particularly worrying for self-funded retirees.

The general approach of the Tax Office these days is much more conciliatory. It is willing to discuss problems with people who are finding it difficult to meet their tax obligations. Indeed, the Tax Office would much rather that people approach them first with their tax problems than that they ignore the difficulties in which they find themselves. The Tax Office is not the 'bogey man' that it is often made out to be.

Taxation is the largest expense for most investors, so it is sensible to investigate strategies that will legally reduce the amount of tax you have to pay. This is easier said than done, as tax laws are complicated. For a start, there are three volumes of the Income Tax Act. In addition, there are Tax Rulings which are issued virtually daily and seem to be the way the Tax Commissioner administers the Act. Moreover, tax experts frequently disagree on the content and interpretation of these rulings.

So why even attempt to be at all knowledgeable about tax? There are several reasons. Firstly, there are certain basic rules you need to know in order to minimise your income tax liability. Secondly, even if you engage a tax agent, accountant or financial planner to advise you on taxation matters, he or she may miss something. Always remember that you sign and are liable for your own tax return, not the person who prepared it. Finally, you can better understand tax issues raised in the media if you have a working knowledge of basic tax laws.

Taxation is a burden

A large number of investments are taxed at your highest marginal rate of income tax. This means that if your marginal rate is 46.5 per cent nearly half of your investment income goes in tax. If you have an investment earning 6 per cent and you pay tax at 46.5 per cent, you are earning 3.21 per cent after tax. If inflation is running at around 3 per cent, you are earning a real rate of return of 0.21 per cent. Clearly, this is not the way to accumulate wealth over the long term.

A brief overview of the tax system

A comprehensive coverage of taxation is beyond the scope of this book. What follows covers some important aspects of the system.

In Australia the financial year is from 1 July to 30 June. You pay tax on your 'taxable income', which is your 'assessable income' minus 'allowable deductions'. Assessable income covers such things as: salary, wages, commissions, professional fees, dividends, rent, distributions from managed funds, interest, your share of any partnership income and certain capital profits (see below).

You do not have to physically receive income for it to be liable for tax. Interest credited to your savings account is assessable. So are dividends received under dividend reinvestment schemes (whereby you can elect to have a company dividend reinvested in its shares rather than paid to you in cash).

You commence paying tax when your taxable income exceeds the tax-free threshold. For a resident of Australia, the tax-free threshold for 2009–10 is $6000. However, because there is a low-income tax offset of up to $1500 (from 1 July 2010), tax is not payable by an individual until he or she earns $16 000 per annum.

Personal income tax rates

Table 7.1 shows tax rates for all levels of income for Australian-resident taxpayers for 2009–10.

Table 7.1: personal income tax rates 2009–10 resident individuals (excluding the Medicare levy)*

Up to $6 000	Nil
$6 001 to $35 000	Tax is 15% of the part over $6 000
$35 001 to $80 000	$4 350 + 30% of the part over $35 000
$80 001 to $180 000	$17 850 + 38% of the part over $80 000
$180 001 and over	$55 850 + 45% of the part over $180 000

* Does not take into account the low-income tax offset, family tax benefit or child-care tax benefit.

Deductions

The Tax Act states that all losses and outgoings (that is, expenses) incurred in gaining or producing assessable income are allowable tax deductions. On this basis there are many items of expenditure which qualify as tax deductions; from travel between two places of work (but not between home and work except in unusual circumstances) to the interest payable on a loan taken out to buy an investment property. Some deductions can be claimed in total immediately while others are allocated over the life of the investment, or five years in some cases. You cannot deduct expenses or losses if they are of a private or domestic nature. This is why the cost of travel between home and work is not usually an allowable tax deduction.

There are certain items of expenditure which have nothing to do with gaining or producing assessable income, but which are specified as allowable deductions. For example, donations of $2 or more to registered charities are allowable tax deductions.

The monetary value of a tax deduction depends on which income tax bracket you are in. If you are paying the top marginal rate of tax of 46.5 per cent (including the Medicare levy), every $100 in extra tax deductions saves $46.50 on your tax bill. Net capital gains (capital gains less capital losses) are added to your taxable income. Net capital losses cannot be deducted from your income. However, they can be carried forward and deducted from future capital gains.

Tax offsets

Deductions refer to amounts that can be subtracted from your income before income tax is calculated. Tax offsets, formerly called tax rebates, directly reduce the amount of tax payable by you and hence are worth more than tax deductions. Subject to certain limitations, tax offsets may apply for the cost of spouse or child-housekeepers, housekeepers, senior Australians, mature-age workers, parents or parents-in-law, invalid relatives

16 years or over, students of any age under 25, non-students under 16, sole parents and entrepreneurs who earn less than $50000.

There is also a low-income tax offset and a medical expenses tax offset. From 1 July 2010 the low-income tax offset is up to $1500 and it is payable in full on a taxable income of $30000 or less. For a taxable income over $30000 a proportion is paid based on the amount by which your taxable income exceeds $30000. At a taxable income of $67500 the low-income tax offset is nil.

The medical expenses tax offset enables you to obtain a tax offset of 20 per cent of eligible medical expenses in excess of $1500. The definition of medical expenses includes payments to a legally qualified medical practitioner, nurse, chemist or optician, or to a public or private hospital or to an approved nursing home, or dentist, in respect of an illness or operation pertaining to you or any of your dependants. Expenditure that does not qualify includes payments to chiropractors and naturopaths or for travel or accommodation incurred in order to obtain medical treatment. Also you cannot claim for such things as over-the-counter–type pain killers often sold in supermarkets, even if they are sold in a chemist. Where payments are subject to a Medicare or private health fund rebate, you have to reduce the figure for medical expenses by that amount before you apply the 20 per cent tax offset.

Medicare and your private health fund (if any) will happily send you a tax statement after the end of the financial year which shows the net amount you have paid for medical expenses claimed through them. Likewise, your chemist will prepare a statement for you showing how much you have paid for prescriptions during the year. For this reason it is a good idea to use one chemist for your prescription purchases.

Tax offset for private health insurance

A tax offset of 30 per cent of the premium paid to a registered health fund for appropriate private health insurance cover is allowed. Your level of income does not affect the tax offset. The tax offset can be claimed in one of four ways:

- as a reduction in your private health insurance premium

- as a cash or cheque rebate from Medicare

- as a refundable tax offset through your tax return

- as a combination of the above.

If you obtain a full rebate from your health fund or Medicare, you cannot claim a tax offset in your tax return.

Medicare levy surcharge

The usual Medicare levy is 1.5 per cent. A Medicare levy surcharge of one percentage point applies to single people with no or one dependent child and a taxable income of more than $70000, and couples with no or one dependent child with combined taxable incomes of more than $140000, if they do not have hospital cover through private health insurance. The thresholds increase by $1500 for each dependent child after the first. Also, the thresholds are indexed to the Consumer Price Index and increase in $1000 amounts.

Is it better to pay the Medicare surcharge or take out private patient hospital cover? The Medicare surcharge applies to individuals earning more than $70000 per annum and families earning more than $140000 who do not have hospital cover. There is no phasing in of the surcharge; once your taxable income reaches the threshold the surcharge is applied to all your taxable income. So a single person earning $70000 pays $1050 (assuming a levy of 1.5 per cent), but if you earn $70001 you pay $1750.03 (2.5 per cent of $70001).

A similar situation applies where family income increases from $140000 to $140001. You also need to keep in mind that you only need to take out hospital cover—not hospital and ancillary cover—to avoid the levy, and also that you are entitled to the 30 per cent rebate for private health insurance.

The cost of hospital insurance varies between different funds and states, but it is around $1950 per year for a family and $975 for an individual. After the 30 per cent rebate is taken into account the costs are about $1476 and $738 respectively. So for an individual the cut-off point where it becomes cheaper to take out private patient hospital insurance than to pay the surcharge is $73800. At a taxable income of $73800 you would be paying a surcharge of $738—the same as hospital insurance. For a family the break-even point is $147600. These break-even points are not greatly higher than the threshold limits set by the government. Note that one view is that you get better health care through the private system so taking out private health insurance may well be worthwhile.

Refunds of tax offsets

Subject to the exceptions outlined below, it is important to note that in general tax offsets cannot exceed the tax otherwise payable. That is, you cannot get a refund greater than the amount of your tax liability. For example, suppose your tax bill was $1000 and you had tax offsets of $1200. You would not be liable to pay any tax, but you do not get a $200 refund from the Tax Commissioner. Nor can excess tax offsets be carried forward to offset tax payable in future years. Exceptions to the above include:

- the 30 per cent private health insurance rebate where any excess is refunded

- the franking tax offset where any excess is refunded (see below).

Capital gains tax

Capital gains tax (CGT) took effect from 20 September 1985. Subject to some important exceptions, the basic rule is that if you derive a capital gain from a 'CGT event' you are liable to pay tax on it at your marginal rate of tax. The most common CGT events occur if you sell assets such as shares, property, units in a managed trust and collectables. In general terms you are deemed to have made a capital gain if the proceeds from the sale of an asset exceed its 'cost base'. Any gain made on the sale of your principal place of residence—your home—is exempt from CGT, as is any gain on the sale of assets acquired prior to 20 September 1985. There are also other exemptions listed in the Tax Pack Supplement.

Before 1 October 1999, provided a CGT asset was held for at least 12 months its cost base was adjusted for inflation. For example, if the CPI was 100 when an asset was purchased and 110 when it was sold, the cost of the asset would be adjusted upwards by 10 per cent [(110 − 100) ÷ 100]. This had the effect of theoretically reducing the profit on disposal and hence CGT.

New rules came in from 1 October 1999. Assets sold after this date and held for at least 12 months could be assessed for CGT using the old method with indexation frozen at 30 September 1999 or, alternatively, a 50 per cent CGT discount could be applied. For example, if there was a capital gain of $1000 and the asset had been held for at least 12 months, the gain for CGT purposes could be deemed to be $500 ($1000 × 50%). This amount was then taxed at the taxpayer's marginal rate of income tax. Alternatively, your 'real' or inflation-adjusted profit might have been $700 and you could elect to be taxed on this amount. It is quite in order for you to choose the method that yields the lowest tax—in this situation it was the '50 per cent discount' method. Assets purchased after 30 September 1999 can only be assessed for CGT using the discount method.

Where a CGT asset is held for less than 12 months, CGT is payable on the whole of the capital gain at your marginal rate of income tax.

Excess imputation credits

Dividend imputation is explained later in this chapter. Basically it ensures that shareholders are not taxed twice, initially when a company earns profits, and later when shareholders receive a dividend. Shareholders are entitled to a refund of excess imputation credits. For example, suppose a resident individual with a 15 per cent marginal tax rate receives a dividend of $700 with $300 worth of imputation credits attached. Assuming the total income tax payable is $150, the taxpayer is entitled to a cash refund of $150, equal to the difference between the company tax paid and the individual's income tax liability ($300 – $150).

Life insurance

Any amount received as a bonus on a life insurance policy, other than a reversionary bonus, is assessable income. A reversionary bonus is one where the entitlement to the bonus only accrues upon maturity, forfeiture or surrender of the policy. A reversionary bonus is added to the value of a policy and is payable at maturity of the policy or on the death of the life assured, or it may be cashed in under certain circumstances. A reversionary bonus received under a short-term life insurance policy is assessable income. A reversionary bonus is assessable in full if it is received within the first eight years of the commencement of a policy. If the bonus is received in the ninth year, two-thirds of the bonus is assessable, and if it is received in the 10th year, one-third of the bonus is assessable. If received after the 10th year, the bonus is tax-free.

Insurance companies and friendly societies rely on the above pro-visions when marketing investment bonds to the public. An investor pays a yearly premium, which the relevant organisation invests. Investment earnings are credited each year and fees are taken out. The organisation pays tax at a rate of 30 per cent per annum. After 10 years an investor receives the proceeds from investing in the bond tax-free. Because the insurance company or friendly society has paid tax on the earnings of the bonds, they are more correctly referred to as 'tax-paid' rather than 'tax-free' investments. During the currency of the bond, the investor's life is insured for the amount specified in the policy. The investment returns from these bonds are not particularly high and you can usually do better investing yourself. However, they are good for saving for a particular purpose such as a child's education, and meanwhile you have life insurance cover for the amount in the policy.

Dividend imputation

Dividend imputation was introduced on 1 July 1987 to overcome the effect of the double taxing of dividends. Before that time dividends were taxed twice. Firstly, when a company earned the profits out of which the dividends were paid. Secondly, in the hands of shareholders. Dividends may now be 'unfranked', 'fully franked' or 'partly franked'. Dividends are included in your assessable income in the same way as other income.

Unfranked dividends are paid out of profits on which no tax has been paid. A franked dividend means that the company has already paid some tax on your behalf. The amount of franking depends on the company tax rate and whether the company paid the full company rate. The company gives this information to you when you receive a dividend payment. The credit balance of a company's franking account reflects the amount of company profits that are able to be distributed as franked dividends. In turn, shareholders are given a credit or rebate for the amount of tax paid on these profits. This is referred to as an 'imputation credit'.

How dividend imputation works

In general terms, your imputation credits are determined by the size of the dividend and the company tax rate. For example, if the dividend is $100 and the company tax rate is 30 per cent, the imputation credit would be:

$$30 \div 70 \times 100 = \$42.86$$

You then add back the imputation credit, sometimes referred to as 'grossing up', giving you a taxable income from the dividend of $142.86. Essentially, the company had to earn profits of $142.86, and pay tax at a rate of 30 per cent, in order to pay you a fully franked dividend of $100.

Next you calculate the amount of tax payable at your marginal rate of tax. Finally, you subtract the amount of the imputation credit from this figure. Assuming your marginal rate of tax is 46.5 per cent and your taxable income from the dividend is $142.86, your tax on the dividend is $66.43.

Your tax payable is: $66.43 – $42.86 (imputation credit) = $23.57.

So, if you are on the top marginal rate of 46.5 per cent you will still have to pay some tax on franked dividends. This is because the company tax rate of 30 per cent is below 46.5 per cent and you will have to pay tax on the difference. That is why franked dividends are only tax-free in the hands of some shareholders; some still have to pay some tax. Also dividends may be partially franked, rather than fully franked.

Tax file numbers

All individuals and companies need a tax file number (TFN) before they can lodge an income tax return. TFNs are obtained by making an application to the Tax Office. In the case of a company a copy of the Certificate of Incorporation will need to be sent. There is nothing complicated about this procedure, but it must be done. In the case of individuals, tax may be deducted on some investment income at the top rate of 46.5 per cent if you do not provide your TFN — or claim an exemption from providing a TFN — to the institution where your money is invested. If you are not in the 46.5 per cent tax bracket you will get some of this tax back when you submit your income tax return.

Negative gearing

Negative gearing is most commonly used with investment property (see chapter 20), but as you will see it can be used with any asset that has the potential to appreciate in value.

Like dividend imputation, negative gearing is a term that is confusing to many investors. Also, like dividend imputation, the basic concept of negative gearing is straightforward. All it really means is that you have borrowed money to buy an asset and that the income generated is less than your interest payments and other outgoings. In other words, you are making a running loss on your investment.

The reason why a sensible investor would do this is tied up in the tax system. Under the current tax rules, any loss made through negative gearing is a tax deduction and can be offset against any other income you receive. Therefore, if you are on the 46.5 per cent tax rate, the government subsidises nearly half your loss.

However, you are still making a loss, so how does it make sense to negatively gear? The answer is that you are getting the use of someone else's money at a rate subsidised by the government and that you get the total capital gain if the asset rises in value (minus any capital gains tax of course).

The dangers of negative gearing

The main risks with negative gearing are:

* the value of the asset drops

* interest rates on the loan may go up

- cash flow may dry up so that you have trouble making up the difference between the interest payments and the net income received.

If any of these things occur, they have little impact on an investor who has not borrowed to buy the asset. On the other hand, investors who have borrowed to buy the asset could find themselves in financial difficulties if asset prices do not go up as much as expected. This was a disastrous problem for many investors who had negatively geared share portfolios during the GFC when sharemarkets fell by 40 per cent.

Another point to remember is that although you get a tax deduction on a loss arising from negative gearing, you have to pay out money before you get the benefit of the tax loss. Thus, you need to have ample cash flow from other sources to ensure you do not get caught with a short-term liquidity problem.

Negative gearing and shares

Although most investors associate negative gearing with property it can, as noted, be applied to any asset. Indeed, combining dividend imputation with negative gearing gives the possibility for some excellent returns.

Under the present tax laws, interest on money borrowed to invest in shares or equity and property trusts is tax deductible. Moreover, if you invest in shares paying fully franked dividends, some of the income you receive is tax-free. The end result is that you generate a tax loss on your sharemarket investments which can be used to reduce tax on income from other sources.

However, the GFC emphasised the dangers of negative gearing to buy shares. During the GFC many companies either reduced their dividends or decided not to pay any dividends. In addition, their share prices fell dramatically. This proved to be a major financial headache for many investors when they had to renegotiate their loan as the value of their share portfolio was around 40 per cent less than when they first took out the loan. This even applies to a portfolio of 'blue-chip' shares, as was shown by the substantial falls in share prices across the board during the GFC.

Negative gearing and other investments

The situation regarding the negative gearing of investments other than property, shares and managed funds is somewhat of a grey area, and it is strongly advised that you get a professional tax opinion before investing. For example, in the case of insurance bonds and friendly society bonds, the Tax Office has argued that the cost of borrowed funds used to finance these capital growth investments is not tax deductible.

The main winners from negative gearing

The main beneficiaries of negative gearing are investors who have a solid and reliable cash flow from other sources to make up the yearly shortfall between the income received from the investment and the cost of servicing the loan. Negative gearing also gives more benefits to people on high marginal tax rates. Table 7.2 clearly demonstrates that investors on low marginal rates of tax have to personally finance a greater portion of a negatively geared investment.

The main reason for this is that people on lower marginal rates get a smaller benefit from negative gearing's tax deduction. It is only when you are in the top tax bracket, and remain in this bracket after your negative gearing deductions, that what you get as a tax deduction (45 per cent) approaches your own contribution (55 per cent). But remember, you still have to pay out before getting the benefit of a tax deduction.

So you really need to be able to fund the entire shortfall from negatively gearing an investment if you are to remain in control of the situation.

Table 7.2: negative gearing benefits (not including Medicare levy)

Gross income ($)	Tax funded (%)	Investor funded (%)
20 000	15	85
40 000	30	70
90 000	38	62
185 000	45	55

Property trusts

Listed and unlisted property trusts are considered in chapter 21. If you decide to invest in a property trust, some of the income you earn may be tax-deferred. This means that in the initial years you will not be required to pay tax on part of your income from the trust. The problem is that eventually you will have to pay tax on it; you just do not have to at the beginning. The prospectus of a property trust must clearly outline the circumstances and the extent to which tax is deferred, and you should read it carefully. However, because of the time value of money, it is preferable to pay tax later rather than sooner, so tax-deferred income is a benefit to you.

Foreign income

A resident of Australia is generally liable to pay tax on all sources of income whether earned in or out of Australia, although there are exemptions. For many years the federal government has recognised that an unfair situation arises where a resident Australian individual or company earns money in a foreign country and is taxed on the income in both the foreign country and Australia. Consequently, there are Double Tax Agreements in place with over 40 countries, including all of Australia's major trading partners. Potentially you could receive foreign income from a variety of sources so your situation may become complicated. For further information read the Tax Pack and Tax Pack Supplement, contact the Tax Office (<www.ato. gov.au> or telephone 13 28 61) or find a good adviser. You can start by contacting the Tax Agents' Board (<www.tabd.gov.au> or telephone 1300 362 829).

Investing overseas

Australians are increasingly investing more money overseas, as by investing overseas you are diversifying out of the Australian economy. Early in 1993 the federal government introduced the Foreign Investment Funds (FIF) legislation. This legislation introduced a tax on the increase in value of investments in overseas-based trusts and some overseas companies as well. The legislation applies to both individuals and companies.

You may be taxed under FIF legislation on several bases. For example, if you invest in a unit trust managed in Australia which 'feeds' its money into an overseas-based unit trust you will be taxed under FIF legislation. For other situations, contact the Tax Office and ask for a copy of the *Foreign Investment Funds Guide 2008–09*.

Ownership of investments

You are subject to CGT on most capital assets that you own bought after 20 September 1985. Important exclusions to this are your home and car. It is essential that you keep good records for CGT purposes because the Tax Office requires that all information relating to the purchase, term and sale of a capital asset be kept for the life of the investment.

Companies listed on the ASX now issue holding statements, not share certificates. These should be kept in a safe place because they are generally your only proof of ownership. Also it is essential that you not reveal the holder identification number (HIN) or security reference number (SRN) of your shareholdings to other people.

Income splitting

As a taxpayer there is scope for reducing your liability to pay income tax through diverting some of your income to your spouse or children. The strategy applies to either husband or wife, depending on who the main breadwinner is.

In the case of you and your spouse, let's assume that your taxable income is $91 000, including $10 000 of interest income, and your spouse's income is $10 000. Your marginal rate of tax is 39.5 per cent including the Medicare levy. Your spouse's marginal rate of tax is 16.5 per cent including the Medicare levy.

Now say that you can divert the $10 000 of interest income to your spouse by putting the investment in his or her name. This will reduce your tax bill by $3950 ($10 000 × 0.395). But it will only increase your spouse's tax bill by $1650 ($10 000 × 0.165). The net result is a reduction in tax of $2300. This is perfectly legal.

It is also possible to divert income to children under the age of 18 years (minors), but once the income of a child exceeds $416 not including the low-income tax offset it may become liable to tax at penalty rates, of 66 per cent up to $1307 and 45 per cent on the excess, depending on where the income has come from. If it is the result of a straight diversion of income it will certainly be subject to penalty tax. For other situations you should consult your accountant or tax adviser.

An important question you should always ask before investing is: in whose name should this investment be held? Resolving this issue before you invest can save you and your family thousands of dollars in tax. Remember, if you decide to transfer investments to another family member at a later date this could result in a capital gains tax liability, the reason being that the transfer will involve selling the investment by one family member and the other family member buying this investment.

Never invest solely to reduce your tax

In some cases you may make a decision to invest, at relatively short notice, in an area that has tax advantages. For example, as the end of a tax year approaches, numerous schemes are marketed that have tax minimisation as their purpose. In recent years the Tax Office has applied stringent criteria in deciding whether to approve these schemes. As part of this process the Tax Office has issued product rulings that specify the extent to which a scheme qualifies as a tax deduction. You should not invest in one of these schemes unless there is a product ruling available. Similarly, you should not invest if the promoter of the investment claims that a tax ruling is 'pending'. Just as importantly, you should never make an investment solely to reduce your tax. An investment must also stand up to commercial scrutiny.

Investing in Australian films

Under the Film Licensed Investment Company Act, a tax deduction used to be allowed for amounts paid to subscribe for shares in a film licensed investment company (FLIC) during the period the FLIC was licensed to raise share capital that will qualify for the deduction. The deduction was allowed in the income year in which the shares were issued. This Act ceased to have effect from 1 July 2007, and consequently the principal tax incentives for investments in Australian films and telemovies are contained in sections of the Tax Act. There are currently three tax offsets available:

- a location tax offset

- a producer tax offset

- a post, digital and visual effects tax offset.

All offsets are refundable. The location offset is 15 per cent of a company's production expenditure on a film to the extent to which it is incurred or attributable to goods and services provided in Australia, the use of land in Australia or the use of goods located in Australia at the time they are used in the making of the film.

The producer tax offset is 40 per cent of qualifying expenditure (with the same meaning as for location tax offset) if it is a feature film and 20 per cent if it is not a feature film. To be eligible a film has to have significant Australian content, or be made under government arrangement with a foreign country or authority, and be a feature film, a single episode program, a series, a season of a series or a short-form animated drama. A documentary may qualify as a feature film.

The post, digital and visual effects (PDV) tax offset is 15 per cent of qualifying expenditure incurred in relation to PDV production for a film. It does not matter where the film is shot but there must be at least $5 million of qualifying expenditure on PDV. PDV production is defined as the creation of audio or visual elements, the manipulation of audio or visual elements or activities that are necessarily related to these activities.

Investment advice

The Tax Office has issued a ruling on the extent to which investment advice is an allowable tax deduction. An initial consultation with a financial adviser, making initial investments and restructuring a portfolio are all items of a capital nature and therefore are not allowable tax deductions. However, at the end of 2009, the Parliamentary Joint Committee on Financial Products and Services recommended that the federal government examine this further.

Ongoing management fees or retainers, as well as fees paid in connection with changing your mix of investments, are allowable deductions in limited circumstances. With regard to the mix of investments, the Tax Office will only allow a deduction where the fee paid is part of day-to-day management of investments in accordance with an investment strategy. On this basis, a subscription to an investment newsletter may be an allowable deduction, but you should get a formal ruling from the Tax Office before embarking on this course of action, especially if you are considering subscribing to several newsletters.

Australia's Future Tax System Review

The Australia's Future Tax System Review (AFTSR) Panel was established in 2008 to examine Australian and state government taxes. The panel submitted its final report to the federal government at the end of 2009, and the government has said it is reviewing the report and that it will make it public in 2010. At the same time it will publish its initial response. The AFTSR's terms of reference were far ranging and included:

- to review revenue raising through taxation to ensure that it is done so as to do least harm to economic efficiency, provide equity (horizontal, vertical and inter-generational) and minimise complexity for taxpayers and the community

- to create a tax structure that will position Australia to deal with the demographic, social, economic and environmental challenges of the 21st century and enhance Australia's economic and social outcomes

- to enhance overall economic, social and environmental wellbeing, with a particular focus on ensuring there are appropriate incentives for:

  - workforce participation and skill formation

  - individuals to save and provide for their future, including access to affordable housing

  - investment and the promotion of efficient resource allocation to enhance productivity and international competitiveness

  - reducing tax system complexity and compliance costs.

The AFTSR reflects government policy not to change the GST and to preserve tax-free superannuation payments for the over 60s and announced personal income tax goals. It is intended that the AFTSR report form the basis of government taxation policy for the next 25 years. For further information go to <www.taxreview.treasury.gov.au>, or telephone the Australia's Future Tax System information line on 1800 614 133.

Key points

o The impact of the GFC was widespread and many people had difficulty paying their tax bills. It is wise to discuss your problems upfront with the Tax Office if you are having difficulties meeting your tax obligations.

o Taxation is complicated and the average person can never hope to be an expert. It is therefore imperative that you have good advice, especially if your tax return is not straightforward.

o Often the Tax Office will give you advice over the telephone or make a formal ruling in writing. A formal ruling can be invaluable if you are unsure of how a particular item should be treated because the ruling is also binding on the Tax Office.

o Never act on verbal advice from the Tax Office—always get the advice in writing.

o You are the person responsible for your tax return, not the person who prepared it. So it is essential that you check that all the details are correct.

o Negative gearing can be used in conjunction with any income-producing asset, but it is most commonly used with property. Be careful when using it in conjunction with shares and ensure that you can afford to make a loss if share prices decline.

o Never invest solely to reduce your tax.

o If you hold an investment for more than 12 months you get a 50 per cent discount on your capital gains tax bill.

o Splitting income with other family members is an effective and legal way of reducing your family's tax liability.

o Keeping accurate tax records is a legal requirement but it can also ensure that you do not pay more tax than is absolutely necessary.

o The Australia's Future Tax System report and the government's response will almost certainly fundamentally change the Australian tax system.

Investment options

Part II looks at various investment options. There is a review of share-market investing that incorporates an analysis of sharemarket tables and a consideration of such things as P/E ratios and dividend yields. This is followed by a review of more sophisticated sharemarket products, including warrants, contracts for difference and hybrid securities such as convertible notes, and margin lending. Listed investment companies (including REITS) are discussed at length, and the peculiarities of these types of companies are looked at. In chapter 12 you will learn about new floats and how to read a prospectus — invaluable skills for all investors.

The advantages and disadvantages of different types of managed funds are discussed and explained. This is followed by an examination of hedge funds and their place in an investment portfolio. Many investors want to reduce risk by investing in fixed-interest securities. Chapters 15 and 16 reveal that fixed-interest securities might not be as low risk as is generally believed; they have different risk and return characteristics. Chapter 17 analyses the more risky options and futures, and there are worked examples to assist your understanding of these complex products.

Chapters 18, 19, 20 and 21 deal with real estate investments. To start off most people need to be conversant with investing in residential property as this is the most common avenue for property investing. Important issues covered in these chapters include how to evaluate direct property as an investment and how to select appropriate residential properties. Factors that need to be considered to select a commercial property are also considered. This is followed by an analysis of the tax implications of real estate investing. Finally, different property investment structures, and the advantages and disadvantages of each, are discussed.

Chapter 22 evaluates the investment markets for collectables, and some key pointers on traps to avoid are given. The book concludes with a review of the advantages and disadvantages of investing in superannuation, how superannuation is taxed and how to select the best investment option in a super fund.

8

Investing in the sharemarket

After world sharemarkets began their decline in March 2000, many investors realised that making money from shares was not as easy as they thought. For most of the 1990s, world share prices rose significantly, giving the impression that share prices only moved in one direction—up. But this impression was dispelled in 2000 and with the GFC when share prices fell dramatically in 2008 to early 2009. However, many investors who suffered in 2000 also fell into the trap with the GFC, plus new investors had come into the sharemarket by then. These phenomena highlight that successful investing in the sharemarket can involve considerable risks and there are no guaranteed 'get rich' schemes. This book may not make you a million dollars out of the sharemarket. What it will do is give you an understanding of how the sharemarket really works so you can give yourself a better chance of selecting good-quality shares and minimising your losses.

The sharemarket has an important role to play in the economy because it is the means by which companies can raise money to finance their operations. They do this by issuing shares to the public. When you buy shares you become a shareholder in a company and get the benefits of its growth via dividends and a capital gain when the share price rises, or lose money if it performs badly.

If a company in which you are a shareholder goes bankrupt and cannot pay all its debts, your liability is limited to the amount you originally invested. For example, if a company with 10 000 shareholders went bankrupt and still owed $10 million, there is no legal obligation on shareholders to contribute another $1000 each. For this reason, most companies listed on the ASX are called limited liability.

Before companies are allowed to list their shares on the ASX they have to comply with regulations laid down by ASIC and the ASX itself. To remain listed they must comply with the ongoing requirements of the exchange.

Although companies listed on the Australian sharemarket are subject to ASX regulation and supervision, this is not a guarantee that you will make money on your share investments or that the companies you invest in will not get into financial difficulties. Indeed, in past years, notable company failures have included Hooker Corporation, Budget Corporation, Qintex, Bond Corporation, HIH, Pasminco, OneTel, ABC Learning Centres and Timbercorp. In all cases, shareholders lost considerable amounts of money.

Company floats

Companies are 'floated' or listed on the ASX by issuing a prospectus and selling shares to the public. These are called 'ordinary shares'. Before a prospectus can be issued it is vetted by ASIC and the ASX, but this in no way guarantees that the company will be successful once it is listed. There is also no guarantee that the price of the shares when quoted on the ASX will be greater than the price that you paid for them.

There are various reasons for a company wishing to be floated. In some cases the existing owners of an unlisted company may wish to turn some of their ownership (equity holding) into cash. Another possibility is that the existing owners may require capital for expansion and this is easier for a company listed on the ASX. A further possibility is that a company wishes to sell-off an operating unit that it no longer wants. In recent years there have also been privatisation schemes whereby the federal and state governments have floated such organisations as GIO of NSW, the Commonwealth Bank, Qantas, Tabcorp in Victoria, TAB Limited in NSW and Telstra.

Stockbrokers and/or investment banks underwrite the vast majority of floats. This means that, if there are not enough buyers for the shares, the underwriter guarantees to buy any shares not bought by the public. In return for doing this the underwriter is paid a fee. Company floats and prospectuses are considered in detail in chapter 12. A well-prepared prospectus will provide potential investors with a corporate history, the names and experience of the company's directors, financial information and a general overview of the company's activities, plus details of the main risks involved in buying these shares. Once a float has been completed and all requirements have been met, the shares can be listed on the ASX.

Dividends

Under the Corporations Law companies may pay dividends to shareholders out of current profits or retained profits, including retained capital profits. This means that a company can still make a loss in the current year but, provided that it has sufficient retained profits, it may pay a dividend. The overriding consideration is that dividends paid not reduce paid-up capital. Directors need to be prudent in judging whether a dividend can be paid, but the preceding explains how a dividend can be paid that exceeds current earnings. In the terminology used later in this chapter, dividend per share can be greater than earnings per share, but directors can be held to account for their actions.

Bonus issues, rights issues, share placements and purchase plans

After companies are listed on the sharemarket they can increase the number of shares via bonus issues, rights issues, share placements or share purchase plans.

Bonus issues

A bonus issue is a free hand-out of shares to existing shareholders in proportion to the number of shares already held. If a company makes a one-for-one bonus issue it will double the number of shares on issue. So if you originally bought 1000 shares you would now be given another 1000 as a bonus. But if nothing else changes, you would expect the share price to halve. If a company maintains its dividend rate on the increased number of shares, shareholders are much better off.

Rights issues

A rights issue is when a company offers new shares to existing shareholders. They are entitled to receive new shares in proportion to their existing holding, at a price that is usually less than the current market price of the shares. Hence it is usually worthwhile for shareholders to accept the offer. A 'renounceable' rights issue means that you may buy new shares by 'taking up' your rights or you may sell the rights in the market. With a non-renounceable rights issue the rights cannot be traded. You either take them up by paying for them or they lapse. A company must issue a prospectus when it offers shares via a rights issue and this will outline how the money being raised will be spent.

Share placements

A company can issue up to 10 per cent of its existing shares as a share placement. These shares are normally issued to investing institutions such as insurance companies and sometimes to clients of the underwriting stockbroker or investment bank.

Share purchase plans

Share purchase plans (SPPs) give existing shareholders the opportunity to buy additional shares at a price fixed by the company—usually at a discount to the current market price—without paying brokerage or commissions. The maximum you can usually invest is $15 000 and there is usually a minimum investment of around $2000, but some SPPs give you the opportunity to apply for more than $15 000—without giving any guarantee that you will receive more than $15 000 worth of shares. This means that you can buy up to $15 000 worth of shares and be guaranteed of receiving them. You can apply for more shares, and whether you receive these depends on whether other shareholders take up their full entitlement. If other shareholders take up their full entitlement you will not be able to buy any more than $15 000 worth.

Types of shares

The sharemarket trades in different types of securities, including ordinary shares, preference shares, convertible preference shares, options and convertible notes. Before you begin to invest in the sharemarket it is important to understand the main features of these different types of shares.

Ordinary shares

Ordinary shares are the units into which the share capital of a company is divided. In initial floats, usually only ordinary shares are offered for sale.

An ordinary shareholder is entitled to a share in the company's profits in the form of dividends, and a subordinated claim over the company's assets if the company goes bankrupt. Shareholders are also allowed to vote on certain matters concerning the company's affairs. However, ordinary shareholders do not have a day-to-day say in the management of a company's activities.

Contributing shares

Ordinary shares may be fully paid—that is, paid for in full on purchase—or contributing, sometimes called partly paid. Contributing shares are only partly paid for, and at a future date you will be required to pay the balance outstanding. Contributing shares are said to have an uncalled liability. So a share may be issued at $1, but you are only initially required to pay 50¢. You may be required to pay the extra 50¢ at some time in the future. In 2010 fewer than six limited liability companies have contributing shares. There are also 'no liability' (NL) companies which are generally mining and oil companies, and they may have contributing ordinary shares as well. What this means is that you are not obliged to pay your uncalled liability. If the company makes a call and you do not pay it, you forfeit your shares. In 2010 there are about 25 NL companies.

Preference shares

Preference shares differ from ordinary shares in several ways. They usually have preferential rights with regard to the payment of a dividend, the return of capital on winding-up, or both. Companies must pay dividends on preference shares before they pay dividends to ordinary shareholders. Preference shares usually pay a fixed dividend, rather than one subject to change, and this often starts out higher than an ordinary dividend. Also preference shares are often not listed on the ASX.

There are different classes of preference shares. These are considered below.

Redeemable preference shares

Redeemable preference shares come with an option for the company to buy them back at a stated price. A company is only likely to do this if it has excess cash or if it can obtain money more cheaply elsewhere. The other conditions that attach to preference shares still apply, but the shares may not be convertible into ordinary shares (see below).

Cumulative redeemable preference shares

Cumulative redeemable preference shares are said to be 'cumulative' because if in one year a company misses paying a dividend the amount owing is carried forward to the next year. It keeps carrying the dividend forward until it is eventually paid. Preference dividends must be paid before any ordinary dividends are paid.

Participating preference shares

Participating preference shares are shares for which, after receiving their fixed dividend, shareholders are entitled to share in any surplus profits along with the ordinary shareholders.

Convertible preference shares

Convertible preference shares are a hybrid between ordinary shares and preference shares in that they enable you to convert your preference shares into ordinary shares at a fixed price. You can decide to be repaid in cash rather than convert into ordinary shares. They involve less risk than ordinary shares and allow you to benefit from any increase in the ordinary share price.

Converting preference shares

Converting preference shares are akin to convertible preference shares, but they convert into ordinary shares at a predetermined date in the future and you do not have any choice about whether to convert or not.

Reset preference shares

Reset preference shares entitle you to receive a fixed rate of dividend until a date specified in the future, known as the 'reset date'. When that time is reached the terms of the security—dividend rate and next reset date—may change. You can either accept the new reset terms or convert into ordinary shares at a discount to their market price; for example, 10 per cent. More about reset preference shares can be found in chapter 10.

Convertible notes

Convertible notes are debt securities that can be converted into ordinary shares at some time in the future. Investors are often attracted by the regular income flow which comes from these securities and the opportunity to convert to ordinary shares at a later time. Convertible notes pay interest, not dividends, and the interest is fully taxable, whereas dividends from shares may be partly or wholly franked.

Deferred dividend shares

Deferred dividend shares have dividends deferred for a number of years. Companies raising finance for long-term projects where income is deferred until the project becomes operational occasionally issue them.

Options

Options give you the right, but not the obligation, to buy or sell a particular share at a specified price up until a predetermined date in the future. Exchange-traded options (ETOs) are considered in chapter 17. However, it should be noted here that some companies, especially speculative oil and mining companies, issue their own options to shareholders to raise money for their activities. These options are issued at a fraction of the price of the company's shares. They confer the right to buy shares only. They are traded on the ASX as opposed to the derivatives market, where ETO trading takes place.

* * * * *

While all listed companies have ordinary shares they may not have all the other types of securities listed above. Ordinary shares are by far the most commonly traded shares on the sharemarket.

Understanding sharemarket tables

To be a competent share investor you need to know how to find your way around the financial pages of newspapers. The information contained in the sharemarket tables of the major daily newspapers is fundamentally similar, although not identical. *The Australian* is used for illustration because it is a national newspaper, although it is not the most comprehensive of the newspapers in terms of the amount of information shown.

Figure 8.1 (overleaf) shows an excerpt of the full details contained in *The Australian*'s industrial sharemarket table. Let's look at each column in turn.

Code

Initially *The Australian*'s sharemarket tables contain a four-digit code. This is the code you can use to ring a number listed at the bottom of the tables to obtain live sharemarket information. There is a fee for using this service.

Name of the stock

Shares are listed in alphabetical order, with some permutations that might confuse you. For example, the Commonwealth Bank of Australia is abbreviated to CBA and appears towards the top of the 'Cs', while

Commonwealth Property Office Fund is abbreviated to Cwlth Prop and appears under 'Cw'. Also note that capitals take precedence over lower case so that ANZ Bank, for which the full name is Australia and New Zealand Banking Group, ranks many companies above Australian Ethical Investment and Superannuation Limited ('AuEthical'). Other newspapers and magazines interpret alphabetical order differently. The result is you may have to look around just to find the company you are interested in.

Last sale

The last sale price is given in the '4 p.m. close' column. This is the last sale price at which a share has traded, regardless of when the sale took place. In some cases this will be the last sale price of the previous day. In other cases it may be the last sale price of several days ago.

Figure 8.1: *The Australian* industrial shares table

INDUSTRIAL SHARES

Code	Stock	4pm close	Move	Vol 100s	Buy	Sell	Year High	Year Low	Div Yield	P.E. Ratio
	A									
5386	Abacus stpld	.42	+.01	37842	.415	.42	.48	.245	13.69	
2721	Aberdeen	1.40			1.345	1.37	1.62	.90	6.43f	18
5598	Acrux	2.05	+.01	2527	2.04	2.05	2.54	.42		
5155	Actinogen	.07			.051	.074	.10	.017		
6905	Acuvax	.014			.013	.015	.05	.012		
7280	Adacel	.44	+.02	30	.43	.44	.84	.325		16
6655	AdcorpAus	.18	-.04	684	.165	.195	.31	.165	5.56f	40
7425	AdelBrtn	2.37		37917	2.36	2.37	3.01	1.445	5.70f	12
3833	ADGGlobal	.071	+.01	1914	.07	.071	.123	.058		
8427	ADGGlobal opt11	.01			.01	.029	.01	.01		
1393	Admerex	.008			.007	.008	.016	.004		
7443	Adtrans	3.50		36	3.50	3.60	3.60	1.65	5.71f	13
9866	Adultshop	.01		15000	.01	.011	.014	.004		
7500	Adultshop op11d	.003			.003	.006	.005	.002		
2019	AdvanShar	.39			.365	.39	.435	.15	7.05f	12
8582	AdvBrakin	.021			.021	.023	.038	.005		
2829	AdvEgySys	.05			.025	.034	.085	.02		
7555	AdvEngine	.055			.05	.056	.093	.031		
7642	AdvMag	.056		216	.056	.06	.124	.016		
5392	AdvSurgic	.52			.52	.53	.64	.28		
4789	Aeris Env	.09	-.01	100	.09	.095	.185	.05		
6786	Aevum	1.25	-.01	299	1.25	1.27	1.67	.545	3.20	30
8786	AFT Corp	.001		60749	.001	.002	.002	.001		
8095	AGLEnergy	14.37	+.57	27026	14.36	14.37	15.46	12.96	3.76f	4
7860	AgriLandT ordun	.17			.17		.21	.13	14.24	
7856	AHC	2.25			2.25	2.40	2.45	1.295		16
6610	AHG	2.38	-.02	82	2.34	2.41	2.60	.56	7.14f	8
3013	Ainsworth	.155			.145	.15	.22	.05		
8015	Ainsworth ucn11	.765			.805	1.00	.95	.62	14.59	
1858	AlnvTrust ordun	1.03		10	1.03	1.07	1.45	.575	45.63	
8602	Air NZ	.995	-.02	2114	.995	1.01	1.12	.55	5.25	62
9818	AJ Lucas	3.00	-.02	2327	3.00	3.06	5.60	2.03	1.83f	1
5551	Alchemia	.675	+.02	810	.64	.67	.81	.14		
9206	Alcoa cdi	45.25				45.20	47.10	44.00	.27	
2837	AleGroup stpld	2.24	+.03	446	2.21	2.24	2.43	1.416	12.05	2
2839	AleGroup ufrn	103.00			103.00	104.95	105.00	86.00	7.06	
2306	Alesco	4.37	-.14	2474	4.35	4.37	5.91	.60	3.20f	
1696	AlintaErg stpld	.079		3720	.079	.08	.13	.032		
7181	AllBrands	.135	-.01	2055	.135	.14	.245	.10	3.70f	5
9039	AllBrands opt10	.001				.001	.005	.001		
2835	AlphaFin frn12	19.70	-.30	10	18.80	24.00	25.00	5.25	21.31	

Move

This is the amount by which a share has increased or decreased during the previous day's trading. It is determined by comparing the last sale of the previous day with the last sale of the day prior to that and is expressed in cents. For some companies there will be no move because its shares did not trade during the previous day, or because they did trade but there was no net increase or decrease. To determine whether there has been any trading you can look at the 'Volume' column (see below).

Volume in 100s

This is sometimes referred to as turnover. It is the total number of shares that have been traded during the day. Analysts frequently view this as a sign of interest in a particular company. A marked increase in volume may herald an event of importance, which will have an effect — either good or bad — on a company's share price.

Buy and sell

'Buy' is the maximum price that the highest bidder in the market is prepared to pay for a company's shares at the end of the day. But it does not reveal how many shares the buyer wishes to buy. 'Sell' is the minimum price that the lowest seller in the market is prepared to accept at the end of the day. Here again, however, it does not reveal how many shares are for sale. However, this does not mean that these prices will still apply the following day. If overseas sharemarkets rise significantly overnight, sellers might cancel their existing selling orders and offer their shares at much higher prices.

Year's high/low price

This shows the highest and lowest prices a company's shares have traded at during the previous 52 weeks. For example, in February 2010 AMP's high for the past 52 weeks was $6.97 and its low was $3.52. The share price on 1 February 2010 was $6.43. High and low prices should be adjusted for bonus issues to make these comparisons valid. For example, suppose AMP made a one-for-one bonus issue, effectively doubling the number of shares on issue. The amounts shown in the high and low columns should be halved because there is now twice the number of shares on issue. Make sure when you are reading share tables that you note whether they have been adjusted for bonus issues.

Dividend yield

This is sometimes preceded by dividend per share (DPS), which is the number of dividends paid by a company during its financial year divided by the number of ordinary shares on issue. There is no guarantee that this dividend will be maintained in the future. An 'f' indicates that the dividend is fully franked. This means that it may be tax-free in the hands of some shareholders (see chapter 7). A 'p' indicates that the dividend is partly franked. If there is no letter after the dividend yield it means that the dividend is unfranked. Dividend yield, expressed as a percentage, is DPS divided by the company's current share price. So if you buy a share for $1 and receive 5¢ in dividends during the year, the dividend yield is 5 per cent.

Price/earnings ratio

Price/earnings ratio (P/E, PE ratio or PER) is one of the most used, abused and misunderstood sharemarket statistics. Its calculation is straightforward: divide a company's share price by its earnings per share (EPS). EPS is net profit after tax divided by the number of ordinary shares on issue (see below). If a company's share price is $1.50 and it has an EPS of 20¢, then its P/E ratio is $1.50 ÷ 0.20, or 7.5 times.

The main use for a P/E ratio is to give an indication of the relative value of a share. For example, a share selling on a P/E of 5 might be better value than one selling on a P/E of 20. However, 'might' is the key word. The earnings figure upon which the P/E ratio is based is last year's earnings. Next year's earnings are much more relevant. If a company's profits are expected to double next year, it may be selling on a historical P/E of 10 and a future P/E of 5. Conversely, a company may be selling on a low P/E because the market thinks its profits are about to decline, which would increase its P/E ratio.

You need to be careful interpreting P/E figures, but they can be useful for comparing companies in the same industry. If one retailer is selling on a P/E of 10 while the industry average is 15, it may indicate that its shares are undervalued, or it may mean it is the worst performer in the industry. This means you must first make an estimate of what the company will earn next year. When you do this it may turn out that the company selling on a P/E of 15 is the bargain, not the one selling on a P/E of 10.

This is the last column given in *The Australian*'s industrial share tables, although some tables in other newspapers give additional information, looked at below.

Dividend cover

Dividend cover—which is net profit after tax less preference dividend, divided by the ordinary dividend amount—is not always published. Most companies do not have preference shares, but when they do, preference shares rank ahead of ordinary shares and their dividends are therefore deducted from net profit after tax before calculating the dividend cover for ordinary shares.

When dividend cover is published it may be referred to as 'times covered' or 'tms cov'. If the dividend cover is less than 1, it means that a company is paying out more in dividends than it is earning in profits. In turn this means that it would be paying some part of its dividend out of profits of previous years. This is a situation that cannot continue indefinitely and suggests that the company will have to reduce its dividend payments in the future. A dividend cover of—for example—2.5 indicates that a company has scope for increasing its dividend in the future.

Net asset backing

Net asset backing (NAB)—usually referred to as net tangible asset (NTA) backing because it excludes intangible assets such as goodwill, patents and formation expenses—is total net tangible assets divided by the number of shares on issue. It is intended to be a measure of the underlying worth of a company's shares. However, assets may be valued at 'book' values—that is, their historical cost—which is not necessarily their market value. Hence, NAB may not give a true picture of the worth of a company's shares. In years gone by it was not uncommon for a company with a low share price and a high NAB to be taken over as the takeover raider was attempting to buy assets below their true market value.

Earnings per share

Earnings per share is the company's net profit after tax divided by the number of shares on issue. If a company earns a profit of $20 million after tax, and has 200 million shares on issue, its EPS is 10¢.

Mining and oil shares

Mining and oil shares are listed separately on the ASX and also in the financial pages. In *The Australian* (see figure 8.2, overleaf) the information presented in the mining and oil section of the share tables is not identical to the industrials section. For example, the day's high and low are given in the mining and oil section whereas they are not for the industrials.

The P/E ratio and dividend yield are not given in the mining and oil section. For P/E ratio and dividend in cents-per-share you need to consult a different publication such as the *Australian Financial Review*. From the information there you can calculate the dividend yield. Many mining and oil companies do not pay dividends so you cannot calculate a dividend yield.

Figure 8.2: *The Australian* mining shares table

MINING SHARES

Code	Stock	4pm close	Move	Vol 100s	Buy	Sell	Day's High	Day's Low	Year High	Year Low
4487	3D Oil	.25	+.01	492	.24	.25	.39	.07		
4450	3D Res	.02		750	.018	.021	.026	.007		
A										
4924	A1Mineral	.31		3633	.31	.315	.32	.31	.42	.11
1998	ABM Res	.028		870	.028	.029	.028	.028	.07	.006
2795	AbraMin	.16		500	.16	.18	.16	.16	.25	.13
7142	ACap Res	.34	+.01	2514	.34	.35	.34	.33	.60	.105
3201	AccentRes	.19	+.02	976	.175	.19	.19	.17	.27	.071
6726	Acclaim	.022		1264703	.022	.023	.023	.018	.026	.003
4664	Acclaim ordpp	.003			.001	.006				
5301	Activex	.08	+.01	1330	.081	.088	.08	.08	.12	.042
4137	Activex opt10	.011			.011	.02			.06	.001
8858	AdamusRes	.385	-.02	475	.385	.39	.40	.38	.53	.29
7395	Adavale	.028		1039	.028	.038	.028	.028	.065	.016
9328	AdelEngy	.135	-.01	1271	.13	.14	.14	.135	.16	.04
1266	AdelphiEn	.34	+.02	4833	.325	.34	.34	.30	.385	.045
6736	AdelRes	.22	-.01	567	.22	.225	.225	.22	.395	.049
6616	Aditya	.95	-.01	6848	.95	.97	.98	.945	1.65	.096
1945	Admiralty	.012		135891	.012	.013	.013	.012	.037	.011
9085	AdvEnergy	.06			.044	.05			.125	.03
1842	AdvEnergy mat15	1.07				1.05			1.07	1.02
3404	AED Oil	.56	-.03	1198	.55	.57	.575	.55	1.24	.50
2013	AfricanEn cdi	.099		715	.099	.10	.099	.095	.24	.02
8005	AgriEngy	.01		12000	.01	.011	.01	.01	.015	.009
2943	AlamarRes	.185			.18	.24			.245	.14
1148	AlaraRes	.11	-.01	1505	.11	.15	.12	.11	.25	.035
4501	Alchemy	.705	-.01	526	.70	.705	.71	.70	1.27	.042
9239	Alchemy opt10	.45			.43	.50			.96	.002
8384	Alcyone	.034		8500	.034	.035	.035	.034	.06	.029
5694	Alcyone opt11	.021				.001				
9044	Alkane	.31		545	.31	.315	.315	.30	.49	.18
6233	Alliance	.52	-.02	1115	.52	.525	.52	.51	.98	.363
4991	AlliedGol	.28	+.01	1090	.27	.28	.28	.275	.55	.25
4472	AlloyRes	.031			.024	.03			.045	.013
4636	AlturaMin	.195		77	.195	.20	.20	.195	.37	.065
4653	AlturaMin opt10	.018			.006	.018			.08	.01
9922	Alumina	1.505	-.01	270910	1.505	1.51	1.53	1.485	2.06	.683
6769	Amadeus	.22		13659	.22	.225	.23	.21	.43	.205
1956	AmexRes	.175			.06	.18			.25	.08
7924	Ampella	.92	-.02	14527	.90	.92	.955	.89	1.04	.081
3046	Ampella opt10	.80			.72	.77			.82	.03
3110	AnchorRes	.185	-.01	1091	.185	.23	.20	.185	.28	.032

Share categories

Shares are also referred to by such terms as 'blue chips', 'growth' and 'penny' shares. Blue-chip shares are shares of the biggest and supposedly safest companies, such as National Australia Bank, Woolworths, BHP Billiton and Telstra. For the most part blue-chip shares make up the

S&P/ASX's Twenty Leaders Index, which encompasses the ASX's 20 largest companies. Generally, any company which has a market capitalisation of over $10 billion can be considered a blue chip.

Mention has already been made of NAB (net asset backing). Investors often focus on shares that are selling at a price below their NAB. In theory, the NAB of a company represents the amount per share that would be realised if the company was liquidated.

Shares in rapidly expanding companies are termed growth shares. A fast way for a company to expand is through acquiring other companies by way of takeover. Consequently, the term 'growth stock' is often used to refer to companies that have a reputation for making aggressive takeovers. However, it does not follow that increased sales and higher profits go hand in hand with growth stocks.

In terms of appeal to many novice investors, 'penny' shares rank highly. Usually worth about as much as the name suggests, the attraction to some investors is that many of these shares can be bought for a small outlay. Or instead of only being able to buy 100 blue-chip shares, an investor is able to buy many thousand cheap shares. However, most penny shares are not attractive from an investment point of view, mainly because they are usually thinly traded and a handful of participants can significantly affect the price. Also they usually have few assets, little potential earnings and pay no dividends.

The All Ordinaries index

These days nearly every evening news broadcast makes some mention of how the All Ordinaries index (All Ords) behaved during the day. But it is clear that many people watching the news, as well as many investors, do not have a clue what the All Ords actually means.

Most people have the general idea that if the All Ords is going up, the sharemarket is going up, and vice versa. Basically this is true, but it gives no indication of how individual shares or particular sectors of the market are faring.

The All Ordinaries index comprises the 500 largest companies listed on the ASX based on market capitalisation (see below). With over 2000 companies listed on the Australian sharemarket, most are not included in the All Ords. The main groups of companies to miss out are speculative oil and gas explorers and small mining and industrial companies.

Once the shares that make up the All Ords are selected, they are then weighted according to their market capitalisation. This is the company's share price multiplied by the number of shares on issue. For example, National Australia Bank has about 2050 million ordinary shares on issue. At a share price of around $27.50 it has a market capitalisation of about $56.4 billion (2050 million shares × $27.50 per share). Although it is not Australia's largest company, National Australia Bank represents over 4 per cent of the All Ords. Generally speaking, companies in the All Ords make up over 90 per cent of the total market capitalisation of the Australian sharemarket. Naturally these figures will vary depending on the relative prices of shares of companies which make up the All Ords. In turn, the All Ords as a percentage of total market capitalisation will vary according to both movements in the market capitalisation of companies constituting the All Ords and movements in the total market capitalisation of all shares traded on the ASX.

Movements in the All Ords are publicised widely in major daily papers around Australia, as well as via radio, television and the internet. These days you can even get the information via your mobile phone. Hence the information is readily obtainable. However, the All Ords is only a broad indicator of sharemarket behaviour. There are also numerous specific indices which mirror behaviour in particular sectors. These include the S&P/ASX All Industrials, the S&P/ASX Fifty Leaders, the S&P/ASX Twenty Leaders, the S&P/ASX 200, the Energy Index, Financials Index, Health Care Index and so on. These are sometimes published in the financial pages of newspapers.

How to invest

The first step in investing in the sharemarket yourself is to set up an account with a stockbroker. A full list of stockbrokers is available from the ASX—go to <www.asx.com.au> and click on 'Find a broker'. This list does not tell you which stockbroker is best for your level of investment as some brokers only deal with large institutional clients. However, you can use the ASX's service to find a broker that fits your needs in terms of whether you need advice, how much you wish to invest or sell and where you are located. Alternatively, you may already know someone who has a suitable stockbroker.

Depending on the stockbroker you deal with, he or she may be able to advise you on a range of shares to invest in. They do not usually charge for consultations and investment advice. Brokerage is only charged if you elect to buy or sell shares. In the case of some investments, such as some managed funds, stockbrokers may receive a commission.

Once you have acquired a broker you are in a position to buy and sell shares. Stockbrokers make money by adding on (or subtracting) a commission when each client buys (or sells) shares. Commission rates are negotiable and brokers can charge what they like. However, there is competition which serves to keep charges within reasonable limits. In effect, for orders under $20 000 there is not much variation. Most brokers charge a minimum fee ranging from $50 to $100 on each order.

There are also discount brokers that charge lower rates, but do not give any advice.

You will also find that if you are a small investor the service you receive from brokers will vary.

It is possible to buy and sell shares online. Brokers that offer such a service include:

- E*Trade Australia Securities: <www.etrade.com.au>

- CMC Markets Stockbroking: <www.cmcmarketsstockbroking. com.au>

- Westpac Securities: <www.westpac.com.au>

- Commonwealth Securities: <www.commsec.com.au>

- Macquarie Equities: <www.macquarieprivatewealth.com.au>

- National Online Trading: <www.nab.com.au/trading>.

With some of the above websites you will have to follow links before you get to online broking. For example, in the case of Macquarie Equities you need to click on the following sequence:

Products and services > Trading solutions > Australian shares

And then click on 'Apply now'.

One of the benefits of using the internet to buy and sell shares is that you are charged a much lower fee than if you use a traditional broker. But there are dangers — particularly if you unknowingly buy partly paid shares and do not realise that your total liability is much greater than the amount you are about to invest (as we saw in the previous chapter). Chapter 6 has more details on how to trade over the internet.

The dangers of sharemarket investing

The basic danger with investing in the sharemarket is that share prices go down as well as up. Indeed you can lose a significant part of your investment. For example, during the October 1987 crash the Australian sharemarket dropped by around 25 per cent in one day. Also since the technology boom burst at the end of March 2000 many investors have lost considerable amounts of money. More recently, sharemarket investors saw the value of their portfolios fall by 30 to 40 per cent during the GFC. But the potential for handsome short-term and longer term gains also exists.

Your aim with the sharemarket should be to pick the main trend in share prices, with your investment objective being to hold shares when the market is going up and let someone else hold them when the market is going down. This sounds simple, but usually greed gets in the way. It takes a lot of discipline to sell shares when they are still going up, or to admit a mistake and cut your losses. But these are two of the principal characteristics of successful sharemarket investors. You also need to recognise times when it is advisable to stay out of the sharemarket altogether.

It is unrealistic to think you can pick the top and bottom of the entire sharemarket, or indeed a particular share. Yet many investors waste much time and energy trying to do just this. You are far better off buying when a share represents good value and selling when you think it has become too expensive. Of course, the hard part is how to measure good and bad value. Unfortunately, there are no hard and fast rules; if it was cut and dried it would take much of the mystery away from the sharemarket.

How to pick shares

When investing in shares you have three important decisions to make:

- what to buy
- when to buy
- when to sell.

There are two main types of analysis that can help you make these decisions:

- fundamental analysis to pick a share
- technical analysis (charting) to confirm decisions on the timing of purchases and sales.

Fundamental analysis

Fundamental analysis uses analysis of the economy as a whole, and of industries and individual companies, to arrive at an intrinsic value for a share. It tries to assess a vast amount of data concerning everything from product lifecycles and quality of management to supply-and-demand factors. You buy when this analysis tells you a share is undervalued and sell when it is overvalued. Fundamental analysis mainly concentrates on the internal financial strength of a company and the position it holds in the marketplace; that is, is it the dominant company in the industry?

Fundamental analysis looks at:

- *Overall economic activity:* Swings in the business cycle, monetary and fiscal policy changes, inflation rates, unemployment, productivity and so on. It seeks to determine how these factors affect individual industries and companies.

- *Specific industries:* Costs, competition, labour relations, business cycles, industry structure and standards.

- *Specific companies within an industry:* Projected future earnings, quality of management, accounting policy, marketing, research and so on.

Both technical and fundamental analysis have die-hard champions who pour scorn on each other. In practice most sharemarket analysts tend to use a combination of the two methods.

Technical analysis (charting)

A pure technical analyst believes that 'all the information is in the chart'; that is, everything you need to know about a share is reflected in its price and the number of shares bought and sold.

Technical analysts believe that past and present prices hold clues to the future. They believe that charting share prices on graphs creates certain patterns that will correctly forecast future trends and tell you what to buy and sell. The more extreme version, chartism, believes that these patterns are all you need to know—it isn't even necessary to know what business a company is actually in. Charting methods do not attempt to explain why prices are moving in one direction or another.

Of greater importance is the fact that charting methods are often slow in giving an investment decision. Frequently, charting simply confirms the existence of a bullish—where share prices are rising—or bearish—where share prices are falling—trend.

The most important limitation of charting is that it requires recognising a pattern in the chart. These patterns may, on rare occasions, emerge clearly so that most analysts agree. But, much more commonly, interpretation of the patterns is a subjective matter. There may be little agreement between analysts on either the pattern emerging at any point or on its implication for future market prices.

Charting assumes that share prices move in trends which are recognisable, and give guides to future price movements. According to most technicians, there are three time and magnitude trends in charting:

- the primary trend

- secondary or medium-term trends

- daily or short-term fluctuations.

The primary trend usually lasts slightly over four years and is related to the political business cycle. It is divided into bullish and bearish phases. Bull markets, averaging about three years in duration, are periods of generally rising share prices. Bear markets, averaging one year to 18 months, are periods of generally falling price levels, and are usually characterised by deteriorating expectations about economic conditions. The importance of the primary trend cannot be overstated: when the market is going up most share prices go up; when the market falls, most share prices fall. So identifying the primary trend is crucial for successful sharemarket investing.

Secondary or medium-term movements, both rallies and declines, can be found interrupting all primary-trend movements. The typical bull market primary trend will be interrupted from two to five times by declines of short duration (a few weeks to a few months) and limited extent (5 per cent to 15 per cent falls in share prices) before completing its cyclical rise from trough to peak. The typical bear market primary trend move is usually broken by one to four deceptive rallies, also of short duration and limited extent—often called a 'bear trap'. Daily or short-term fluctuations are important for share traders—particularly those dealing in options or futures. These fluctuations may be caused by one-off events such as the calling of a general election or the collapse of a major financial institution. There are numerous internet sites—including the ASX site—that provide share price charts free of charge.

Most professional analysts choose either fundamental or technical analysis while occasionally using other methods to confirm their decisions. Thus fundamentalists may recommend selling Woolworths and buying David Jones, and then check these findings by using technical methods.

If they get a confirmation of their original analysis they will proceed. If not they go back and check again, and perhaps do nothing.

Building your own share portfolio

If you have less than $10000 to invest and you wish to invest in the sharemarket, you are probably better off investing in an unlisted sharemarket managed fund or a listed investment company (LIC), the reason being that stockbrokers charge a minimum fee on each buying and selling transaction. To have a diversified portfolio, say 10 companies, you would be charged a disproportionate amount of money in brokerage fees. Realistically you could only buy shares in two or three companies. As a result you will not be able to get enough diversification. If one of these companies goes bad you will lose a significant portion of your investment.

By investing in a sharemarket managed fund you are buying into a diversified portfolio of shares. Similarly, LICs—such as the Australian Foundation Investment Company—invest in the shares of other listed companies. An added advantage of doing this is you get to see the types of shares a professional manager buys and how they structure their portfolio. This may give you hints on how to eventually build your own portfolio. Investing in LICs is covered in detail in chapter 11. If you have $30000 or more to invest in the sharemarket you can begin to build your own well-diversified portfolio. Unless you see yourself as a speculator, you should have dividend-paying blue-chip shares as the core of your portfolio. One way of starting your portfolio would be to buy 10 different shares according to their importance in the All Ordinaries index.

For example, table 8.1 (overleaf) shows the largest 10 companies on the sharemarket as a percentage of the All Ordinaries index. So BHP Billiton represents 11.50 per cent of the All Ords, Commonwealth Bank and Westpac each 5.91 per cent, ANZ Bank 4.60 per cent and so on. All together these 10 blue-chip companies make up 45.97 per cent of the All Ordinaries index (as at February 2010).

If your share portfolio was constructed along the same lines you could expect to get a similar performance to the All Ordinaries index. As these companies make up nearly 50 per cent of the All Ords you would need to double the percentages shown in table 8.1 to construct your portfolio. Hence you would invest around 23 per cent of your money in BHP Billiton, another 12 per cent in Commonwealth Bank and Westpac, 9 per cent in ANZ and so on.

You would expect a portfolio constructed along these lines to rise or fall by about the same amount as the All Ordinaries index. For the year ending 31 December 2009 a portfolio based on the All Ords increased by around 50 per cent—but in 2008 this portfolio dropped by 41 per cent. As you can see, past performance is no guarantee of future performance. Over the long term you can expect the sharemarket, as measured by the All Ordinaries index, to show steady gains. The main drawback with this approach is that four of the ten companies are banks, so you may wish to replace one or two banks with blue-chip companies from other industries, such as CSR, AGL Energy and Foster's Brewing. The other sectors represented in the largest 10 companies in the All Ordinaries index are: diversified telecommunications services (Telstra); materials (BHP Billiton and Rio Tinto); energy (Woodside); and consumer staples (Wesfarmers and Woolworths).

Table 8.1: top 10 companies as a percentage of the All Ords at Feb. 2010

Company	Market cap ($billion)	% of All Ords
BHP Billiton	145.8	11.50
Commonwealth Bank	75.0	5.91
Westpac Bank	74.9	5.91
ANZ Bank	58.3	4.60
National Australia Bank	56.4	4.45
Telstra	41.7	3.29
Rio Tinto	35.7	2.82
Woodside Petroleum	32.5	2.56
Wesfarmers	31.5	2.48
Woolworths	31.1	2.45
Total		45.97

Source: *The Australian*, annual reports, ASX.

Constantly review your portfolio

One thing to keep in mind when investing in the sharemarket is that from time to time you are going to buy dud shares. It is important that you prune these shares out of your portfolio and reinvest in others with better prospects. Remember that even so-called 'blue-chip' shares can turn out to be duds—good examples of this are the share price performance of AMP, Brambles and Telstra. Also every six months you should revalue your shares at their current price—not at the price that you bought them.

This might show, for example, that BHP Billiton was 23 per cent of your portfolio, but because its share price has risen faster than your other shares it now represents 30 per cent of the portfolio. You then may wish to sell some BHP Billiton shares and reinvest the money in another company to bring the balance of your portfolio back into line.

Once you get the hang of sharemarket investing you could then consider investing in some second-line industrial companies—again it is wise to go for those paying dividends. Perhaps you may even become game enough to take a punt on one or two speculative mining and oil shares. But always remember, these shares are high risk. Do not invest more than you can afford to lose.

Be a contrarian

While at first it might sound strange, successful sharemarket investing often involves not doing what most other investors are doing. This can be neatly summarised by an old sharemarket saying: 'Buy in gloom, sell in boom'. In other words, when everyone else is pessimistic about the prospects of the sharemarket this is often an ideal time to buy. Similarly, when you read in the papers about how ordinary people, even school children, are making money on the sharemarket this is usually a sure sign that it is time to sell.

As an individual investor you are ideally placed to stand outside the crowd. No one can sack you from your job for failing to follow an investment fad. Smart investors often go against the crowd—long experience shows them that the crowd is very often wrong. Of course the difficulty that novice investors have with this strategy is that they do not have confidence that they can be right and so many 'professional' investors can be wrong. But professional fund managers are just as likely to get caught up in the excitement of the moment. A good example of this is that many professional investors were still buying shares a month before the October 1987 sharemarket crash. Also at the beginning of 2002 nine out of ten respected investment banks on Wall Street predicted a good year for the sharemarket in the US, while it actually fell by over 20 per cent. In the lead up to the GFC, professional investment advisers were encouraging their clients to invest right up until the crash.

Key points

o In order to be listed on the ASX a company usually must issue a prospectus and be floated. A prospectus is a complex document and should be studied carefully.

o Start reading the financial pages of a major daily newspaper. Check the sharemarket tables to improve your understanding.

o Investing in the sharemarket is fun, but it can be risky. The golden rule is to never invest more than you can afford to lose.

o History shows that over the long term—for example, 10 years —returns from investing in the sharemarket are good, but you can expect short-term fluctuations.

o Remember, invest in shares that are going up and let someone else hold them when they are going down.

o At times the safest strategy is to stay out of the sharemarket completely.

o Make good-quality shares the core of your portfolio; speculative mining and oil shares are only suitable for people prepared to take high risks with their money.

9

More sophisticated sharemarket strategies

As well as the types of products outlined in the previous chapter, there are also more sophisticated ways of investing in the sharemarket. These include American and European warrants, endowment warrants and margin lending. Warrants are one of the investment success stories of the last 20 years, with tremendous growth since the ASX became one of the first markets to list these products in 1991.

Beginning solely with equity call warrants, other types have been gradually introduced. Different warrants currently available for trading or investment include: equity warrants, instalment warrants, index warrants, currency and commodity warrants and endowment warrants. This makes it difficult to summarise the common characteristics of warrants as they now cover a wide range of risk profiles, investment objectives and potential investment returns. However, it is useful to classify warrants as either having a trading focus—that is, where you expect to hold the warrants for weeks or months—or investing focus—where you expect to hold the warrants for one year or more.

More recently, another new trading product—contracts for difference (CFDs)—has become the fastest growing financial product in the market. A CFD is a highly leveraged product that gives you the opportunity to make money in both rising and falling markets.

Warrants

A share 'call' warrant is a type of long-term options contract usually issued by a third-party financial institution and traded on the ASX's warrants market. Typically it enables you to buy shares at a predetermined price — referred to as the exercise or strike price. The price of this right is also the price of the warrant. There are also 'put' warrants, which enable you to sell shares at a predetermined price. Warrant prices are usually shown in share tables in a separate 'warrants' section.

Warrants are riskier than ordinary shares. Provided you do not need cash urgently you can hold ordinary shares for years — even decades — and they may eventually trade at many times the original price you paid for them. All this time the shares might also be paying dividends. In contrast, a warrant has a definite expiry date, and when a warrant's time has expired it becomes worthless.

American and European warrants

Warrants can be either American (where you can buy the underlying shares at any time by paying the strike price) or European (where you can only buy the underlying shares at the warrant's predetermined expiry date).

For example, if you bought a Telstra $3.00 call warrant you are entering a contract in which you could buy Telstra shares for $3.00 each. If Telstra's share price goes up, the price of your Telstra call warrant would also go up. You need to be aware that some call warrants can be used to buy shares in a one-for-one ratio, while with other warrants you might need two or four warrants for each ordinary share.

Warrant issuers

Currently most warrants traded on the ASX are issued by banks, governments and other institutions, and you are therefore dependent on them delivering the underlying shares to you should you exercise your warrants. Warrant issuers are independent and are in no way backed by the ASX. Consequently, as a warrant investor, you should be aware that you are exposed to the credit risk associated with the warrant issuer. Under the ASX Business Rules, warrant issuers are required to make regular reports to the ASX and to advise the market of any developments that may influence an investor's assessment of the risks involved in dealing with that institution. Importantly, warrants do not have standardised terms and conditions, and these can vary considerably between warrants of the same type and different warrant issuers. The terms and conditions of a particular warrant series are set out in a product disclosure statement (PDS) or an offering circular that is prepared by the warrant issuer.

Advantages of warrants

Compared with purchasing ordinary shares warrants have considerable advantages. To begin with, warrants provide you with the opportunity to derive a 'leveraged' rate of return on your investment. This is because the warrant price is considerably less than the full value of the underlying shares, and when the price of a share in a company increases its warrants increase by proportionately more. In addition, when you buy warrants your risk is limited to the cost of the warrant, not the full value of the shares.

Compared with exchange-traded options, warrants have the advantage of being traded through the Stock Exchange Automated Trading System (SEATS). You are required to settle your warrant transactions within the same settlement period as for shares. Before you buy your first warrant your broker will require you to sign a warrant client agreement form saying that you have read the booklet on warrants published by the ASX. You can also apply for newly issued warrants directly from the issuer.

Hedging

Warrants can be used as a form of insurance to protect an existing share portfolio against a falling market. If you own shares in a company and are nervous about the direction the market is about to take, you could purchase put warrants instead of selling shares. This would allow you to retain share ownership without realising capital gains and without having full exposure to the downside risks.

Warrants also can be used to hedge against future price increases. If you want to purchase shares but do not have immediate access to funds, you could purchase call warrants to capture the benefits of an anticipated price rise. This would allow you to establish a price (the exercise price) at which to purchase the shares in the future.

You can use call warrants to free up capital invested in shares. You can sell existing shareholdings and purchase a corresponding number of call warrants for a fraction of the price. Thereby, you have maintained your exposure to share price rises but have released capital from your share portfolio.

While you can expect warrants to participate fully in gains during a bull market, there is often some degree of protection in a bear market. Because of the gearing effect the initial fall will probably be faster, in percentage terms, than the underlying share, after which a floor may be reached. This is because of the low price of the warrants compared with the shares. If there is a sharp fall the warrants may reach a level at which they can fall no further.

Finally, because the warrants market is less well known than most other speculative markets it can offer more opportunities for the astute investor. Price inefficiencies and short-term anomalies occur frequently and can provide 'windows of opportunity' for profit. Equally, as warrants are relatively under-researched, those investors armed with good information and advice can find themselves in a strong position.

Disadvantages of warrants

The biggest disadvantage of warrants is that leverage can work in reverse. Just as a warrant will outperform the underlying share during share price rises, the opposite happens when the share price falls.

Also, with many types of warrants you do not get paid dividends. Warrants only give you the right to buy shares on the terms stipulated. Since they do not form part of the issued share capital of a company, warrants do not carry voting rights or the right to attend ordinary shareholders' meetings.

There are several variables that determine the price of warrants: interest rates, the expected dividend payments of the underlying share, the time to expiry and the expected volatility of the underlying share. Should any of these factors move in an adverse manner the price of a warrant will be affected accordingly.

Other risks associated with warrants are:

- Warrant prices may be volatile and subject to dramatic change over short periods.

- If you buy a call warrant you may lose your entire investment if the price of the underlying share falls dramatically.

- Even if underlying share prices are steady, warrant prices will diminish as time passes.

- Warrants lapse if they aren't sold or converted before their expiry date.

- Some warrants have 'caps' or 'barriers'. Caps limit the upside profit potential of the warrant, while some barriers cause the warrants to terminate before the original expiry date. So it is essential that you read the warrant disclosure documents carefully and understand whether caps or barriers are a feature of the warrant you intend to buy.

There are various factors that influence the price of an option or warrant. How the underlying share price moves is of course important, however it is not the only influence. What this means is that even if the underlying share price moves in the direction you expected it to, other factors may mean that your warrant or option falls in value.

Each warrant is a contract between the warrant issuer and the holder. You are therefore exposed to the risk that the issuer (or its guarantor, where relevant) will not perform its obligations under the warrant. You must make your own assessment of the credit risk associated with the warrant issuer. To help you evaluate the ability of an issuer to meet its obligations, the offering circular (or PDS) contains information on the financial situation of the issuer.

Trading warrants

Trading warrants is as easy as trading shares. Brokerage charges are identical to share transactions. As with shares you must pay for your purchase in three business days. As previously stated, the ASX also requires that you sign an ASX warrant client agreement form. Among other things you will be asked to state that you have read the explanatory booklet issued by the ASX, and that you are aware that warrants do not have standardised terms of issue and that it is your responsibility to become familiar with them. The ASX also disclaims responsibility in the event of default by the warrant issuer.

A word of warning though: warrants are not as simple as shares, and it is worth finding a broker who understands them. Always make sure that your broker understands exactly what it is you want to buy and sell.

If you buy call or put warrants you are not entitled to any dividends, you do not have voting rights and you do not receive rights or bonus issues. In the event of a bonus or rights issue the warrant exercise price is adjusted so that you do not miss out on any benefit from these issues.

Different types of warrants

There are several different types of warrants traded on the ASX. Some are riskier than others so it is essential that you understand which one is suitable for your investment objectives.

Equity warrants

Call warrants and put warrants are usually issued over shares in listed companies and are currently the type of warrant most traded. The exercise price is usually set reasonably close to the share price at the time of issue and the expiry date is typically anything from six months to three years from the date of issue. These are called equity warrants.

Often, one warrant entitles you to subscribe for one ordinary share, but this is not always the case. It is important to check both this and the price of conversion. Investors normally have to pay in cash to convert warrants into ordinary shares.

The date of conversion also varies considerably, and it is vital to be sure of the precise details. With some warrants conversion can only take place at specific times, and in some cases there is just one specific date on which conversion is allowed.

Index warrants

The value of an index warrant is linked to the performance of an index such as the All Ordinaries index or an overseas sharemarket index, such as the Japanese Nikkei 225 index or the US S&P 500 index. The exercise level is usually expressed in points and generally index warrants are settled in cash. The settlement amount is generally calculated by multiplying the difference between the exercise level and the closing index level by a multiplier to convert the points to a dollar figure. The issuer of the particular warrant determines this multiplier. Some index warrants allow holders to elect to take delivery of the underlying shares instead.

Some index warrants have special conditions if the index reaches specified levels—usually referred to as a 'barrier'. A barrier warrant is a generic term used to describe an ordinary warrant which has a fixed lower or upper barrier (limit) for the underlying security on which it is based.

Like an ordinary warrant, a barrier warrant has an exercise level and expiry date. The key difference is the introduction of a barrier that imposes a defined trading range for the underlying asset such as the All Ordinaries index.

So, if the index trades at or below the barrier in the case of call warrants or at or above the barrier in the case of put warrants, the barrier is triggered and index warrants terminate worthless without any amount being payable to holders. Barrier warrants suit investors who want maximum profits if their view on the short-term direction of the All Ordinaries index is correct and they are willing to take higher risks.

Instalment warrants

An instalment warrant gives the holder the right to buy the underlying share by payment of a number of instalments during the life of the warrant.

Instalment warrants may be similar to the instalment receipts that have been issued by Telstra, the Westpac Office Trust and the Commonwealth Bank. There are, however, some key differences. For example, instalment warrants are issued by a third party rather than the company in question and the final instalment is voluntary, unlike the instalment receipts where you must pay the last instalment. It is important to note that if the instalment warrant is not exercised and the final payment not made, the right to delivery of the underlying shares will be forfeited.

A common feature of these warrants is that you are entitled to any dividends and franking credits paid on the shares during the life of the warrant.

The instalment warrant is one of a number of sophisticated products for equity investors which have sprung up in recent years. Typically, the shares underlying instalment warrants are in blue-chip companies. Instalment warrants are initially issued by a third party (a financial institution, also called the 'issuer') and not by the company that issued the underlying shares to which the warrant relates.

You as the purchaser of such a warrant from an issuer pay an initial amount which comprises a loan fee and some tax-deductible interest in advance, as well as a capital amount. The upfront amount is only a fraction of the price of a fully paid share in the underlying company — it is roughly half for the standard instalment warrant and roughly one-fifth for a more highly geared version. The precise initial amount depends on the circumstances at the time, including the interest rate and the term to maturity; that is, how long the instalment warrant has to run.

You would then expect to pay a further fixed amount on the defined expiry, or maturity, date of the warrant, about 18 months later. This would comprise tax-deductible interest in arrears as well as a further capital amount, representing the balance of the share price. This second instalment is usually a round figure amount, often a whole number of dollars per share.

The approach just described allows you to have an exposure to a particular company of several times that obtainable through a direct purchase of the underlying shares, at least until the final instalment is paid. For example, if the shares were selling for $5.00 and the instalment warrants were selling for $2.50, you could buy twice as many instalment warrants for the same initial outlay. This is useful in a capital gains situation — but it can also magnify capital losses. If the shares fall 20 per cent then your investment will be down by around 40 per cent.

As the quid pro quo for the interest being charged on the loan element you will receive the full dividends on the shares, together with the benefit of any associated franking credits. However, you will not get all the other benefits of direct share ownership, such as the right to participate in dividend reinvestment plans or the right to vote at company general meetings. You should also compare the fees and the interest rate payable under this arrangement with the costs of borrowing in other ways — such as margin lending or borrowing against the equity in your home.

Buying instalment warrants is not cheap. For example, a standard instalment warrant with 16 to 18 months to maturity might cost you as an initial investor about $109 for every $100 of market value ($55 initially plus $54 at maturity). However, more significantly, the implicit rate of interest on the borrowed portion, allowing for the fees, can be as high as 20 per cent per annum.

Once created by the issuer, instalment warrants can be bought and sold on the ASX in the same way as ordinary shares; but be aware, the market could well be a lot less liquid than the market for the underlying shares.

If you still hold the warrants shortly before maturity, you will have a choice of:

- paying the final instalment as originally intended and receiving the unencumbered shares; however, because this is a warrant and not a true contributing share, payment is not compulsory

- deferring that payment by rolling over into another series of warrants, if one is available

- exercising the 'put' option that is part of the contract and receiving cash equal to the difference between the market value of the underlying shares and the unpaid final instalment.

If nothing along these lines has been done then the default mechanism at maturity comes into play — the shares will be sold and the net sales proceeds less the unpaid final instalment will be paid to you.

The loan fee is a tax deduction, but it needs to be apportioned over the tax years involved. Naturally, the cost base of the shares for capital gains tax purposes comprises the capital portions of the two instalments only, and not the loan fee and the interest components, as these are already tax deductions in their own right.

You can also use shares you already own in any of the companies in respect of which instalment warrants are being issued. You can put these up in lieu of putting up cash — in fact you will receive a 'cash back' amount which can be used for further investments or even for non-investment purposes, although the latter use naturally results in the interest being non-deductible.

The transfer of shares in this way does not trigger off capital gains tax as you are retaining the beneficial interest in the shares concerned.

The above description is a summary only. You will still need to study the offer document to get the full details of any specific product that interests you.

Currency warrants

The Australian dollar is one of the world's most actively traded currencies. Yet, until recently, the benefits of trading our currency have been largely unavailable to private investors. While many investors have had a strong view on the A$, they were unable to trade it easily, thereby foregoing potential trading profits and the ability to hedge existing investments against exchange rate fluctuations.

Currency warrants let you take advantage of currency opportunities by allowing you to take a positive or negative view on the A$ against, say, the United States dollar, just like you would a normal warrant or share.

Currency warrants entitle holders to exchange an amount of foreign currency for Australian dollars on or before the expiry date. The value of the warrant rises and falls in line with movements in the Australian dollar against a foreign currency with reference to the exercise price. For example, holders of A$/US$ call warrants benefit from an increase in the A$/US$ exchange rate, and holders of A$/US$ put warrants benefit from a decrease in the A$/US$ exchange rate.

Endowment warrants

With an endowment warrant (EW) you have the right, but you are not obliged, to buy shares in a blue-chip company at some future date based on today's price for the shares.

The main attraction of EWs is that you only have to invest a fraction of the current share price—the cost of the EW will usually be between 30 per cent and 60 per cent of the share price. It's a bit like buying shares using a lay-by system.

This is how EWs work. Let's suppose the company's current share price is $1 and the EW costs 30 per cent of this, or 30¢. Instead of receiving dividends in cash, these are used to pay off the remaining 70¢. When the 70¢ is paid off you can take full ownership of the shares. In most cases it will take about 10 years for the dividends to pay off the outstanding amount. But if the company's dividends increase significantly you could get full ownership earlier than 10 years.

It's one thing to understand how a new financial product works, but the real issue is how to make it work for you. There are at least two situations where you could use EWs profitably:

- *Self managed superannuation funds:* EWs are attractive if you are managing your own super fund. Current rules prohibit super funds from borrowing to invest — usually referred to as 'gearing'. But by using EWs you get access to geared sharemarket investments without putting your fund at risk.

  A super fund is well suited to warrants because of the long-term nature of superannuation. Provided there are at least 10 years to run before the shares would need to be sold, a super fund can outlay $20 000 and have a portfolio of 10 of Australia's leading companies, valued at around $42 000. Once the shares have been paid for through the warrants, the fund then has the option of selling them and paying capital gains tax at the rate of 15 per cent within the fund. (There are also more sophisticated endowment warrant strategies, which are beyond the scope of this book.)

  Trustees of the fund must ensure that the purchase of warrants is in accord with their documented investment strategy and that the warrants do not create an over-exposure to shares compared with the fund's asset allocation guidelines. Also, annual tax planning within the fund with the use of franking credits is not available through these warrants because they produce no income until the shares have been fully paid for.

- *Sharemarket investors:* Because an EW is effectively a deposit on a share with the balance of the purchase price provided by a financial institution, it is possible to get a much higher exposure to shares for a given amount of money. This is referred to as 'leveraging' your investments. If you are a long-term investor you could consider the possibility of selling some of your holdings in individual shares and using the after-tax proceeds to buy warrants in the same shares. For example, you could sell 1000 BHP Billiton shares, invest the proceeds in warrants and get exposure to around 1500 BHP Billiton shares.

  You have to recognise that there will be no dividend income and associated franking credits until you actually take possession of the shares. So warrants are only appropriate where buying shares is viewed as a long-term investment rather than a means of producing ongoing tax-effective income.

Many investors who buy so-called 'growth stocks' that produce little in the way of dividend income may be better off buying some of these warrants, which give exposure to companies with a history of growing dividends and long-term capital growth. For example, over the past 10 years, National Australia Bank has increased its dividend by an average of over 20 per cent each year.

The following are some disadvantages associated with endowment warrants:

- You have less control over your gearing strategy. Your level of borrowing automatically reduces over time and there is no flexibility to re-gear the portfolio as capital growth occurs.

- An investor in endowments is taking a long-term view on the underlying company's dividend policy versus interest rates, with the belief that the dividends will outweigh the interest payments and the outstanding amount will reduce over time.

- You may not be able to sell your warrants for a reasonable price in the market. This could be because there are insufficient orders to buy your warrants, or the price at which others are prepared to buy them is very low.

- The ASX may suspend or remove a warrant series from trading if the warrant issuer fails to comply with the ASX Market Rules. In almost all circumstances, a warrant will automatically be suspended if the underlying share is suspended.

Where to find warrant prices

Warrants are listed in the sharemarket tables of major daily newspapers, usually under a separate heading 'Warrants market'. Different types of warrants are listed together. So call warrants are listed separately from endowment warrants.

There are also several internet sites that have information on warrants, including:

- <www.macquarie.com.au>

- <www.egoli.com.au>

- <www.asx.com.au>.

Evaluating warrants

Evaluating warrants takes two stages. The most important consideration is the underlying performance of the ordinary shares. If the company does badly and the ordinary shares fall substantially then the warrants will not do well, regardless of their own technical merits. The analysis behind this company evaluation will cover future profitability, assets, management record, current and prospective P/E ratios, net asset backing, new products, industry movements and a host of other relevant factors.

The second prong relates to the warrants themselves and requires an analysis of the premium, gearing, time to expiry and volatility. These concepts are all explained below. The perfect warrant would combine a low premium with a long life, high gearing and high volatility.

How to calculate the premium

For all of the benefits warrants confer, such as gearing, there is a price. The warrant will normally (though not always) command a higher price than it is intrinsically worth on conversion. This 'conversion premium' is the premium you pay for buying the warrants instead of the shares, and the lower the premium, the 'cheaper' the warrant. It is important though not to consider the premium in isolation — the time to expiry is important, as is the degree of gearing.

Suppose a call warrant is selling for 40¢ with an exercise price of $1.10 when the share price is $1.20.

The premium is calculated as:

Premium = (Warrant price + Exercise price – Share price)
÷ Share price

Example: ($0.40 + $1.10 – $1.20) ÷ $1.20 = 25%

Premiums do vary considerably, and they are one of the most important technical factors used in the evaluation of warrants.

Factors affecting warrant prices

Let's have a look at the factors that affect the price of a warrant.

Share price

The underlying share price is the key driver of a warrant's price. As the share price increases, the value of a call warrant should increase. The value should fall as the share price falls. The opposite occurs for put warrants.

Put warrants should increase in value as the share price falls and decrease in value as the share price rises.

The direction of the warrant price is directly related to the direction of the underlying share price. Generally, warrants do not move cent for cent with the underlying shares. The relationship between the movement in the share price and the corresponding change in the warrant price is referred to as delta.

A delta of 1 means that the value of the warrant should change 1¢ for every 1¢ change in the underlying share price. A delta of 1 also means the warrant is currently in-the-money and there is a 100 per cent expectation that the warrant will expire in-the-money. A warrant is in-the-money if its exercise price is less than the underlying share price, which means that you would make a profit by exercising the warrant. A delta of 0.5 means that the expectation of the warrant having value at expiry is only 50 per cent. Accordingly, it means that the value of the warrant should change by 0.5¢ for every 1¢ change in the underlying share price.

Effective gearing

The effective gearing of a warrant provides a realistic expectation of how much the warrant should outperform or underperform the underlying shares over a short period of time. Effective gearing is calculated by dividing the share price by the warrant price and multiplying this by the delta.

This provides a measure that indicates the level of additional exposure the warrant holder has to the underlying share price. For example, a call warrant with an effective gearing multiple of 5 implies that every $1 invested in the warrant could equate to $5 invested in the underlying share. Be aware that the effective gearing multiple does change and therefore is only applicable for short periods of time.

Time to expiry

The time to expiry is important because the longer the time remaining the greater the opportunity for the warrant to gain intrinsic value as the share price appreciates. The premium takes this into account and incorporates what is known as 'time value': a measure of the benefit of the time remaining in terms of likely appreciation. When a warrant has several years to run the time value and premium may be considerable. Naturally, time value disappears as the time to expiry diminishes, and the premium will disappear. Hence, when considering the premium, or time value, it is always necessary to consider it in relation to the time to expiry.

Volatility

Volatility is another factor because the more volatile a share the more likely it is that a warrant over this share will be able to show considerable capital gains (or losses). Some warrants move much more frequently and sharply than others.

Choosing a warrant

You should consider the following when choosing a warrant:

- Determine whether you should select a call warrant or a put warrant.

- Look at the nature and performance of the underlying shares. If you aren't enthusiastic about the prospects of the shares you should avoid call warrants.

- If you are pessimistic about the outlook for the company you could consider put warrants.

- Are you taking a two-year view or a six-month view? This will eliminate some warrants from your selection.

- How much gearing are you seeking? The effective gearing of a warrant is determined by the delta (the relationship between the share price and the warrant price) and the gearing ratio. Effective gearing is expressed as a multiple. The higher the multiple, the higher your potential returns or losses from investing in this product.

Tax effectiveness

Given the wide variety of warrant products it is not possible to summarise the tax implications of warrants. Some products, such as instalment and endowment warrants, offer tax benefits to investors. The disclosure document for the particular warrant generally contains information on the tax implications of that warrant. However, it is strongly advised that you seek tax advice that applies to your individual circumstances before you begin trading or investing in warrants.

Contracts for difference

CFDs allow you to make significant gains—and losses—from rising and falling markets with a relatively small capital outlay. A CFD is a contract between a buyer and a seller to exchange the difference in value of a particular investment between when the contract is opened and when it is closed.

There are two types of CFDs: over-the-counter (or OTC) CFDs and ASX-listed CFDs. With OTC CFDs you trade a CFD with your CFD broker; the trade is not made over an exchange or financial market. Therefore, you are not protected by laws which apply when trading on a government-regulated financial market. For this reason, and for other reasons discussed later in this chapter, it is suggested that if you want to trade CFDs you should only trade ASX-listed CFDs.

CFDs are 'leveraged' investment products. This means that you are fully exposed to price movements of the underlying investment without having to outlay the full price of that investment. The following example illustrates this point by comparing buying 500 BHP Billiton shares directly with getting the same exposure to these shares through a CFD.

Suppose BHP Billiton shares are currently trading at $40 and you think that the share price will go up and you decide to buy 500 shares. This means you would have to outlay $20 000 plus brokerage fees. If instead you bought the same number of shares through BHP CFDs, you would only need to put up an initial 'margin' of 7 per cent, or $1400. Suppose BHP's share price rises to $41 the next day and you decide to sell out your position. As table 9.1 (overleaf) shows, your net profit on both these transactions is about the same, but because your initial outlay with CFDs is only 7 per cent of the outlay if you purchase the shares directly, your investment return on CFDs is about 15 times the return you received if you purchased the shares directly. So, CFDs offer the potential to make a higher return from a smaller initial outlay than investing directly in shares. However, it should be emphasised that if BHP's share price had fallen to $37 you could have lost more than your initial margin position with CFDs.

Attractions of CFDs

For short-term traders the main attraction of CFDs is their leverage. Indeed, CFDs are among the highest leveraged products traded on the ASX. As table 9.1 illustrates, CFDs require only a small initial margin, but your investment exposure is many times the initial margin. Another attraction of CFDs is that they give you the ability to profit when prices are going down, not just up. Most CFDs do not have an expiry date so they are referred to as perpetual investments. Consequently, the only way to close a trading position is to complete the opposite side of the position. So if you initially bought a CFD you would sell it to complete the transaction; if you initially sold a CFD you would need to buy it back to complete the transaction.

Unlike other derivatives, such as options and futures, CFD cash flows are paid while the position is open. This allows CFD prices to track the underlying investment rather than trade at a discount or premium, as can be the case with other derivatives.

Table 9.1: comparing CFDs and share purchases

	CFDs	Shares
Day 1		
Opening purchase price	$40.00	$40.00
Quantity bought	500	500
Commission	$20	$20
GST	$0	$2
Value of shares	$20 000	$20 000
CFD margin (7%)	$1 400	$0
Total outlay	$1 420	$20 022
Day 2		
Closing price	$41.00	$41.00
Quantity sold	500	500
Sale proceeds	$20 500	$20 500
Commission	$20.50	$20.50
GST	$0	$2.05
Financing charge	$3.20	$0
Total investment outlay	$1 443.70	$20 044.55
Gross profit	$500	$500
Net profit	$456.30	$455.45
% investment return	31.6%	2.3%

Trading CFDs

When trading ASX-listed CFDs, your order is entered directly via a participant into the ASX-listed CFD central market order book. All orders are executed on a strict price/time priority, so the first order with the best bid or offer price is always executed first. Trading in the ASX-listed CFD central market order book also ensures client orders are always given priority over a broker's house orders.

In contrast, if you trade CFDs through an OTC broker, you do not have your orders in the ASX-listed CFD central market order book. These orders are transacted with the OTC CFD broker. Your order is not protected by the ASX's price/time priority or client order precedence rules. Another risk with trading OTC CFDs is that you are not covered under guarantee arrangements such as the Australian National Guarantee

Fund and you are directly dependent on the creditworthiness of your OTC CFD broker. Finally, because the contract is between you and your broker, you are not able to take your contract to another CFD broker to close out the trade.

Product range
ASX-listed CFDs include CFDs over:

- the top 50 companies listed on the ASX

- key global equity indices

- a range of major foreign currencies

- selected commodities.

A full list of current ASX-listed CFDs is available at <www.asx.com.au/cfd>.

Margins on CFDs
Initial margins apply to both buyers and sellers upon opening a CFD contract. The initial margin is typically set at a level designed to cover reasonably foreseeable losses on a position between the close of business on one day and the next. The amount of initial margin for each contract varies according to the price volatility of the underlying instrument, but typically is about 5 to 10 per cent of the value of the underlying instrument described by the contract. The ASX publishes the initial margin rates for all ASX-listed CFDs. You can find these rates on the ASX website. Initial margins are returned when the contract is closed out.

There are also 'variation margins' which cover adverse movements in position value and ensure all parties meet their accumulated losses. These are paid daily and are based on the daily settlement price of the shares or the relevant index.

Client agreement forms
You will need to sign a client agreement form before you start trading CFDs. This is a legal contract setting out the terms on which your broker will act for you. It is important that you read the client agreement carefully before signing it and retain a copy of the agreement. The ASX does not prescribe a set client agreement but requires minimum terms which the client agreement must contain. Brokers may have other terms provided they are not inconsistent with the ASX's minimum terms.

ASX CFD trading simulator

As trading CFDs can multiply your losses as well as giving you the opportunity for significant profits, before you start trading CFDs it is highly recommended that you try out the ASX CFD Trading Simulator, where you can experience trading in CFDs without actually putting any money on the line. This simulator is available on the CFD page of the ASX site.

Key points

o Before investing in these more advanced sharemarket products, make sure you understand the potential risks you are taking. You should also read the product disclosure document prepared by the warrant issuer.

o First establish why you are using the products outlined in this chapter — are you hedging against price falls or are you speculating on the future direction of share prices?

o Generally speaking, the products discussed in this chapter have the potential to greatly increase your investment return if the sharemarket moves in the direction you expect. They also have the potential to magnify your losses if your judgement is wrong.

o Before investing in warrants make sure you read the brochures on warrants that are available from the ASX so that you are fully aware of the risks you are taking.

o Many of the products and strategies discussed in this chapter allow you to make money when share prices are falling. However, if share prices rise rather than fall when using such an approach, your potential losses can be substantial.

o CFDs are highly leveraged trading products where you can lose more than your initial investment. They are only suitable for experienced personal investors who are able to bear the risks involved.

o It is highly recommended that you take advantage of the ASX CFD trading simulator before you try to actually trade CFDs.

10

Hybrid securities and margin lending

An enduring feature of financial markets is that new products are continually being invented to accommodate changing conditions. In the late 1990s when share prices were rising strongly, companies raised new money by issuing ordinary shares either via new floats or rights issues. When share prices began a downward spiral in March 2000 investors were not so keen to put more money into shares given the prospects of further share price falls. So an old sharemarket product was dusted off, given a couple of new twists and marketed with a variety of catchy names. The end result is the emergence of a 'new' investment product known as 'hybrid securities'. In fact, these securities are just a re-modelling of a product that has been around for decades, known as convertible preference shares.

Hybrids are the general name for a group of securities which are listed on the ASX that combine some features of fixed-interest securities and some characteristics of shares, just as a hybrid car is one that can run on both petrol and electric power. Hybrids pay a predictable (fixed or floating) rate of return or dividend until a certain date. At that date the holder has a number of options, including converting the hybrids into ordinary shares.

Therefore, unlike a share, if you buy a hybrid there is a 'known' cash flow, whereas you do not really know what dividend you will be paid on a share. Also, unlike fixed-interest securities, hybrids have an option to convert to the underlying share. It is important to note that hybrid securities vary considerably from one company to another. This means that while the prices of some hybrids behave more like fixed-interest securities, others behave more like the underlying shares into which they convert. In 2010 there were over 100 securities trading on the ASX fixed-interest market, most of which would be classified as hybrids.

Modern hybrids have a number of features that distinguish them from preference shares and convertible notes issued in the 1980s and 1990s, including:

- Instead of paying interest that is fully taxable, they often pay fully franked dividends, which are much more tax-effective for investors.

- The rate of return is not fixed forever but can be 'reset' at specified intervals. This is an important change as you might invest in one of these hybrids when market interest rates are low and then find that you are disadvantaged if market rates rise and you are locked into a fixed rate of return. Hence the name reset preference shares (RPSs).

- Instead of converting into ordinary shares at a fixed ratio — for example, one hybrid equals one ordinary share — the conversion ratio is determined when the hybrid matures by a formula contained in the prospectus. This conversion technique is explained in more detail later in this chapter.

How a typical hybrid works

Hybrids pay regular distributions or dividends. The calculation to determine the amount of the distribution begins with the 90- or 180-day bank bill swap rate, which is the rate at which major financial institutions lend money to each other. This rate is usually just above the Reserve Bank cash rate. An interest rate margin is then added to this; for example, the distribution might be 3.5 per cent above the 90-day bank bill swap rate. This margin differs from company to company. Generally, the more financially sound the company the lower the margin above the bank bill swap rate. Consequently, hybrids tend to trade at different prices depending on the size of the margin above the bank bill swap rate and the financial soundness of the company issuing the hybrids. When each distribution is paid, the rate for the next period is set — or reset. For example, if the bank bill swap rate has gone up since the last reset date, then the distribution for the next period will also increase. The actual distribution is calculated on the face value, not the market price, of the hybrid.

For almost all hybrids, distribution payment is conditional. Typical conditions include the obvious such as the company/institution having sufficient funds, the Australian Prudential Regulation Authority not objecting to the payment and the directors at their sole discretion permitting the payment. The flipside is a dividend stopper, which applies to dividends or distributions on all the issued securities — this makes the bank pay a coupon on the hybrids if dividends are being paid on the ordinary shares. Distributions are often non-cumulative, so if a distribution is not paid there is no requirement for the company to make up missed payments.

The generic RPS structure incorporates a franked dividend set for a specified period, usually five years, at a rate higher than prevailing interest rates. At the end of that period, the dividend rate and other conditions may be reset. You can either roll over your RPSs at the new terms or convert into the issuer's ordinary shares. Alternatively, the issuer may exercise its option to redeem the RPSs through either cash or ordinary shares.

The 'new' RPSs are described by a variety of names, depending on the issuer and the investment bank that advises them. For example, the Commonwealth Bank (CBA) hybrids are called 'PERLS', the Bank of Queensland hybrid issue was called 'Reset Convertible Preference Shares' ('ReCaPS'), Seven Network's were TELYS and Fairfax's PRESSES, to name a few. Despite the variety of names, all these hybrids have the same essential features. Perhaps this is best illustrated by an example of the CBA's PERLS (Perpetual Exchangeable Resaleable Listed Securities) V, which were issued in September 2009:

- PERLS V entitle holders to quarterly distributions, expected to be fully franked, that are subject to the payment tests. These distributions are expected to comprise interest on the notes.

- The distribution rate will be calculated each quarter as the bank bill swap rate plus the margin of 3.40 per cent, together multiplied by $(1 - \text{Tax rate})$.

- Assuming the bank bill swap rate is 3.2800 per cent, the cash distribution received by a holder would be 4.6760 per cent per annum (assuming distributions are fully franked). The fully franked distribution rate of 4.6760 per cent per annum would be equivalent to an unfranked distribution rate of 6.6800 per cent per annum if the potential value of the franking credits is taken into account in full.

- Holders should be aware that the ability to use franking credits will depend on their individual position and that the potential value of franking credits does not accrue at the same time as the cash distribution is received.

- Distributions are non-cumulative. If a distribution or part of a distribution is not paid on a distribution payment date, holders have no claim or entitlement in respect of non-payment nor any right to receive that distribution at any later time.

- Distributions are discretionary. If distributions are not paid on PERLS V, a dividend stopper will restrict the CBA from paying dividends, interest or distributions or returning capital on CBA ordinary shares and certain other securities.

- PERLS V are expected to be exchanged on 31 October 2014 (being the initial conversion date) by one of the following methods:

  - Resale: the CBA may arrange a resale, where the purchaser will acquire all PERLS V for $200 each.

  - Conversion: if resale does not occur, PERLS V will convert into a variable number of CBA ordinary shares worth approximately $202.021 if the conversion conditions are satisfied.

  - Repurchase: if resale and conversion have not occurred, CBA may, subject to the Australian Prudential Regulation Authority's prior written approval, elect to repurchase all PERLS V for $200 each.

- If PERLS V are not exchanged on the initial conversion date, the same possible outcomes will apply to each subsequent distribution payment date until exchange occurs.

- PERLS V do not have a fixed maturity date and are effectively perpetual investments. However, on 31 October 2014, PERLS V may be resold for $200 each at the election of the bank, or PERLS V will convert to CBA ordinary shares (if the conversion conditions are satisfied).

This is just a summary of the main features of PERLS V. So, as you can appreciate, before investing in a hybrid you need to read the product disclosure document carefully.

Common terms

Although hybrid securities are reasonably easy to understand they are surrounded by a considerable amount of financial jargon and it is essential that you understand what these terms mean. The typical RPSs are called 'convertible' as they give the option of swapping them for ordinary shares at specified dates. If you decide not to convert to ordinary shares you generally have two choices: either receive the face value of your investment back or continue or roll over this investment with new terms and conditions. In contrast, a 'converting' security gives you no choice other than to convert into ordinary shares.

Other common terms you need to be aware of include:

- *Cumulative:* If a dividend is missed you are still entitled to be paid the dividend if the company's fortunes improve.

- *Non-cumulative:* If a dividend is not paid you have lost it forever.

- *Face value:* The issue price of the RPS—usually $100.

- *Coupon rate:* This is the rate of dividend or interest that is being offered and it is calculated on the face value. For example, if the rate of dividend is 8 per cent and the face value is $100, you would receive an $8 dividend per year. If you buy the RPSs for $104 after they are listed on the ASX you still only receive $8 in dividends per year.

- *Redeemable:* At certain times you may have the option to redeem or 'hand back' the securities to the company and be paid the face value. The company may also have the ability to redeem these securities in certain circumstances.

- *Non-redeemable:* The securities cannot be redeemed under any circumstances.

- *Reset/resettable:* A resettable security means that after a certain period—usually between three and five years—the current terms and conditions are reviewed and a new interest or dividend rate is set for a new term. At this 'reset' date you can either accept the new terms or convert into ordinary shares.

Trading hybrids

Hybrids are listed on the ASX and you buy and sell them in exactly the same way you do shares. Unlike warrants and options, there is no need to sign a client agreement with your broker. Before you buy or sell these securities you should check when the next dividend is due to be paid and whether these securities are trading 'cum dividend'—you will receive the next dividend payment—or 'ex-dividend'—you will not receive the next dividend payment. For example, an RPS paying an 8 per cent dividend twice a year with a face value of $100 might be due to pay its next $4 dividend in a few weeks. If its market price is $105, $4 of this reflects the dividend payment and you would expect its price to drop by around $4 when it goes ex-dividend. It is usually better to buy ex-dividend, as otherwise you will receive part of your initial investment back in a taxable form soon after you invest. In the *Australian Financial Review* there is a separate table headed 'Hybrid securities' which gives buy and sell quotes, the high and low prices for the year and other information such as the next reset date.

Risks of hybrids

The yields on hybrids are usually higher than other fixed-interest investments, but so too are the risks. As always when you invest in the sharemarket you are exposed to two types of risk: market risk and non-market or company-specific risk. Although RPSs are resettable, you could be in trouble if market interest rates rise significantly soon after you invest. The result is that you are locked into an investment which now has a relatively low return until the reset date.

The risks associated with RPSs also vary from company to company. For example, ABC Learning Centres, Allco, Timbercorp and Great Southern all issued hybrids, and investors in these companies lost substantial amounts of money—irrespective of whether they bought the ordinary shares or the hybrids.

The company's credit rating and size are clearly important factors, because you need to be confident there will be a ready market for these shares if you decide to convert. In addition, you need to be sure that the company has the financial strength to be able to pay the dividends it has promised for its RPSs. One issue you need to check before investing is under what conditions can a dividend payment on an RPS not be paid. In some cases, if a company decides not to pay dividends on its ordinary shares then it also will not pay dividends on its RPSs.

Choosing which RPS or portfolio of RPSs is appropriate for you depends in part on what risks you are willing to take. If you are willing to take higher risks in search of higher returns you could consider a blend of higher yielding but higher risk RPSs. One possible drawback of investing in lesser-known RPSs is that they usually do not trade as often as those issued by blue-chip companies. In addition, the 'spread' between buyers and sellers is also likely to be larger. This means that if you want to sell these securities you might have to accept a much lower price because there are fewer potential buyers. If you are a more conservative investor then it is best to stick to the better-known names, such as the major banks, although this does not guarantee that you will not lose money.

On a more positive note, because RPSs are 'preference' shares they rank ahead of ordinary shareholders if the company goes bankrupt. Unfortunately, this is often cold comfort to investors as most companies that go bankrupt do not pay anything to either their preference or ordinary shareholders.

Conversion terms

Although hybrids are partly like a fixed-income security and partly like an ordinary share, there are some hybrids that perform more like fixed-income securities and their prices are influenced more by the overall level of interest rates. In contrast, there are other hybrids that are linked more closely to the ordinary shares of the issuing company and their share prices are influenced more by factors affecting the company's ordinary shares. It is essential that you are aware of this difference, otherwise you could end up buying a hybrid that does not suit your investment needs and objectives.

Basically there are two types of hybrids: those offering fixed conversion into ordinary shares and those offering dollar value conversion into ordinary shares. While this difference might appear to be inconsequential, it is a crucial element in determining how the price of a hybrid will perform.

Fixed conversion

Before the invention of modern RPSs, most hybrids had a fixed conversion ratio into ordinary shares and this ratio was established at the time the hybrid was issued. Many such hybrids—for example, securities known as convertible notes—are still being traded on the ASX so it is important that you do not confuse the two and end up buying the wrong hybrid. For example, a fixed conversion ratio would be if one convertible note converted into one ordinary share. This fixed ratio suggests that the price of this type of hybrid would be closely tied to the movements in the price of the underlying ordinary shares. However, you would expect that in a bear market the price of convertible notes might not fall as far as ordinary shares as they eventually become priced in comparison to other fixed-interest securities. In other words, you would expect that the price of convertible notes would find some support when the yield you receive on them begins to compare favourably with interest returns on government bonds and fixed-term deposits.

Another distinguishing feature between convertible notes and RPSs is that convertible notes pay a fixed rate of interest that is fully taxable and not resettable. Consequently, they are a far less flexible investment than RPSs, but some high-yielding convertible notes might be attractive to investors in low income tax brackets. Keep in mind that high yield normally goes hand in hand with high risk.

If you are buying or selling convertible notes you need to know if you are trading on a 'cum distribution' or 'ex-distribution' basis. This can be very important for tax purposes. For example, suppose you bought a convertible note for $3 and sold it just before it went 'ex-distribution' for $3.60. Further suppose that the distribution was 30¢ per note, so you expect that the price of the convertible note would fall by around 30¢ when it started trading ex-distribution. If you sell at $3.60 you make a capital gain of 60¢ per note, and if you held these notes for more than 12 months you pay capital gains tax at a maximum rate of 24.25 per cent. In contrast, if you sold ex-distribution for $3.30 you would have a 30¢ per note capital gain plus a fully taxable distribution of 30¢ per note. Depending on your rate of income tax, it could be more tax-effective to sell 'cum distribution' as the overall tax on your investment would be lower. A list of convertible notes is available in the *Australian Financial Review*.

Dollar value conversion

One of the innovations with modern RPSs is that they usually have a dollar value conversion—but you need to read the prospectus to ensure that this is the case. In this situation, the number of ordinary shares you would receive when you convert your RPSs is determined at the maturity or reset date, which could be five years after the RPSs are issued. The face value of the RPS, usually $100, buys you shares at a discount—usually 5 or 10 per cent—to the market price of the ordinary shares at the date of conversion. The conversion terms also have maximum and minimum limitations on the quantity of ordinary shares you can receive. The minimum number of shares issued on conversion is set so that you receive ordinary shares at least equivalent in value to the hybrid's original issue price.

At conversion, the number of ordinary shares you receive is calculated by the application of a conversion formula, by which ordinary shares are issued at a discount to the prevailing ordinary share price of the issuer, with the number of ordinary shares obtained being calculated with reference to that ordinary share price. In practice, the conversion formula uses the issuer's ordinary share price during a period after the conversion trigger date and before the actual conversion occurs (the 'reference price'). This means that if you want to sell the shares once you have received them you will receive a price close to the reference price.

Alternatively, you can decide to retain the resulting ordinary shares, in which case you will then have all the opportunities for gain and risks of loss of an ordinary shareholder.

You are not liable for capital gains tax when you convert your hybrids to ordinary shares, and any capital gains you achieve when you sell the shares will be taxed at the discount capital gains tax rates so long as you held the hybrids and shares for more than 12 months.

Essentially, the issue of ordinary shares at conversion operates like a money-back mechanism, simply requiring you to sell the ordinary shares after conversion to receive cash. Since the number of shares you will receive on conversion and their value are determined by a formula set out in the offer documents for the issue, you can normally be confident that you can exit your ordinary shares and receive the original value paid for the hybrid, unless of course the company goes bankrupt before the conversion date. In turn, this means that the market prices of these hybrids are not as closely tied to the company's share price as are those with fixed conversion ratios.

The main feature that varies between RPS issues is the strike price that determines the minimum number of shares RPS holders receive on conversion. In this way, RPS holders can participate in some upside of the equity price. Remember that some hybrids also allow the issuer to redeem for cash before conversion.

Valuing hybrids

Hybrids are often priced according to the size of their yield. Unfortunately, there are a couple of methods of measuring yield:

- Running yield is the distribution rate divided by the face value. Suppose a hybrid pays 8 per cent on a $100 face value, but is selling for $80. Then the hybrid's running yield is: $8 ÷ $80 × 100 = 10%.

- Yield to reset is the running yield of the distributions plus the difference between the market price and the face value, assuming the principal is returned on the reset date. So if a hybrid is trading at $95 and will pay two $8 distributions and then be redeemed for $100, the yield to reset accounts for the capital gain of $5 when the hybrid is redeemed at $100.

In financial markets, perpetual securities are normally valued using a running yield as there is no actual redemption date. Hybrids, like government bonds, are usually valued on a yield to reset basis. The yield to maturity for different hybrids is calculated in the hybrids table published in the *Australian Financial Review*.

There are a number of factors you should consider when deciding whether hybrids should be included in your portfolio and what represents a fair price for a particular hybrid. Firstly, if you intend to add some hybrids to your investment portfolio, what will they replace? Are you going to count them as part of the fixed-income component of your portfolio or part of your exposure to equities? The answer to this depends in part on the type of hybrid you are considering: is it more like an ordinary share or more like a fixed-income security?

Be aware that if you are diverting money from government bonds or fixed-term deposits to hybrids you might increase the potential income return from your portfolio but you are also increasing the risks. On the other hand, if you are diverting funds from ordinary shares to invest in hybrids you are reducing the risks of your portfolio but you are also reducing your exposure to a general rise in share prices.

Turning to individual hybrids there are several issues to consider. As was previously stated, if you do not think that the ordinary shares in the company are worth buying then you should steer clear of the company's hybrid offerings. If the hybrid passes this first investment criterion, then you need to examine:

- Does the hybrid pay interest that is fully taxable or dividends that are fully franked? Depending on your marginal income tax rate, a 10 per cent fully taxable return might not be worth as much as an 8 per cent fully franked return.

- What are the conversion terms? If there is a dollar value conversion, what discount do you get on the market price of the ordinary shares?

- Do the conversion terms allow you to participate in any upside in the company's ordinary shares? This is often difficult to establish, but often there is some section in the prospectus that addresses this issue.

- How long before the next reset date? The longer the time the more chances you have of being locked into the current dividend return.

- How often is income paid — is it quarterly or half-yearly? The more frequently the better.

- How often and in what quantities are these hybrids traded? As with any investment it pays to think about how easy it will be to sell.

Margin lending

Margin lending means you are borrowing to buy shares. With margin lending the shares you buy are normally used as security for the loan. However, as many investors have learned the hard way by losing tens of thousands of dollars, there are different forms of margin lending documentation in use in Australia. One form of margin lending casts doubt on whether the investor retains any legal or beneficial ownership of the shares purchased under the margin lending agreement. Under this documentation, legal and beneficial ownership of the investor's securities may be transferred to the margin lender, and perhaps then to a third party who has advanced a loan to the margin lender. This has the risk that the shares could be sold without the investor's knowledge and the proceeds used to repay the debt of the margin lender.

The other form of documentation involves a more traditional form of borrowing and mortgage of securities by an investor, so that title to the shares bought using the margin loan remains at all times with the investor unless the investor defaults on the margin lending facility.

Usually the lender will only advance between 30 per cent and 70 per cent of the market value of the shares. This is called the loan-to-valuation ratio. The rest you have to put in yourself. Lenders also have an approved list of shares they are prepared to lend money against — this would not include speculative mining and oil companies.

Another key feature of margin loans is that you must keep your equity in the share portfolio at a predetermined level. For example, suppose you borrow $70 000 through a margin loan, put in another $30 000 of your own money and buy a share portfolio worth $100 000. Suppose the value of these shares falls to $90 000. Your equity has now dropped to $20 000 ($90 000 – $70 000). The lender would then require you to 'top up' your equity to keep it at 30 per cent of the current value of the share portfolio. Thirty per cent of $90 000 is $27 000 — so your lender would require that you pay off $7000 of the original loan immediately. This is referred to as a 'margin call'.

You could sell some shares and use the proceeds to reduce the loan. Normally you have to respond to a margin call within 24 hours. If you do not, the lender can sell some shares on your behalf. It is therefore wise to make suitable arrangements in advance if you are ever going to be difficult to contact.

Margin loans are available from banks and other financial organisations—a list of these organisations can be found on the InfoChoice website: <www.infochoice.com.au>. The minimum loan is usually around $50 000. You cannot use margin loans to buy just any listed shares. They must be on the lender's list of approved companies—basically non-speculative companies. Some listed property trusts may also be acceptable. The shares can be held in the names of individuals, companies, partnerships or trusts.

Margin loans are granted on an 'interest-only' basis and you can combine a margin loan with negative gearing to maximise the tax-effectiveness of the arrangement. The interest rate is likely to be higher than in the case of loans secured by mortgages on property, but because of the simplicity of the transaction the establishment fees are likely to be less. A choice of fixed and variable rates is usually available. You receive all dividends and franking credits, plus entitlements to rights and bonus issues. You can also participate in dividend reinvestment plans, shareholder discount schemes and similar arrangements. To purchase shares subject to a margin loan arrangement you normally need to set up a separate account with your broker.

Whether such a loan is suitable for you depends on your willingness and ability to take risks with your investments. The main attraction of margin loans is that they enable you to acquire a much bigger portfolio of shares than if you used only your own money. If the shares go up then you will make a much bigger profit. But if the shares go down then you will also make a much bigger loss.

One danger with margin loans is that in a volatile market there is an increased likelihood of you being asked for margin calls. If you do not have sufficient money to pay these calls you could find yourself sold out of the market. This was the position that thousands of margin lending clients of Opes Prime, Storm Financial and Lift Capital found themselves in during 2008 and 2009. Some retail investors exposed to margin loans lost their homes when the sharemarket plunged 40 per cent during the global financial crisis. You should never take out a loan against your home in order to buy shares.

As a result of the collapse of these margin lending organisations, the federal government announced a major crackdown on margin loans. New laws to provide national regulation of the $21 billion margin loan industry will also prevent investors from using the family home as security for taking on risky levels of debt to buy shares.

As part of the overhaul, margin lenders will be regulated by the Australian Securities & Investments Commission, required to hold an Australian Financial Services Licence and be forced to fully disclose fees and commissions on the products they sell. Previously, margin lending in Australia was not regulated.

Key points

o   Reset preference shares are called hybrids because they are a cross between a fixed-income security and an ordinary share.

o   Before making any investment in a hybrid, you should check the specific terms of issue by reading the prospectus.

o   You need to be comfortable that you understand the mechanics of the conversion process, especially if you wish to cash out your investment at conversion.

o   Hybrids can be a good investment but you need to monitor them like shares. If the company's ordinary shares are not highly regarded by other investors it could be time to sell the hybrids.

o   Some hybrids pay interest that is fully taxable while others pay fully franked dividends—make sure you clarify this before you invest.

o   'Older style' hybrids such as convertible notes usually do not pay fully franked dividends and so have become less attractive than RPSs for many investors.

o   A list of hybrids and a summary of their main terms and conditions is available on the ASX website: <www.asx.com.au>.

o   Margin lending is often recommended by financial advisers as a means of getting greater exposure to the sharemarket. But many investors in 2008 and 2009 learnt the hard way that margin lending has considerable risks when share prices fall.

o   You should never use your home as security in order to take out a margin loan.

11

Listed investment companies

Listed investment companies (LICs) are legally constituted companies which are listed on the ASX. At the start of 2010 there were 45 LICs listed in the S&P/ASX LIC Composite Index, of which 33 are in the S&P/ASX LIC Domestic Index and 12 are in the S&P/ASX LIC International Index. LICs invest predominantly in shares in other listed companies. This is very much what equity managed funds do, and LICs have many of the attributes of equity funds for this reason. But there is a fundamental difference between the two. LICs have all the characteristics of companies, such as limited liability. On the other hand, equity funds are governed by a trust deed and need to have a responsible entity. Also equity funds are not listed on the stock exchange, although there are many listed property trusts.

LICs have been in existence for much longer than equity funds, although they are much fewer in number. For example, Milton Corporation was incorporated in 1937 and Australian Foundation Investment Company in 1928. Although managed funds have been in existence as a form of retail investment since 1936, they did not become a popular form of investment until the 1980s. Table 11.1 (overleaf) shows the largest 15 Australian LICs based on S&P/ASX LIC Composite Index weight at February 2010.

As with all companies, the constitution of an LIC is its memorandum and articles of association. Since they are listed companies, their shares are traded on the ASX. Hence you can buy and sell LICs through a stockbroker. A prospectus is required for initial listing and rights issues.

LICs are subject to the usual ASX listing and reporting requirements. In contrast, with unlisted equity funds you buy and sell units through the fund manager.

Table 11.1: top 15 LICs based on composite index weight at Feb. 2010

Company	Index weight (%)	Domestic or international
Australian Foundation Investment Company	28.15	Domestic
Argo Investments	21.99	Domestic
Milton Corporation	9.03	Domestic
Djerriwarrh Investments	5.24	Domestic
Australian United Investment Company	4.00	Domestic
BKI Investment Company	2.99	Domestic
Diversified United Investments	2.71	Domestic
Carlton Investments	2.65	Domestic
Choiseul Investment	2.63	Domestic
AMP Capital China Fund	1.85	International
Mirrabooka Investments	1.46	Domestic
Platinum Capital	1.39	International
Hunter Hall Global Value	1.38	International
Global Mining Investments	1.33	International
Magellan Flagship Fund	1.28	International
Total	88.08	

Source: ASX.

Why invest in an LIC?

There are several reasons why you would consider investing in an LIC in preference to buying units in an equity fund:

- There are tax implications. Currently equity funds do not pay tax on their income provided that all of it is distributed to unitholders. LICs pay company tax and then pay dividends from their after-tax profits. Dividends from LICs may be partly or wholly franked, or unfranked.

- The management of the two types of entity is different. But some organisations, such as AMP Capital Investors, have both LICs and unlisted equity funds.

- LICs may offer you better liquidity in that you can sell shares on the sharemarket and get your money in around three business days.

With an equity fund there may be delays before redemption is completed, such as occurred with some equity funds in the aftermath of the October 1987 sharemarket crash and the GFC.

- Management costs are generally lower with LICs than with unlisted equity funds because there are no upfront fees, and ongoing management fees are lower. But you do pay brokerage when you buy and sell.

- You can often buy shares in an LIC at a discount to their net asset backing. In contrast, you usually pay a premium to buy units in a managed fund when you take upfront fees into account.

Unlisted equity funds and LICs invest in similar securities, normally Australian listed shares. Nevertheless, there are some significant differences between the structures of unlisted equity funds and LICs. If you are considering investing in these areas, it is important that you understand these differences before choosing one structure over the other.

Liquidity

LICs and unlisted equity funds can differ markedly in their liquidity characteristics. The liquidity of LIC shares depends on the trading volume of the shares. Generally speaking, if you try to buy or sell $10 000 to $20 000 worth of shares in these companies, you should encounter few problems. The liquidity of an equity fund is heavily dependent on the underlying value of the fund's net assets, the ability to realise those assets when necessary and the amount of liquid assets of the managed fund. If a large number of investors want to redeem their units, the fund manager may have to dispose of assets to meet these redemptions. This was a particular problem during the GFC for some managed funds. For example, AXA, Perpetual, Colonial First State and Australian Unity froze redemptions covering around $4.1 billion from their mortgage funds, which was especially difficult for self-funded retirees who relied on income from these funds for their daily living expenses. A freeze on redemptions does not necessarily mean the investors in these funds will lose money. Indeed it could be a prudent longer term strategy by the trustees of those funds as they have delayed redemptions until liquidity improves. The alternative would be to sell down assets at 'fire sale' prices. The prices of shares in LICs certainly fell during the GFC but you could at least sell them and get access to some of your money.

The assets of an unlisted equity fund are owned and held by the responsible entity. The manager invests these assets on your behalf. If you wish to dispose of your units the manager arranges to pay you directly from the fund, at a price which reflects the underlying value of the fund. With an LIC the assets are owned by the company and you are a shareholder in the company. You buy and sell shares in the company like any other listed company. But there will only be a sale if there is a buyer for your shares. That means that there has to be another investor who wishes to buy the shares at the price you are willing to sell at. There is no guarantee that you can sell your shares at the price you wish to, which is a problem many investors encountered during the GFC. Like any other shares, the share prices of LICs can rise or fall — not particularly surprising as the assets of LICs are listed shares. So if the overall sharemarket is rising you would also expect the share prices of LICs to increase. If the overall sharemarket is falling so too would the share prices of LICs.

These differences between an LIC and an unlisted equity fund can become significant in a rapidly declining market, such as occurred during the GFC. If an equity fund manager is forced to sell investments to meet higher than expected levels of redemptions, this can have an adverse impact on the remaining unitholders, as the fund may be forced to sell investments at unfavourable prices.

As noted previously, many fund managers froze redemptions of units during the GFC for this reason. As LICs are traded on the sharemarket, they do not need to sell assets to meet redemptions, although the financial crisis saw the value of their investment portfolios fall by 30 to 40 per cent. Normally, during a fall in the overall sharemarket, investors in LICs wishing to dispose of their shares may be forced to sell at a significant discount to the company's net asset backing, which usually would not be incurred by an investor exiting from an unlisted equity fund. This is because the redemption price of most equity funds is related to the net asset backing of the funds. However, during the GFC the net asset backing of units in funds also fell significantly, so the redemption price of units dropped alarmingly. Fund managers simply did not have the cash to make redemptions at the rate at which investors were applying for them. In addition, the problem that investors in LICs have when selling at a discount to net asset backing may become exacerbated if the LIC has a low trading volume.

Due to this structural difference between unlisted managed funds and LICs, cash flow becomes important. An unlisted equity fund will usually hold 5 to 10 per cent of its portfolio in cash to meet redemptions from the fund's assets. During the GFC this was insufficient to satisfy all unitholders who wished to redeem their units. On the other hand, LICs can remain fully invested. You and other investors can sell your shares through a stockbroker at any time. Thus, it is not necessary for the company to maintain cash reserves for redemptions.

Fees

When you invest in an unlisted equity fund you will usually pay an entry fee in the range of 4 to 5 per cent. When you invest in an LIC you will pay standard brokerage charges, which are generally around 1 per cent of each transaction, buying and selling. If you buy shares online, brokerage is around $20 to $30 for transactions up to $10000. The ongoing management fees levied on an equity fund generally range between 1.0 and 1.8 per cent per year. The ongoing management fees of an LIC are generally below this level.

Regulation

Equity managed funds are included under the classification of prescribed interest products. As such they are governed by the rules of their respective trust deeds, and are regulated by ASIC. LICs are subject to the rules outlined in their memorandum and articles of association, and to the requirements of the Corporations Law. As they are listed companies they are also subject to the rules and regulations of the ASX.

Risk

All types of investments carry some degree of risk. A risk that applies to unlisted equity funds and LICs alike is market risk. This is the risk that the sharemarket in general will fall, such as happened during the GFC, causing the underlying assets of the fund or LIC to fall. In turn, the unit price or LIC share price will decline. There is also non-market risk. This is the risk that an unlisted equity fund or an LIC will invest in poorly performing companies. Generally, this risk is not significant as most LICs and equity funds have a diversified portfolio of shares which reduces the level of non-market risk. Nevertheless, before you invest in either an LIC or equity fund you should ask to see the latest share portfolio to satisfy yourself that the LIC or equity fund is not exposed to the performance of a small number of companies.

The price of an LIC is also influenced by a number of other factors. These include the market's perception of the company's management, the attractiveness of the sector or sectors in which it invests—such as Asian shares, resources or media—and its relative dividend yield.

Net tangible asset backing

The underlying value of an LIC is its net tangible assets (NTA). This is the value of its tangible assets minus its liabilities divided by the total number of shares on issue. In an LIC all assets are usually tangible assets. They do not have such things as goodwill, patents, promotion expenses and so on.

Depending on market sentiment, shares in an LIC may trade at either less than the underlying value of its NTA or more than the underlying value of its NTA. When it trades at less than the underlying value it is said to be trading at a discount. When it trades at more than the underlying value it is said to be trading at a premium.

For example, the NTA of Argo Investments at 31 December 2009 was $6.56 per share. If the company's price on the sharemarket exceeded $6.56 it would mean that the company was trading at a premium. In turn, this would mean that the market was valuing the company at more than the value of its net tangible assets. If the company's shares were trading below $6.56 it would mean that it was trading at a discount. This would mean that the market was valuing the company at less than the value of its net tangible assets. In February 2010 Argo was trading at $6.75, so it was trading at a premium to NTA. The premium is calculated as: ($6.75 − $6.56) ÷ $6.56 × 100 = 2.9%.

LICs are now required under accounting standards to publish their NTA at market value, taking into account possible capital gains tax if their portfolios are sold. If this provision was deducted at 31 December 2009, Argo's NTA would have been $5.83 per share.

With an equity fund, on the other hand, units are continuously being revalued so that they mirror the latest valuation of the underlying assets of the fund. However, units will be valued at slightly less than the underlying value of net assets because some costs are deducted. The formula that is the basis for determining the value of units is contained in the trust deed.

The premium/discount factor

The premium/discount factor is the amount by which an LIC's shares are selling at a premium or discount, expressed as a percentage of its NTA. For example, as was seen with Argo, the company's shares were selling at a premium of 2.9 per cent. This is known as the premium factor. When an LIC's shares are selling for less than NTA the reverse is true and there is a discount factor. It is important to have up-to-date NTA per share figures to calculate the current premium/discount factor. This information is usually published monthly by LICs and announced to the ASX.

The premium/discount factor can have a significant impact on investment performance. This is because the premium or discount component of the share price of an LIC has the potential to magnify general sharemarket movements. For example, when a market downturn occurs, as happened during the GFC, investors in LICs suffer a fall in the value of the underlying investments, as well as a possible adverse movement in the premium/discount factor.

A list of LIC premiums/discounts to NTA can be found on the ASX website: <www.asx.com.au>. This information includes premiums/discounts on a pre-tax and after-tax basis.

Investing in listed investment companies

The rationale for buying shares in an LIC is to obtain an interest in a diversified portfolio of shares for a relatively small investment. This portfolio could consist of either Australian shares or shares from a particular region, such as Asia/Pacific. An equally important consideration is to have a highly liquid investment. At the outset it is clear that the nature of the assets of an LIC will differ from most other types of companies. For example, LICs do not have property, plant and equipment as assets. Hence, the criteria generally used in evaluating companies for investment purposes may not be appropriate with LICs. For example, NTA per share usually has more significance with LICs than with many other companies.

Having decided to make an investment in an LIC, the problem then becomes: which one? One solution is to seek the advice of an investment adviser, such as a stockbroker. This may be available to you even if you do not do your broking business through the firm. Some advisers can steer you in the right direction. Unless you have acquired a fair degree of expertise in investment analysis, it is often preferable to seek professional advice as a first step.

For further information you can go to the ASX website and use the search engine. You can obtain share prices, NTA information, ASX announcements, charts, performance details and more. Note that in some parts of the ASX website LICs are referred to as listed managed investments (LMIs). Beware if you consult an investment adviser about investing in LICs. Many advisers receive commission for recommending unlisted equity funds, but no commission if you buy an LIC through a stockbroker. Hence you will probably not receive totally disinterested advice.

LIC performance

The performance of selected LICs is shown in table 11.2.

Table 11.2: performance of selected listed investment companies

Company	Return (% p.a.)*		
	1 year	3 years	5 years
Australian Foundation	37.92	4.48	12.41
Argo Investments	33.74	−0.79	9.21
Milton Corporation	31.59	−1.76	7.15
Djerriwarrh Investment	38.02	4.47	11.37
Clime Investment	100.72	−15.12	−4.85
Wilson Investment	53.23	−5.78	0.64
Bentley Capital	17.92	−10.31	−2.75
Aberdeen Leaders	44.09	−2.30	10.22
Global Masters	−18.82	−10.10	NA
Australian United	45.55	1.20	10.54
All Ordinaries accumulation index	39.58	−0.62	8.23

* Returns include dividends and capital gains or losses.
Years to 31 December 2009.
Source: Morningstar, ASX.

As you can see, the performance of LICs varied markedly. In the 12 months to 31 December 2009 the All Ordinaries accumulation index increased by 39.58 per cent, so you would not expect any LIC to earn a negative return during this period, yet Global Masters Fund Limited earned a return of −18.82 per cent. The best performing LIC during 2009 was Starpharma Holdings Limited which earned a return of 256.53 per cent, but over five years it earned a return of −1.23 per cent per annum. This just emphasises that in the investment world past performance is no guarantee of future performance.

Table 11.2 highlights the fact that there are significant differences in the individual performances of LICs. There are two main reasons why this may occur. Firstly, a particular LIC may have been selling at a substantial discount to its NTA and investors realised they can buy assets relatively cheaply. As a result of increased buying activity the share price goes up and the gap between share price and NTA narrows. This has the effect of increasing the LIC's return.

Secondly, the performance of an LIC is directly related to the type of shares it has in its portfolio. If an LIC mainly invests in resource companies and commodity prices fall, you would expect this to have an adverse impact on the LIC's investment portfolio and hence its NTA.

Some LICs have fewer shares on issue and have a more stable group of shareholders. This means that there are fewer shares available to be traded. When the sharemarket is rising this usually means that a small increase in demand for these shares will have a disproportionately larger impact on the share price. With larger LICs, such as Argo Investments and Australian Foundation Investment Company, it takes a much larger increase in demand to move the share price significantly.

An LIC will not perform identically to a unit trust that invests in the same selection of shares. This is due to the premium/discount factor with LICs and the fact that LICs may borrow to make investments. Unit trusts are not prohibited from borrowing, but they usually do not do so — but you should also check whether this is the case before you invest. Provided the cost of borrowing is less than the return from investing, an LIC will earn a higher return than a unit trust investing in the same shares. This gearing may entail exposure to foreign currency movements. Gearing, combined with the wider range of investments available to LIC managers, means that some LICs are inherently more risky than similar unit trusts.

It is important for you to determine the reasons for the existence of a premium/discount factor, as this may have a significant bearing on the attractiveness of the investment. For example, you may conclude that there is questionable value in buying shares in an LIC that is trading at a large premium over its NTA, particularly if strong fundamental share price analysis does not support the optimistic market sentiment regarding the future prospects of the investment. This means you should be wary of investing in an LIC which is trading at a premium — unless you consider that the investment manager deserves this premium ranking. An LIC's P/E ratio and dividend yield are not as important as the discount/premium factor. On the other hand, an LIC trading at a discount to its NTA may represent good value, allowing access to the underlying investments at less than their market value.

LIC investment portfolios

In evaluating LICs you should review their investment portfolios to establish what they hold and whether it is an appropriate balance compared with the weightings in the All Ordinaries index. Table 11.3 (overleaf) shows the top 10 investments held by Argo Investments at 31 December 2009.

Table 11.3: top 10 investments held by Argo Investments at 31 Dec. 2009

Company	Market value ($ million)
BHP Billiton	304.7
Westpac Banking Corporation	218.8
Rio Tinto	179.3
Macquarie Group	173.1
Wesfarmers	144.0
Milton Corporation	140.4
National Australia Bank	136.5
Australian United Investment Company	128.3
Commonwealth Bank	120.6
ANZ Bank	110.9

Source: Argo Investments.

Note that the above list is not unrepresentative of the top 10 companies in the All Ordinaries index (see chapter 8) except for the fact that two of the investments are in other LICs—Milton Corporation and Australian United Investment Company. Also, there are substantial holdings of the big four banks, so if bank shares fare badly Argo could be adversely affected. Other holdings of Argo include Telstra ($109.4 million), Woolworths ($107.5 million), Woodside Petroleum ($72.0 million), AMP ($48.3 million) and another LIC, Diversified United Investment ($47.6 million).

Sunset clauses

Some LICs have a 'sunset clause'. This is a clause in their memorandum and articles of association that says that shareholders will have an opportunity to vote on a winding up of the company if its shares trade at a predetermined discount to NTA over a prescribed period. For example, every predetermined number of years, if an LIC's shares trade at a weighted average discount to NTA of 10 per cent or more a special meeting of shareholders can be called within 90 days to vote on a voluntary winding up of the company to realise the true value of the company's assets. In cases like these, if you purchase shares in an LIC at a reasonable discount to NTA and the underlying value is realised, you can earn an attractive return. However, sunset clauses are not as popular as they used to be and you should check with the LIC in which you are interested in investing.

Even if an LIC selling at a discount is not wound up and the underlying value of its shares realised, the company may adopt other measures to give you access to its NTA. For example, an LIC may conduct a buy-back of its shares whereby shareholders could sell their shares to the respective companies at their NTA. If you buy these shares when they are selling at a significant discount you can earn attractive returns with a relatively low risk.

Premium/discount factor volatility

The premium/discount factor is an important indicator of the investment attractiveness of different LICs. These factors can also be volatile. This means that the measure can change significantly over a short space of time.

Because of constant fluctuations in premium/discount factors you need to be continually aware of an LIC's NTA and the relationship to its share price. The companies usually make this information available on a monthly basis.

LIC annual reports

As LICs have to conform to the rules of ASIC and the ASX, there is certain basic information that must be provided in annual and interim reports and ASX announcements. An important piece of information which it is not compulsory to show in an annual report is a complete portfolio of investments of the company. In practice, most companies will disclose this information. If they don't you should ask them for it. You should also ask for an up-to-date portfolio of investments periodically because it will change as time goes by. However, most companies will only disclose this information at their balance date, usually 30 June. Another piece of information which LICs normally provide is an up-to-date NTA backing. This is critical for calculating current premium/discount factors and comprehensive information, including premiums/discounts on a post-tax basis, and is available free on the ASX website.

Listed investment company floats

As has been seen, an LIC is a company that invests in the shares of other companies listed on the ASX. When an LIC is formed and its shares are offered to the public by way of a float (see chapter 12), you can generally expect that the shares will trade at a discount to the issue price when first listed. This is because an LIC invests in other companies, and after deducting the expenses incurred in conducting a float the amount invested in other companies per share issued is less than the issue price. Another way of saying this is to say that the NTA of the shares at the date of listing will necessarily be less than the issue price. For example, if the issue price is $1 per share and the costs of getting listed are 5¢ per share, the company's asset backing will be 95¢ when it lists. So you would not expect that such shares would list at a premium. Indeed it is quite likely that the shares of an LIC will list at a discount. It may then be worthwhile to buy LIC shares after the company has been listed at a discount to net asset backing.

Taxation and LICs

LICs pay tax on profits at the company tax rate of 30 per cent. The income of LICs generally consists of dividends, which may be partly or wholly franked or unfranked. LICs get the benefit of franking credits (if any) when calculating their income tax liability. The dividends LICs pay to shareholders may similarly be partly or wholly franked or unfranked. You should include the dividends in your income tax return in the same way as other dividends.

Managed funds distribute all of their profits to unitholders and the distributions are taxed in the unitholders' hands. Any franking credits are passed on to unitholders. In the case of capital gains, unitholders can claim a discount of 50 per cent on investments held for more than 12 months. Within LICs, there is no capital gains tax discount because companies are not entitled to claim this discount. However, superannuation funds can claim a 33.3 per cent discount on investments held for more than 12 months. Of course, shareholders in LICs can claim a discount when they sell their shares providing they have held their shares for longer than 12 months.

Key points

o   The investment portfolios of a listed investment company and an unlisted equity trust may be similar, but they are fundamentally different structures.

o   An LIC does not need to keep a cash balance to make redemptions so it can be fully invested at all times, if it so wishes.

o   Liquidity is generally better with LICs because you can trade shares on the stock exchange and obtain payment in three business days.

o   The costs of running an LIC are lower than an unlisted equity trust so management fees are lower in LICs.

o   Net asset backing is more relevant with LICs than it is with most other types of companies.

o   Before investing in an LIC it is important to know whether it is trading at a premium or a discount to net tangible assets. Generally, it is not wise to invest in an LIC that is trading at a premium to its NTA.

o   The performance of LICs varies widely so it is essential that you analyse the company's current share investments before you invest.

o   You generally should not invest in a new float of an LIC because it is likely to trade at a discount shortly after listing on the stock exchange.

12

New floats

As well as buying shares in companies that are already listed on the ASX, you can also buy newly issued shares through subscribing to company floats, also called initial public offers (IPOs). Company floats are the means by which companies raise money and finance their activities by issuing shares to the public. In the 12 months to February 2010 there were over 40 company floats in Australia.

During the GFC in 2008 and 2009 there were well over 70 company floats in Australia. The increased number was due to the fact that companies sought to reduce their debt levels and turned to the investing public as a way of doing this, mainly because it was harder to obtain a bank loan. However, floats were not as successful during this period as they had been at other times. For example, in the year 1 January 2008 to 31 December 2008, average float prices were 17.75 per cent below the prices at which shares were issued—hardly surprising as the overall sharemarket declined during this period.

At certain times—for example, during the internet boom in the late 1990s and in the lead up to the GFC—buying shares in a float virtually guaranteed that you would make money. At such times new floats almost always sell on the ASX at a higher price than the price paid for them. This is referred to as selling at a premium to the issue price. But during these times investors are so keen to buy into new floats that it is often difficult to get in on the action.

A stockbroker and/or investment bank underwrites many floats. In return for a fee, an underwriter guarantees to take up any shares that are not bought by the public. In effect an underwriter guarantees that all shares in a float will be sold. It works this way. Say a company is issuing one million shares, but only receives applications for 900 000 shares. If the company has an underwriter, the underwriter would buy the 100 000 shortfall. Before stockbrokers or investment banks take on the role of underwriter they seek to satisfy themselves that the float will be successful and that they will not be left with a shortfall. If a float does not have an underwriter, you should steer clear of it because it generally indicates that no organisation is sufficiently confident of the float that it will guarantee a shortfall in subscriptions (though there are some floats that are so attractive that it is apparent no underwriter is required).

In general, in a heavily subscribed float, unless you are a client of the underwriter or the sponsoring broker, you will not receive any shares, and even if you do receive an allocation it will often be scaled back (that is, you won't receive as many shares as you applied for).

At other times—for example, in a bear market—investors shun floats. At these times stockbrokers will readily offer you an allocation of shares. But in these times you are likely to lose money if you invest in these floats as they usually list on the ASX at a price lower than their float price.

The float process

The process by which a company becomes listed on the ASX is not straight-forward, and when evaluating a float you need to identify the reasons why the company is listing. In some cases—such as Qantas, Telstra and the Commonwealth Bank—the government wishes to sell off all or part of its ownership. This is a widely accepted reason for a float. Alternatively, the owners of a family company or partnership may wish to turn their interests into cash. This rationale requires closer examination.

In some cases a company may wish to sell off a business which is no longer core to its mainstream of operations. An example is BHP selling off first OneSteel to the public in 2000, and BHP Billiton selling off BHP Steel in 2002. In recent times this has become more common and is a reversal of a trend towards conglomeration that began in the 1960s. In the case of Myer, which floated during 2009, the venture capitalist that had taken over the company wanted to take a profit.

However, the most common reason for a float is that a company requires additional capital to expand an existing business. Companies may prefer raising money from the public to alternatives such as a bank loan because it is cheaper and because it is easier to obtain a bank loan once equity capital has been raised. Where a float is being made for this reason you should ensure that you know what the money raised will be used for.

Once a company has decided to list it will usually prepare a prospectus and approach an underwriter. It is not essential to have an underwriter, but many view the appointment of one as a screening process. It can be considered a test of whether the float will be successful. If no one will take on the role of underwriter, it could give the impression that no one is prepared to accept the risk that the float will be unsuccessful. In some cases there may be more than one underwriter. Underwriting fees vary, but 2.5 per cent of the amount raised can be taken as a guide. There may also be sub-underwriters who receive a lesser percentage.

The next step in the listing process entails the underwriter marketing a company's shares to its clients and/or the general public. In some cases the underwriter will look no further than its own client base and investors are often offered a 'firm'—that is, guaranteed—allocation of shares in the float. In other cases an IPO may be freely marketed to the public—such as the case with Telstra and the Commonwealth Bank—and anyone who applies is likely to receive shares. However, if there is strong demand for the shares, you might not get as many shares as you applied for.

A closing date is set for applications at the time the marketing phase begins. After the closing date, shares are allocated to applicants and, where necessary, money is refunded to applicants who were allocated fewer shares than they applied for. Once this is completed, and providing all formal requirements have been met, the company lists on the ASX.

Winners and losers

The general aim when investing in a float, as with any sharemarket investment, is to buy shares in a company at a cost—the issue price—that is lower than the price at which you sell them. Hence, if all goes according to plan, you make a profit. Some investors buy shares in a float with the intention of selling them immediately the shares are listed on the ASX. The object of this practice, known as 'stagging', is to take a quick trading profit. However, the reality is that the share price when a company's shares are first listed is frequently below the issue price. In these cases those stagging newly floated shares make a loss.

Table 12.1 (overleaf) shows information for numerous floats that listed on the ASX in the year to February 2010. As you can see, investors who stagged the shares had mixed results. Premiums on the issue price, which measure the extent to which the list price exceeds the issue price, were as high as 100 per cent. Discounts on the issue price, which measure the extent to which the list price is below the issue price, were as high as 64.4 per cent. Clearly there are opportunities to both make and lose money quickly.

Table 12.1: selected company floats 12 months to February 2010

Company	Date listed	Issue price	Close 1st day (stag) price	Premium or (discount) on issue price	Price at Feb. 2010
Southern Hemisphere Mining	5 Jan. 2010	$0.25	$0.38	52.0%	$0.52
General Mining Corp	21 Dec. 2009	$0.20	$0.175	−12.5%	$0.185
Luiri Gold	16 Nov. 2009	$0.20	$0.40	100.0%	$0.37
Digislide Holdings	24 Aug. 2009	$1.25	$0.445	−64.4%	$0.295
Myer	2 Nov. 2009	$4.10	$3.75	−8.53%	$3.51
Apollo Gas	15 Dec. 2009	$0.20	$0.40	100.0%	$0.60
Metrocoal	4 Dec. 2009	$0.40	$0.185	−53.75%	$0.225
Dragon Energy	18 Feb. 2009	$0.20	$0.24	20.0%	$0.11
NT Resources	1 Feb. 2010	$0.20	$0.20	None	$0.20
Raisama	2 Dec. 2009	$0.35	$0.53	51.42%	$0.40
Azurn International	19 Aug. 2009	$0.20	$0.17	−15.0%	$0.095
Ethan Minerals	4 Dec. 2009	$0.20	$0.195	−2.5%	$0.18

Source: InvestSMART.

A disparity also exists between the price shares trade at on the first day of listing and what they may trade for later on. For example, Azurn International's shares traded at $0.17 on the day of listing, a discount of 15 per cent. By early February 2010 the shares had fallen to $0.095, a fall of 44.1 per cent compared with their price on the first day of listing.

As can be seen from table 12.1 there are opportunities to derive substantial gains by participating in a float either by stagging shares immediately they are listed or by holding them for a longer term. There are also notable risks. Shares offered in floats frequently list at below their issue price, and may sink further.

The basic problem when deciding on whether to invest in a float is how to sort out the potential winners from the unprofitable ones. This is not easy because, among other things, there is a limited amount of information with which to work and it may not be readily digestible. Indeed, some companies provide information in such a way as to confuse you so that you will merely fill out an application form and be done with it.

Evaluating a float

To apply for shares in a float you must fill out a form in the company's prospectus. A prospectus is a lengthy document that contains in-depth information about a company that is seeking listing on the ASX. A prospectus is partly a legal document in that it has to be registered with ASIC. It also has to be lodged with the ASX. A tick of approval for the prospectus from ASIC and the ASX means that the law and ASX rules have been adhered to; it does not mean that either body considers that a float has merit.

A prospectus is also a marketing document because it is designed to attract investors. You can therefore expect it, as far as possible, to portray a company and its management in a favourable light.

When you are evaluating a float, one of the first things you need to do is to distinguish between those that are being made by companies that are starting up—such as an oil or mining explorer—and those being made by already established companies—such as Telstra, the Commonwealth Bank, Qantas and Myer. An important difference between the two is that with an already established company it is possible to conduct fundamental analysis to determine the company's financial strength and review its historical earnings. As a first step you should look at traditional criteria such as net tangible asset backing and whether the company has a profitable trading history.

Irrespective of whether a company is just starting up or already trading, profit projections are important because if they are not met a company's share price is likely to nosedive. You can rely on profit projections in a majority of cases, but each case should be considered on its own merits. Make sure that the assumptions upon which projections are made are stated and that they are realistic. An example of over-optimistic projections was contained in the prospectuses of private tollways where the estimates of the number of vehicles that would use the tollways were generally far too high.

Where a profit projection has been made you can, on the basis of the number of shares contained in a float, calculate forecasted earnings per share (EPS) (see chapter 8). You can then use the P/E ratio for the sharemarket as a whole, and for the industry in which a company operates, to evaluate whether the shares are over- or under-priced. For example, say forecast EPS is 10¢ and the P/E ratio for similar companies in the same industry is 10. A company's forecast share price using these two pieces of data would be $1.00 (10¢ × 10). This price can be compared with the issue price and used as a guide as to whether you should apply for shares.

For some floats the companies concerned may not expect to make profits for some time; for example, technology companies. In these cases profit projections may be inappropriate and sales projections substituted. However, if a company is not likely to earn a profit in the near future there is no accepted way of establishing an appropriate share price. These companies would be classified as highly speculative—particularly if the company is marketing a new product with few current sales.

How to read a prospectus

An essential rule when you are evaluating a float is to read the entire prospectus. Although there is usually a 'Summary' at the beginning that facilitates an understanding of key points, much useful information can be buried in 'Additional information' and other parts of a prospectus.

A summary section should cover such things as the principal activities of the company, what the funds raised will be used for, a company's future direction, likely markets and competitors, possible joint ventures and distribution arrangements. If a company is an oil or mining company a guide should be given to existing deposits and exploration leases. Information given in the summary is usually expanded on in other parts of the prospectus.

You should familiarise yourself with the business that a company is in and form a view of the likely prospects for the company's industry. It is advisable to avoid a company if you do not understand the business it is in. In particular you should:

- consider industry growth prospects and the ability of the company to take advantage of this

- look at a company's competitive strengths and weaknesses, potential barriers to entry into the industry and the impact of technology

- examine the markets for a company's products, taking into account such factors as size, ease of servicing and location (for example, whether the company depends on exports)

- assess the risks that a company faces in conducting its business.

Your overall aim is to assess whether a company is in a go-ahead industry and whether it has a competitive advantage over other companies in that industry.

Details of the offer of shares will be contained in a separate section. You will generally be told in this section how the funds raised by the float will be used. It is a good idea to stay away from floats where the sole purpose of the issue of shares is to pay off debt, or the buy out of existing owners (referred to as vendors) of the company. Ideally, funds raised should be used to expand a company's business, otherwise all an issue does is facilitate a change in financial structure and ownership.

When looking at the details in the prospectus you should be wary if there is a high number of vendor shares. Vendor shares are shares issued to the existing owners of a company, often at no cost. When such an issue is made it results in a transfer of wealth away from new investors to existing owners because the existing owners become shareholders in the newly listed company but have not had to pay the issue price for their shares. Sometimes vendor shares have to be held for a certain period of time — for example, 12 months — before they can be sold. This is often a danger period for the share price if the vendors decide to sell a large parcel of their shares.

An element of risk is present in all investments and risk should be formally addressed in the prospectus. Generally a potentially high rate of return goes hand in hand with a high rate of risk. A prospectus should outline the risks you are taking when you apply for shares. The nature and extent of risk factors will vary between industries and companies. Some industries such as transport, food and banking are relatively stable and less subject to cyclical fluctuations. Others such as building, automobiles and mining are more volatile.

When you are offered a much greater than average return, it is usually a sign that you will be taking a much greater than average risk. Successful investors seldom take great risks with the prospect of only a moderate return. When investing in speculative ventures, the degree of risk may be clear cut and a prospectus is required to say that the shares being offered are speculative. On the other hand, risks might not be so obvious with, for example, companies that have been trading for a few years. However, they involve taking risks as well; for example, investing on the basis of a short trading history is taking a risk. A company should be forthright in disclosing risks. Unfortunately, many prospectuses list a large number of generic risks that apply to all companies without specifically outlining how a particular risk will impact on the company's profits.

An evaluation of the company's management is required before you invest in a float. This can be difficult as the company's management team is often unknown even to experienced investors and stockbroker analysts. As an individual investor you will have to rely on the often glowing descriptions of management contained in the prospectus. You should look at management's track record and establish whether it has a proven history of success in the industry in which the company operates. You should avoid companies where management is highly dependent on one key executive.

A reputable company will be forthright with any matter that is worthy of special consideration; for example, a pending law suit. Other companies may lump relevant information in as additional information. These are generally companies that are best avoided.

In a different section there will be an independent accountant's report and also there may be reports by other relevant specialists and experts; for example, a geologist for a mining company. Make sure you understand any assumptions they make. If you do not, ask the company for an explanation, and if you are not satisfied do not invest.

Investment versus speculation

When you are evaluating a float you need to establish whether you are investing for the long term or whether you are speculating and hoping to make a quick profit. If you are speculating, much will depend on the general state of the sharemarket. For example, in a bull market even mediocre companies can list at a premium and there is an opportunity to stag shares with good results. Stagging requires that you watch the market closely. It is important not to be greedy and to sell out when you have made a reasonable profit. If you are faced with a loss, it is usually better to sell and accept the loss rather than extend your investment time horizon in the hope that the shares will eventually come good.

If you view buying shares in a float as a long-term investment, you will be less concerned with the state of the sharemarket at the time of listing and more concerned with the future prospects of a company. You should focus more on such things as potential earnings growth, dividend income, gearing and prospective P/E ratios.

Bear in mind that many successful investors never subscribe to floats, preferring instead to delay a decision to invest until a company has an established record of profitability. They then look for companies that are undervalued. The moral of their story is not to speculate on floats.

Subscribing to a float with the intention of stagging the shares is a form of gambling and involves substantial risks. If you adopt this strategy, treat it as a highly speculative investment and never invest more than you can afford to lose.

Floats and sharemarket cycles

The general nature of floats, and the demand for them from investors, changes according to the phase of the sharemarket cycle. In effect, the market for floats moves in cycles that can be related to movements in the overall sharemarket. For example, in a bull market there is a noticeable increase in the number of floats. Initially they tend to be sound, well-managed companies that are attractive to investors, who in turn make profits because shares list at premiums. This motivates less sound companies to float, and they tend to be more speculative which means that investors are asked to ignore fundamental values for these floats. Instead these 'investors' are relying on the 'bigger fool' theory: I will buy these overpriced shares and hope that an even bigger fool buys them from me at a higher price. This trend continues until the quality of new floats bottoms out and the risks investors are required to take become unreasonable. Towards the end of a bull market, there are usually numerous new issues of small and unproven companies at inflated prices. It is wise to avoid putting any money into such companies.

When the sharemarket is going up after a bear market it is worthwhile applying for shares in a float because the issues are frequently made by good-quality companies and are reasonably priced. The second phase, characterised by lower-quality companies and higher asking prices, may also present profitable opportunities—particularly if your objective is to sell out on listing—because the momentum of the sharemarket is upwards and more often than not new issues list at a premium. By the time floats consist of small, poor-quality companies with high issue prices it is clearly time to say 'no'.

In a bear market companies tend to postpone listing on the ASX because the demand for floats is low and the price they can obtain for their shares is much lower than when the market was booming. Those companies that still continue with a float may have difficulty in attracting subscriptions. As a result, they frequently extend the offer period to give investors more time to decide. This happened often in the second half of 2002 after the 'dotcom' bust. During the GFC many companies sought to raise capital by way of floats to pay off debt—despite the poor state of the overall sharemarket. As a result, there was a wide range of premiums and discounts on issue prices, from a premium of 195 per cent for Phosphate Australia Limited to a discount of 60 per cent for Queensland Mining Corporation Limited.

If you are tempted to invest in a float and the closing date is extended, stay clear because it will most probably be a flop. Usually, the promoters of the company are trying to fill subscriptions. Another warning sign is when your stockbroker starts telephoning you a few days before an IPO is about to close, saying that this is your final opportunity to get shares in the float. If the float has been ignored by other investors, it is a clear signal that it is likely to list at a discount to its issue price.

Although it is not possible to generalise about the quality of floats because there are always exceptions, if you follow an overall strategy consistent with the above guidelines and also evaluate each float on its merits you will profit more often than you will lose from investing in floats. This strategy may sometimes entail buying into a float with the sole intention of stagging shares. In other cases you may be a long-term investor. This is not contradictory. Your aim is to buy into floats at the right time, and the sharemarket in general may be such that it is appropriate to buy shares and sell them upon listing at a profit. At other times you may consider that the issue price in a float is below fair value and that a company warrants investment over the medium or long term. It is a case of adopting different strategies for different sharemarket conditions and differences in the individual floats.

Sources of information

The internet is the most fruitful source of information on floats. The ASX website at <www.asx.com.au> has special sections on floats, including upcoming floats, recent floats and offer documents. Another website that contains information on floats is that of Shaw Stockbroking: <www.egoli.com.au/investing.asp>. It contains current information on floats. InvestSMART, <www.investsmart.com.au>, contains detailed statistics on floats going back to 1993. Information includes: the name of the company, market capitalisation at date of listing, date of listing, issue price, current price, premium/discount at the beginning of the day of listing and premium/discount at the end of the day, premium/discount at the end of the first week and premiums/discounts at 1 month, 3 months, 6 months and 12 months. The website also includes information on upcoming floats. You do not need to be a client of InvestSMART to use its site, but you do need to register, which is free.

You need to be wary of 'research reports' published by stockbrokers that are underwriters to a float. Clearly, there can be a potential conflict of interest here as this stockbroker has a financial stake in the success of the float.

Floats and taxation

The usual tax rules apply when you participate in a float. If you stag shares you will not be entitled to a CGT discount because you have not held the shares for longer than 12 months. Any loss you make on stagging can be offset against capital gains, but not your other income. If you hold the shares for longer than 12 months, you can claim a 50 per cent CGT discount (superannuation funds 33.3 per cent). Dividends you receive (if any) may be partly or wholly franked or unfranked.

Key points

o   History has shown that there is potential for making significant profits or losses by buying shares in floats—also known as initial public offers.

o   One test that you should apply when evaluating a float is whether the company being floated has an underwriter and is currently reporting profits.

o   Distinguish between companies that are starting up and companies that are already trading profitably. In the case of the latter you can undertake fundamental analysis. Investing in start-up companies usually entails higher risks.

o   Reading an entire prospectus might be daunting, but it is important that you do so thoroughly because it can be your only guide to a company's profit prospects.

o   The market for floats moves in cycles and is related to what is happening in the sharemarket. During boom times, sharemarket euphoria is such that most floats will be successful, while in a bear market companies tend to postpone listing.

o   In prosperous times you may not be able to obtain an allocation of shares in some floats unless you are a client of the underwriter or sponsoring broker.

13

Investing in managed funds

Managed funds, also referred to as unit trusts and collective investments, are where you pool your money with a group of other people into a single fund that then invests in a specified range of securities. The person who decides where the money is invested is called a fund manager. Managed funds can invest in shares, property, interest-bearing securities, options and futures, or a combination of all of these. Funds can also specialise in one area of the market—such as industrial shares, small companies, mining shares or only in gold companies. Just where a particular managed fund is allowed to invest is contained in its prospectus.

So instead of owning shares or property directly, you own a part of the managed fund—these parts are known as units. If the value of the investments owned by the fund rises so too does the value of your units in the managed fund. If the value of the underlying investments drops, the value of your units drops correspondingly.

The value of a unit at any given moment is simply the market value of the fund's investments divided by the number of units issued by the fund, less any debt. This is known as the net asset value or NAV. So if a managed fund has issued 10 million units and the fund's investments are worth $20 million, each unit in the fund would be worth $2. If the value of the fund's investments rose to $40 million, each unit would be worth $4.

Investors joining the fund after its launch pay a price based on the NAV. This can be either higher or lower than the original price depending on how the fund's investments have performed.

One of the advantages of a managed fund is that it allows you to pool your capital with others to diversify and reduce your investment risk. You can sell at any time, or others can buy units into the fund, at the current market price of the unit. This is particularly appealing if you only have a relatively small amount to invest. For example, if you want to invest $2000 in the sharemarket you would normally only be able to buy shares in one or two companies. If one of these companies gets into financial difficulties you could lose a substantial portion of your investment.

Alternatively, if you invested this $2000 in a managed fund, you are buying a share of a portfolio that could consist of 40 or more companies. If one of these companies goes bad it would not have such a damaging impact on your investment.

Another reason you would buy units in a managed fund is to get the benefit of a professional manager, who presumably has a better knowledge of investment markets than you do. Unfortunately, having a professional manage your money is no guarantee that you will make a profit. Many professional fund managers lose money for their investors. Others do not lose money, but the rate of return they achieve on investors' money is poor.

Sometimes managed funds make exaggerated claims about their performance, based usually on accurate but highly selective statistics. There are now a number of publications that give regular data and commentaries on the investment performance of managed funds. But these tables often use technical jargon that can confuse even the most seasoned investor.

It's important that you know how to interpret the figures in these tables so that you can accurately measure the performance of one fund against another. You also need to know how to evaluate whether you are getting good value for money from the fund manager.

Measuring risk

There are two important pieces of information you need to know about all managed funds:

• What returns are you likely to get?

• And, just as important, how risky is your investment?

When analysing the performance of a managed fund it is not sufficient to know that last year the return was 20 per cent. What you also want to find out is: was this a 'normal' rate of return and what risks did the fund manager take to achieve this return?

The usual method of assessing risk is to measure volatility; that is, the extent to which investment returns vary from one period to another. When surveys purport to measure risk, they usually measure standard deviation—a technical term which basically means how far the returns deviate from their 'expected' or normal return. The expected return usually is predicted from historical data, but this presents a problem for a newly established fund. Standard deviations show whether a managed fund's returns vary considerably from year to year. Thus, the higher the standard deviation, the more volatile (or risky) you can expect a fund's returns to be.

For example, if you invest money in a fixed-interest deposit with a bank at 6 per cent per annum you can be reasonably confident that the return you will get will be 6 per cent. On the other hand, if you invest in a sharemarket fund you might get a 40 per cent return in one year and a minus 15 per cent return in the next year.

The size of the fund

Another important consideration is the size of the fund. If a fund manager has only a small amount of money to invest, say less than $50 million, a significant increase in one or two shares can cause a sharp jump in investment performance. In contrast, a fund with over $5 billion invested is not so susceptible to short-term movements. Consequently, the performance of a fund in its first few months, when it has a relatively small amount of money to invest, may not provide a good indication of its long-term investment potential.

It is also important not to get carried away with one month's or one quarter's performance. Many commentators believe that a fund's performance should not be judged on anything less than a three-year period. Selecting investment managers on the basis of large, short-term growth figures is a sure way to get your fingers burnt.

These are just some of the issues which you have to address when reading the performance tables in newspapers and magazines. Fund managers and research houses are constantly seeking new ways to report performance, and this, of course, is laudable where the aim is to make the investing public better informed. However, sometimes there are attempts to obscure the truth by making information too technical or complex. In other instances, the major aim is to develop a marketable competitive edge in statistics. Neither of these approaches is helpful to the average investor.

If it all gets too much, seek an objective professional opinion from someone with no vested interest in either flattering the performance or trying to appear clever through the use of unnecessarily complex techniques.

Performance tables

The three main organisations in Australia that 'rate' fund managers and their managed funds are:

* Morningstar: <www.morningstar.com.au>

* Standard & Poor's: <www.fundsinsights.com>

* ASSIRT Software: <www.assirtplanningsoftware.com.au>.

These sites give details of their ratings methodology for assessing managed fund products and the ratings process followed. The three rating systems are not identical and should not be compared with each other. All three organisations use a combination of quantitative—such as the historical risk-adjusted performance of the fund—and qualitative methods—where they assess the fund manager's research team and investment processes. As Morningstar's data are the most widely published in newspapers and magazines, this chapter will concentrate on how to interpret these figures.

Interpreting performance tables for managed funds is not as simple as it may appear. For example, some performance tables give 'gross' investment returns while others report 'net' returns. Gross returns are returns before deducting fees and charges, while net returns are returns after deducting all fees and charges. Some performance tables calculate performance on the basis of a fund's net annual return after deducting upfront fees.

The returns/performance figures Morningstar publishes are net (after) the annual management fee, but do not take into account any transaction (entry/exit) fees that you may have to pay.

Also, the performance figures are before tax; that is, tax is paid by the individual investor. But the performance figures for superannuation funds take into account the 15 per cent superannuation tax; that is, they are net of tax.

There are, in fact, sensible arguments for using either gross returns for evaluating managed funds or net returns. When gross returns are used there is no distortion due to fees or charges. These are taken into account when calculating net returns and they vary from investor to investor depending upon such things as whether you used a discount or fee-for-service adviser. It is argued by many that the purpose of performance tables is to reflect the value of underlying assets in the fund and not the return to any particular investor. Those who argue for deducting charges and showing a net return contend that this method gives a fairer and more accurate view of the actual return on funds invested.

Star ratings

Most researchers end up summarising their views on managed funds by using a 'star' rating system. For example, an 'excellent' quality fund may be assigned five stars (★★★★★) while a 'very poor' quality fund might be assigned one star (★). The Morningstar star rating from one to five stars measures a fund's risk-adjusted historical performance compared to peers. A fund with a Morningstar rating of four or five stars has produced higher returns while taking less risk (being less volatile) than similar funds. A fund with a Morningstar rating of one or two stars has produced lower returns while taking more risk (being more volatile) than similar funds. To get a Morningstar star rating, a fund must be at least three years old, and be in a peer group which has at least 10 funds with three-year track records.

Investors generally interpret this to mean that a fund with a high number of stars is much better than a fund with a low number of stars. But be wary of drawing this conclusion. Because funds are rated within their respective categories, not all five-star funds are interchangeable or equal. For example, a five-star fund that invests in emerging markets may have the best risk-adjusted return compared with similar funds within that category, but it may be riskier than a diversified Australian equities fund.

Another problem with measuring how well a fund has performed compared with other funds is that there is no consideration for how well it has performed with regard to other investment opportunities. As a result, the question of whether you should be investing in a managed fund at all (instead of something else) is not addressed.

In addition, it is not just the return that a particular fund has achieved that is important but the risks it has taken in order to achieve that return. So you must be mindful about how a research organisation measures risk when evaluating a managed fund. Morningstar adjusts for risk by calculating a risk penalty for each fund. The basic assumption is that investors are more concerned about a possible poor outcome than an unexpectedly good one. Therefore, they are willing to give up a small portion of an investment's expected return in exchange for greater certainty.

Consider a simple example. A fund's expected return is 10 per cent each year. Though you are likely to receive 10 per cent, past variations in the fund's returns suggest that you might end up with anywhere from 5 to 15 per cent. While receiving more than 15 per cent would be a pleasant surprise, most investors are more likely to worry about the downside — receiving less than 10 per cent. So they're probably willing to settle for a slightly lower return — say 9 per cent — if they could be more certain of receiving that amount of return.

This concept forms the basis of how Morningstar adjusts for risk. A 'risk penalty' is subtracted from each fund's total return, based on the variation in the fund's month-to-month return, with an emphasis on downward variation. The greater the downward variation, the higher the risk penalty. If two funds have the same return, the one with more variation in its return is given the greater risk penalty. However, the actual risk penalty is not clear in the Morningstar published figures.

Past performance is no guarantee of future performance

The main limitation of investment performance tables is that they tell you what happened in the past. What you are really interested in is how a particular fund will perform in the future. Research, both locally and overseas, shows conclusively that past performance is a poor indicator of future performance.

If you believe the glossy ads for managed funds you'd think picking the right managed fund is easy. You simply buy the fund that gave the highest return last year. Yet all too often this is a trap. Many investors fall for it — they try to pick this year's best-performing managed fund by buying last year's star. They assume that history will conveniently repeat itself. In fact, there's a good chance history will not repeat itself.

In 2003, ASIC commissioned a review of Australian, UK and US academic studies into the correlation of past performance with future performance. This report — titled *A Review of the Research on the Past Performance of Managed Funds* — concluded that good past performance is, at best, a weak and unreliable predictor of good future performance over the medium to long term.

About half the studies found no correlation at all between good past and good future performance.

Where correlation was found, it was usually over one to two years — but this is of little help for longer term investors. However, many studies did find that bad past performance increased the probability of bad future performance. Moreover, a strategy of frequent swapping to best-performing funds was viewed as being ineffective because of the costs of buying and selling managed funds and the capital gains tax implications.

How to use performance figures

Of course the main question remaining when you are reviewing perform-ance figures is: how can I judge whether these figures are good or bad? To answer this question you have three major alternatives:

- You can compare the fund's after-tax return with the rate of inflation.

- You can compare the fund's performance to a 'benchmark' rate of return such as the rise or fall in the All Ordinaries index.

- You can compare the fund's performance with that of other funds in the same category.

All three alternatives give you useful information about whether this managed fund is right for you. By comparing after-tax returns with the rate of inflation you can assess whether the purchasing power of your capital has been eroded. Comparing the fund's performance against a benchmark gives some indication of whether the fund manager is 'adding value' to your investment—are they really earning their fees? This is probably the fairest measure of a fund manager's performance. You can also get a measure of a particular fund manager's ability by comparing returns with other funds investing in the same general area. In this situation, you would not compare funds investing in Australian mining shares with funds investing in Australian industrial shares.

These tables are not meant to be used as a means of selecting which funds are best for you. What you can do is use these tables to identify how your particular managed funds are performing against comparable funds. If their performance is below average, ask your financial adviser or the fund's manager to explain why. If you are not satisfied with these answers it may be time to switch your money into another fund.

The potential return from a managed fund depends on many factors. Among them are the skill of the fund manager, the risks taken by the manager, the overall state of the economy and where the fund invests. Generally speaking, the more specialised the investments of the fund are—for example, if the fund only invests in gold shares—the more volatile the returns are likely to be. Also, some fund managers perform better in bull markets, when share prices are rising, than in bear markets, when prices are falling.

The costs of investing in a managed fund

The costs of investing in a managed fund vary with the type of fund. It is usual for an upfront fee to be payable when first buying units in a managed fund. An annual management charge is payable thereafter. Typically cash management funds and mortgage funds do not have entry fees. Other unlisted funds may have an entrance fee of around 6 per cent, most of which is used to pay commissions to investment advisers. There are no entry fees for managed funds that are listed on the sharemarket, but there are brokerage fees for buying or selling. With an unlisted fund the amount of upfront and management expenses can be found in the fund's prospectus. In addition, the fund's manager is entitled to be reimbursed for certain expenses from the fund, but these expenses must be reasonable and properly incurred.

The fund's management expense ratio (MER) is the percentage of your investment the fund manager receives each year to pay for the management and marketing of your fund. The MER is usually expressed as a percentage of your investment account balance and is deducted from the fund's assets or investment earnings. The MER for retail managed funds can range from around 0.70 per cent per annum to more than 2 per cent per annum. Many funds also have a 'trail' commission payable to your adviser which is charged to your account. Typically a trail commission can be up to 0.6 per cent annually. Also, fund managers may be entitled to a performance-based fee if the fund achieves a particular investment return — check the prospectus to see whether this is applicable.

The spread

When you buy a unit in a managed fund you pay the 'entry' price. The 'exit' price is the price that you get when you sell. The difference between the entry and exit price is called the 'buy/sell spread'. When money is received or redeemed from a managed fund the fund manager either buys or sells securities to accommodate either money coming into or out of the fund. As a result there are transaction costs incurred, such as brokerage, and this is recouped through the buy/sell spread. This spread is generally somewhere between nil and 0.50 per cent depending on the type of fund.

Selecting funds

Selecting the right managed fund is just as difficult as picking the shares that will rise most in price on the sharemarket. There is no magical formula to use, but considering the following factors may help eliminate managed funds that do not match your investing aims and objectives:

- One of the first things you need to do is set a minimum size for the funds in which you will consider investing. If you set a minimum of around $100 million you will eliminate funds where performance may be distorted because of the influence of only a small number of elements that make up the fund; for example, shares in particular companies in the case of an equity fund.

- Next look for consistent performance over a period of five to ten years; the longer the better. In particular, examine whether a fund has consistently met or exceeded its stated benchmark. For example, if you are considering investing in a diversified shares fund, compare its return with the All Ordinaries accumulation index. If the fund's returns are less than this benchmark, do not invest.

- Consider the stability of the management team that runs a fund. It may be that a fund has generated high returns under investment managers who are no longer employed by the fund. Also consider how likely it is that the same management team will stay with the fund in the future.

- Fees and managed funds go hand in hand and are unavoidable. Using a discount broker can often eliminate upfront fees. Identify a fund's ongoing fees and compare them with other funds that meet your criteria. High upfront fees and excessive MERs can significantly decrease your overall investment returns.

- From a shortlist of funds, consider the investment strategy and philosophy of the fund manager and determine whether it suits your style of investing. For example, note if the fund manager concentrates on investing for income or growth or some other objective, and whether this fits with the means by which you would like to receive returns.

Alternatives to managed funds

It is important to keep in mind that performance tables showing managed fund information naturally focus on managed funds. As such, they only compare the performance of managed funds with other managed funds. But this information in itself will not tell you whether managed funds are good investments. When reviewing managed funds you need to compare the return for the managed fund sector with the market index for that sector. For example, if you are interested in equity funds you will need to compare the average return from all equity funds with the All Ordinaries index or another relevant share index. Initially this will tell you whether equity funds are a worthwhile investment compared to the market as a whole. After that, you should review what you could have earned by investing in other income-producing assets such as government bonds, finance company debentures and bank fixed deposits. When these comparisons are made the performance of many managed funds is poor. For example, over a long period of time, few managed funds have performed as well as the All Ordinaries index, indicating that investors would have been better off 'buying' the index instead of investing in managed funds.

Exchange-traded funds

Exchange-traded funds (ETFs) in Australia are analogous to unit trusts or managed funds, with the important difference that they are listed on the ASX. Hence you can buy and sell them through a stockbroker in the same way as you buy and sell ordinary shares. With traditional managed funds, units are bought and sold through the fund manager based on the net asset value of the units at the time of the transaction. In turn the NAV of a unit is determined by dividing a fund's total NAV by the number of units issued.

Money invested in ETFs in Australia has grown from $48 million in June 1998 to more than $2 billion under management in late 2009. The turnover of ETFs on the ASX is around $15 million a day, and that puts ETFs in the top 50 stocks in terms of daily turnover on the ASX. It is clear that they have become a major vehicle in the investment marketplace and are worthy of thought for inclusion in your portfolio.

ETFs and managed funds are similar in that they both tend to have diverse portfolios, although there are sector-specific types of both investments. The difference is that ETFs provide equity exposure to these portfolios. ETFs comprise shares representing specific indices, such as the S&P/ASX 50 index, the S&P/ASX 200 index or the S&P/ASX 200 A-REIT index. ETFs have a simple structure which is particularly appealing to investors because, like unlisted managed funds, they provide diversification across the Australian equities market in a single transaction.

As well as ETFs over Australian indices there are international ETFs, sector ETFs and exchange-traded commodities (ETCs). International ETFs were launched in 2007 and provide exposure to both established and emerging markets. They seek to replicate the performance of an overseas sharemarket index and are traded in Australian dollars. Fluctuations in the exchange rate can affect the value of these portfolios. Sector ETFs provide investors with coverage of companies in particular sectors, which may include consumer staples, healthcare, telecommunications and listed property. ETCs are like ETFs that track the performance of an underlying physical commodity or commodity index. There are a number of ETCs, including those that track gold, silver, platinum, palladium and a basket of precious metals.

The advantages and disadvantages of ETFs

One of the main advantages of ETFs is liquidity. You can also follow the movement of prices each day and buy and sell them during ASX trading hours. This is more convenient than buying and selling units in a managed fund through the fund manager. Also, your money is available in three days as these transactions are part of the T+3 settlement system of the ASX. Offset against this, however, is the fact that ETFs may sell below their NAV. Also, while it is generally true that there is active trading in ETFs, the depth of the market is not guaranteed. This is acknowledged by the ASX with respect to sector ETFs and ETCs, where it has contracted 'market makers' who receive fee rebates when they consistently achieve two-sided markets.

ETFs are generally a lower cost investment than unlisted managed funds. Brokerage is payable on purchases and sales but there are no entry fees, exit fees or trailing commissions. Also the management expense ratio is lower for ETFs than it is for unlisted managed funds. An Australian equity managed fund should have an MER around 2 per cent per annum, whereas the MER for an ETF can be as low as 0.09 per cent per annum. ETFs are also more cost efficient than investing in the same exposure of individually purchased shares.

ETFs are a superior vehicle for deriving diversification across the sharemarket, but in this respect they are no different from many managed funds. However, with both these investment categories you may not get direct exposure to the industries you would like. For example, if you wanted exposure to the banking or mining sectors, you are currently unable to do this by way of an ETF. You would have to invest directly in bank or mining shares.

As the majority of ETFs are over sharemarket indices, the capital gains tax liability within an ETF is minimised. Generally speaking, ETFs replicate an index and periodically their portfolios are reviewed and purchases and sales of shares are made to bring the ETF back in line with its relevant sharemarket index. This happens regularly but not immediately each time the index changes. Hence the extent to which capital gains are crystallised is minimised. This compares with actively traded managed funds where a CGT liability is recognised each time shares are sold at a profit. The extent to which capital gains are realised in a sector ETF is greater than with an ETF over an index, but usually less than with an actively traded managed fund.

ETFs are a transparent investment in that the fund manager regularly informs the market of shareholdings of the ETF and its NAV. This is easier than obtaining information on shareholdings from the manager of a traditional managed fund.

ETFs have become very popular with Australian investors. For the year to January 2010 total turnover of ETFs in Australia increased by 141 per cent to a market value of A$3.5 billion. They were originally designed as a flexible market tool for institutional investors but they have now gained broad acceptance with the investment and financial planning community.

Tax and managed funds

Your investment return from an unlisted managed fund consists of two parts:

- The distributions you receive from the fund—this can include both income and capital gains or losses.

- Any capital gain or loss you incur when buying and selling the units in the fund.

When you receive a statement from your managed fund, it will itemise what part of the distribution comprises income and what part is a capital gain or loss. It will also display whether there are any franking credits associated with the income component of the distribution. Income from managed funds is taxed at your marginal tax rate. If distributions have been franked, you will receive franking credits. You will be taxed on 50 per cent of the capital gain component of your distribution if the fund has owned the asset for more than a year. The managed fund statement does not include any capital gains or losses you may have made when you sold off any of your units.

Key points

o Do not be fooled by the performance figures mentioned in advertisements for managed funds. Past performance is no guarantee of future performance.

o You need to be convinced that the fund manager has outperformed the relevant market index or the return you could get from alternative investments with a similar risk profile.

o Remember, fund managers will always encourage you to invest in their funds, regardless of economic conditions. But it is essential for you to make your own decision about whether this is the right thing to do, and also whether it is the right time to invest.

o Before investing in a managed fund, list your own investment objectives carefully.

o Select the sector or sectors—for example, cash management, shares and property—that match your investment objectives.

o Check the volatility values of the funds in your chosen sector to find the ones that appear to have given the best returns without taking excessive risks.

o It is wise to contact the fund manager of the fund and request an up-to-date list of the fund's investment portfolio.

o ETFs are similar to unit trusts or managed funds, with the important difference that they are listed on the ASX.

o The chief disadvantage of ETFs is that you cannot always derive exposure to the industries in which you are interested. For example, some industries are not represented at all by ETFs except as part of an index, so you will need to do your own research and analysis and buy individual shares to achieve exposure to these industries.

o Liquidity with some ETFs may be an issue, and there is no guarantee that you can buy and sell at the price you would like.

14

Hedge funds

At the end of 2009, global hedge fund assets under management (AUM) were around US$1.6 trillion, up more than threefold from US$0.5 trillion in 2002. In Australia there are no accurate figures, but AUM are estimated as being between A$65 billion and A$90 billion. The sector has taken a buffeting during the global financial crisis, along with traditional investment sectors. For example, in the December quarter of 2008 hedge fund redemptions were 25 per cent of AUM. However, hedge fund investments are sizeable and their impact on the investment environment is significant. The chief attraction of hedge funds to investors is that, in theory, they have the potential to make profits in both rising and falling markets. The reality is that some do and some do not achieve this aim—indeed some lose money in both rising and falling markets—so you need to understand the different hedge fund strategies before you invest.

A brief history of hedge funds

There is no universally accepted definition of a hedge fund, but they may be viewed as funds that employ strategies with a broad range of risk and return objectives, the common element among which is the use of investment and risk management skills by the hedge fund managers to seek positive returns irrespective of what the overall market is doing.

It is generally accepted that the first hedge fund was created by Alfred Jones in 1949. Jones was born in Melbourne of an American father, and the family returned to the US when Jones was four. The first hedge fund was a long/short equity fund. Jones went 'long' with some shares, buying those he believed would increase in value. In addition, he 'short sold' — that is, he sold shares that he did not actually own — companies he believed would fall in value. Assuming he picked correctly, the hedge fund would make profits in both rising and falling markets. This was a prime attraction of the early hedge funds, and for many years hedge fund managers advertised that they could profit in falling markets. The bubble burst in 2000–01 when world sharemarkets fell and most hedge funds reported negative returns. This phenomenon was reinforced during the GFC.

Jones also brought in other fund managers to choose shares and opportunities, and thereby created the first 'fund of funds'. In the 1950s hedge funds grew in popularity, but the 1960s and 1970s proved to be difficult times and AUM declined. There was a resurgence in the 1980s, and by the 1990s hedge funds had become large enough to warrant government scrutiny in many countries. In the 2000s they have continued to flourish, although they have received a setback with the GFC.

How hedge funds work

The word 'hedge' when used in the context of a hedge fund is a misnomer because it implies that someone is hedging risk when in fact the strategies of hedge funds are often very risky. With a long/short equity fund the risk of going long is that the shares the hedge fund buys actually fall in value. That is no less risky than any other share purchase. At least the potential loss is limited as the lowest the share price can fall to is zero. With short selling there is the risk that the price of the shares short sold will increase and the hedge fund manager (HFM) will have to buy back in at these higher prices. Here the potential loss is unlimited because in theory there is no upper limit to which a company's share price can rise.

How short selling works

Short selling is fundamental to numerous hedge fund strategies and it is widely employed to make profits in falling markets, although anyone can do it in Australia over a restricted number of shares — you don't have to be in a hedge fund to adopt this strategy. Short selling can be applied to shares, commodities, currencies or anything for which there is a market bringing together buyers and sellers. Here it is explained with regard to a company's shares.

Say an HFM sells Company X's shares at $10 each in the expectation that the price will fall. The HFM does not own the shares it sells so it will have to borrow the scrip in order to settle the transaction. Say the share price then falls to $6. The HFM can now buy the shares in the market for $6 each, repay the scrip lender and profit by $4 a share, less a small fee payable to the scrip lender for its service. The risk to the HFM is that the share price of Company X could increase and it will have to buy back in at a higher price. For example, if a company was unexpectedly the target of a takeover bid its share price could rise rapidly. In managing this risk much depends on the skill of the HFM.

The Australian Government outlawed short selling from September 2008 to May 2009 because it accentuates price falls, and during the GFC short selling was considered to be a destabilising influence on the overall sharemarket. Not surprisingly, hedge fund managers thought that this ban should never have been imposed.

Other hedge fund strategies

Arbitrage is a hedge fund strategy that is frequently employed in one of a variety of forms. This strategy aims to take advantage of different prices for similar investments in different markets. For example, a company's shares might be selling for a price of $5, but an option to buy these shares for $4 might be selling for 50¢. If you are quick you could buy the $4 options for 50¢, convert them into shares and then make 50¢ per share profit by selling the shares for $5. Because other investors can do the same thing, such a discrepancy is quickly 'arbitraged away'.

One of the most successful hedge fund strategies on a global scale in the 12 months to 31 December 2009 was convertible arbitrage. A convertible arbitrage strategy involves taking long positions in convertible notes and hedging those positions by selling short the underlying shares. Convertible arbitrage is much bigger in the US than in Australia because only a few Australian companies have convertible notes.

Another hedge fund strategy is fixed-income arbitrage. For example, an HFM can form a view on the likely direction of future interest rate movements. If interest rates decrease, the price of bonds will increase, and vice versa. However, the price of long-dated bonds will increase more than the price of short-dated bonds because of the difference in times to maturity (see chapter 15). So if an HFM expects interest rates to decrease it can take a long position in long-dated bonds and finance the purchase by taking a short position in short-dated bonds. Ideally, the HFM would just like to take a long position in long-dated bonds but it needs to get the money from somewhere in order to do this.

Another hedge fund investment strategy focuses on understanding, assessing and predicting the outcome of macroeconomic events in world financial markets. For example, an HFM could take a position on future currency or interest rate movements using derivatives such as futures and options. A famous example of this global macro strategy occurred in 1992 when George Soros short sold 10 billion pounds sterling and bought the position back for 9 billion pounds, pocketing 1 billion pounds in two months. Other hedge fund strategies include merger arbitrage, hedged arbitrage, distressed securities, emerging markets, region-specific opportunities, market timing, aggressive growth funds, yield curve trades, relative value and multi-strategy approaches.

Table 14.1 provides an indication of the returns earned by hedge funds globally.

The performance of these indices varies widely, both over one year and three years. In addition, except for the China Index, there is little or no correlation between returns over three years and those over one year. This is another example of where past performance is no guarantee of future performance. The performance of some hedge funds has been consistently poor over three years and no better in the year to 31 December 2009 when the sharemarket increased by 50 per cent.

Other hedge fund features

Some hedge funds have a 'long bias' — meaning that the underlying view of the HFM is that the market is trending upwards and so it is better to be long. Conversely, a fund may have a 'short bias', in which case the underlying view of the HFM is that the market is trending downwards and it is better to be oversold. Where there is no bias the fund is said to be 'market neutral'.

A feature of hedge funds is that they gear or leverage their portfolios, often quite highly. This has the effect of magnifying gains and losses. Gearing is the rule rather than an exception, ever since Alfred Jones started doing it in 1949. However, hedge funds usually do not state the level of gearing that is allowed.

Another feature of hedge funds is that the fees payable by investors are higher than they are for traditional equity funds. Part of the reason for this is that there is a higher number of transactions. In addition, HFMs usually charge incentive fees as well as traditional management fees. For the majority of hedge funds an incentive fee is based on the fund's annual increase in net asset value. If you invest in hedge funds you should ensure that these incentive fees are only paid when the fund manager's performance is exceptional—it should not be a reward for average investment returns.

Table 14.1: global hedge fund performance

	Returns to 31 December 2009 (% p.a.)	
Index	1 year	3 years
HFRX Distressed Securities Index	−5.60	−12.05
HFRX Fixed Income Asset-Backed Index	26.69	10.50
HFRX Convertible Arbitrage Index	42.46	−16.25
HFRX Global Hedge Fund Index	13.40	−3.20
HFRX China Index	50.40	17.72
HFRX Commodity Index	−3.04	8.06
HFRX Russia Index	64.94	1.84
HFRX Short Bias Index	−20.55	2.20
HFRX Volatility Index	−3.04	0.03
HFRX Yield Alternative Index	27.42	1.90
HFRX Merger Arbitrage Index	8.14	5.54
HFRX Macro Index	−8.76	−0.20
HFRX Latin America Index	40.91	6.68
HFRX Market Directional Index	29.34	−1.44
HFRX Special Situations Index	19.57	−1.82
HFRX Credit Arbitrage Index	26.07	6.64
HFRX Fixed Income Corporate Index	20.47	−1.75
HFRX Absolute Return Index	−3.58	−3.67

Selected indices in US$.
Source: Hedge Funds Research, Inc.

You invest in a hedge fund via a prospectus, which will contain basic information on minimum investments and additional investments, minimum withdrawals, minimum balance and details of redemptions. Apart from that there may not be a great deal of transparency in terms of what the fund proposes doing with your money. This compares with a traditional equity fund where you are better able to assess the risks that the manager is taking with your money. For long/short equity funds and fund of funds (see below) the minimum investment is generally A$5000. For single-strategy hedge funds—for example, arbitrage—the minimum is usually A$100 000, and for some wholesale funds it may be as high as A$1 million.

Types of hedge funds

In Australia, hedge funds may be broadly classified as equity-based funds, non-equity-based funds, fund of funds (FOFs) and single-strategy funds. As the name suggests, an equity-based fund invests in equities using such strategies as distressed securities, long/short equity and merger arbitrage. The last strategy seeks to take advantage of mis-pricings in the securities of two companies engaged in a merger. Non-equity-based funds engage in strategies which are not based on equities. Examples include fixed-income arbitrage, macro strategies and yield strategies. FOFs are hedge funds that invest in a selection of other hedge funds, each managed by a separate manager. An FOF may invest in 20 or more hedge funds. Usually these funds are single-strategy funds, but they can also include other FOFs. FOFs tend to be aimed at retail investors and have minimum investment levels of around $5000. A single-strategy fund engages in one hedge fund strategy and it may be equity-based or non-equity-based. Often a single-strategy hedge fund is a wholesale fund with a high minimum investment.

The general performance of the above types of hedge funds for the year to 31 December 2009 is shown in table 14.2.

The All Ordinaries index increased by around 50 per cent in 2009, so hedge funds were a relatively poor investment when taken as a whole. The hedge fund industry prefers to use the S&P/ASX 200 index as a benchmark because hedge funds are large and if they invest in smaller companies it has a disproportionate effect on securities prices. So they tend to invest in the largest 200 companies only. Even on this basis returns were not particularly high. In fact only 20 per cent of the hedge funds in table 14.2 outperformed the S&P/ASX 200 index in 2009.

Table 14.2: Australian hedge fund returns to 31 December 2009

Type of fund	Number of funds	Return (%)
All Australian hedge funds	241	17.54
Equity-based funds	127	24.94
Non-equity-based funds	114	8.71
Fund of funds	60	6.92
Single-strategy funds	181	20.81
S&P/ASX 200 index	–	30.84
S&P 500	–	23.45
MSCI World Index ex-Australia in A$	–	26.14

Source: Australian Fund Monitors.

It should be noted that some hedge funds have outperformed the share-market, and according to the Alternative Investment Management Association there is a danger with lumping all hedge funds into the same basket. For example, investors in Fortitude Capital received a return of 9.83 per cent in the year to 30 June 2009, 19.78 per cent for two years and 35.23 per cent for three years. These sort of returns tend to be the exception, and note that past performance is no guarantee of future performance. The performance differences between hedge funds are primarily due to the skill and ability of managers and traders—and sometimes an element of luck.

Hedge funds and risk

In the past there has been a lot of hype associated with hedge funds, especially when they were heavily marketed to everyday investors. HFMs have identified risk as an area where investing in hedge funds is superior to investing in, say, the sharemarket. It is common to see statistics that show that the actual returns from investing in hedge funds are less volatile than the actual returns from investing in the sharemarket. This means that actual returns from investing in hedge funds vary less from the average return than do returns from investing in the sharemarket. Based on this, HFMs advance the argument that investing in hedge funds is less risky than investing in the sharemarket.

By adopting this stance, HFMs are basically equating risk with volatility where volatility is defined as the extent to which actual returns fluctuate compared with the average return and is measured by the standard deviation. The problem with using standard deviation to measure risk is that returns above the average contribute to standard deviation, and hence risk, as much as returns below the average. Investors generally are quite happy if they receive a return above the average and would not consider this as being a contributor to risk. So using standard deviation to measure risk is inappropriate—more correctly it measures volatility. But HFMs equate volatility with risk. It also assumes that average returns from hedge funds are higher than the average return from the sharemarket—but that is not always the case.

There are other concepts of risk that are more relevant when assessing hedge funds. For example, according to Post-Modern Portfolio Theory, downside risk is the risk that a minimum acceptable rate of return will not be achieved. This concept has the advantage of differentiating risk from volatility, but what is an acceptable rate of return will vary between investors. Consequently, the same investment in a hedge fund may carry different degrees of risk for different investors.

For some investors the prospect of a negative return in a particular month is unpalatable. To assess this risk it is possible to calculate the probability of a negative return in any given month based on past experience. HFMs frequently provide this information in prospectuses. When evaluating such information it is important to ensure that the information is compiled over at least five years. For example, the results over just two or three years can be misleading. Also the GFC had a profound effect on recent historical performance because it represented the greatest economic upheaval since the Great Depression.

There is also the risk of losing your capital, a risk that is present with all investments. In the period 1995 to 1998 there was a relatively high attrition rate of hedge funds in the US. For example, according to Van Eyk Research, 14.6 per cent of hedge funds went out of business in 1995, 19.6 per cent in 1996, 33.0 per cent in 1997 and 42.3 per cent in 1998. These are fairly high attrition rates, and indicate that the risk of total collapse is higher for hedge funds than managed investments. During the GFC there were many hedge fund collapses in Australia, including an $800 million failure of Basis Capital which suffered fallout from the sub-prime mortgage crisis in the US. Investors in Basis Capital have received some of their money back, while in the cases of other collapses investors lost all their cash.

It is wise to steer clear of hedge funds that are highly leveraged; that is, that borrow significant amounts of money to invest or deal mainly in highly leveraged products such as futures and options. A useful rule of thumb is that leverage should be no more than 2:1, meaning that a hedge fund should borrow no more than twice as much as it takes in from investors. Frequently it is difficult to establish what the degree of leverage is in a hedge fund. This is particularly so with FOFs where the leverage of the underlying funds is rarely disclosed.

Hedge fund managers can shift ground

In the past it was difficult not to be cynical about hedge fund performance. In 2001 most HFMs were predicting double-digit returns, some as high as 30 per cent per annum. Hedge fund managers publicised high target returns as a means of attracting funds from the investing public. They did not say this was subject to a favourable investment climate or indeed subject to any conditions. In fact, they also stated that they could make profits in falling markets through, for example, short selling.

Then when performance was generally nowhere near what was publicised, the same HFMs pointed to declining world sharemarkets, especially the US, and took satisfaction in saying that their funds performed better than the returns generated by these markets. This is little consolation to those investors who invested in hedge funds on the basis of high target returns and who saw them turn out to be very low or even negative. The conclusion is that investors were led to believe they would receive high returns, without qualification, and then when this didn't eventuate, managers blamed investing conditions and implied that investors should be happy because hedge funds performed better than world sharemarket indices.

The above scenario was repeated to some extent during the GFC. Some HFMs again took satisfaction in saying they had 'lost less' than other participants in investment markets. Bear in mind that HFMs are supposed to make money in falling markets as well as rising ones.

Hedge funds and investment time frames

In a similar way to many traditional managed funds that invest in Australian and international shares, hedge fund performance has been variable and this is likely to continue. Most HFMs advocate investing in their funds for several years. HFMs are tight-lipped about predicting the future, except to say that investors can expect short-term volatility. For this reason they maintain you should take a longer term view.

Bear in mind that, just as it was in the interests of HFMs to encourage people to invest with them in the first place, it is also in their interests to encourage investors not to withdraw their money. This is because of the fees they earn. Apart from short-term volatility, managers offer no justification for having an investment time horizon of several years, and you should consider whether your money may be better invested elsewhere, such as in the sharemarket or in cash.

Fees

Hedge fund fees are higher than those of traditional managed funds. One reason for this is that hedge funds do more trading, and transaction fees are higher as a result. Another reason is that hedge fund managers receive incentive fees, which traditional fund managers do not. An incentive fee, also referred to as a performance fee, is payable to a manager when the NAV of the fund exceeds its previous highest level, referred to as the 'high water mark'. Often the incentive fee is calculated as a percentage of the amount by which NAV exceeds the high water mark.

For example, if at the end of a year NAV was $82 million, the high water mark was $77 million and the incentive fee was 15 per cent, the incentive fee payable would be:

($82 million − $77 million) × 15% = $750 000

If NAV declines, no incentive fee is payable and losses have to be recouped in the future before an incentive fee is again payable.

In some cases the incentive fee is payable with reference to a hurdle rate, such as a bank bill index. For example, say the hurdle rate is 5 per cent; using the above illustration, the incentive fee would be:

[$82 million − ($77 million × 1.05)] × 15% = $172 500

Because there is a hurdle rate the incentive fee payable has decreased significantly. Using a hurdle rate is the less common way of calculating incentive fees, but in one sense it is the preferred method from an investor's point of view. A problem with using a straight percentage of increase in NAV is that an incentive fee may be payable for poor performance. For example, it would generally be agreed that an increase in NAV of, say, 4 per cent, which does not constitute good performance, would not warrant the payment of an incentive fee. In fact, providing NAV increases beyond the high water mark, poor performance leads to the payment of an incentive fee. Using a hurdle rate overcomes this limitation, but as noted above, most hedge fund managers are not paid on this basis.

HFMs argue that incentive fees help to align the interests of managers and investors because it is in the interests of managers to increase the NAV of a fund, thereby qualifying for an incentive fee. This is true providing that the manager does not take excessive risks in seeking to increase NAV.

HFMs say there is a disincentive to take risks because they have some of their own money tied up in their own funds—but they rarely reveal how much of their own money is at risk.

Another argument is that incentive fees are necessary to attract the 'best and the brightest' management talent to hedge funds, but the recent performance of many hedge funds indicates that there is no proof that this is what happens. Hedge funds engage in investing in more difficult areas than traditional managed funds and therefore some argue hedge fund managers should be compensated accordingly. On the other hand, the incentive fee structures that exist in hedge funds reward mediocre performance and may attract inferior managers. It is yet to be established whether hedge funds attract the 'best and the brightest' managers.

Transparency

Even after reading its prospectus, it is often difficult to determine what a particular hedge fund does. In the case of an FOF, you are lucky if you are given a list of the underlying fund managers and the strategies that they employ. In effect you have to rely on due diligence performed by the FOF manager on a continuing basis, the extent of which is usually not disclosed. This lack of disclosure and transparency of what hedge funds do has been a feature of hedge funds since they began. The chief argument as to why it is this way is that details of what hedge funds do in pursuit of profit is proprietary information and therefore confidential.

As many hedge funds do not reveal very much about their activities, it is difficult to assess the risks that investing with a particular HFM entails. It also makes it difficult to evaluate how carefully an FOF manager has examined individual hedge funds, with a view to investing in them. HFMs point to qualitative and quantitative assessment and the investment in time required when they say that performing due diligence is beyond the scope of an everyday investor. For example, they say that due diligence involves a range of problems for everyday investors, including their lack of access to confidential and reliable market information, their inability to understand and dissect sophisticated investment strategies and the problem of finding and contacting fund managers. Everyday investors also typically do not have access to many of the best funds because they are closed to new investors, and they do not have the ability to perform ongoing monitoring of fund managers.

Balanced against these arguments is a natural desire to know what HFMs are doing with your money so that you can assess the risks for yourself. Also, there is an implicit assumption that the HFM is capable of conducting this due diligence process in a competent manner.

Are hedge funds a good investment?

In the 12 months to 31 December 2009 some hedge funds performed significantly better than the sharemarket. Performance between hedge funds varies, so you need to be selective. Generally, single-strategy hedge funds perform better than FOFs, but on the other hand single-strategy hedge funds are more risky. Also single-strategy funds are often wholesale funds with minimum investment levels of as high as $1 million. To invest in such funds you need to use master trusts and wrap accounts.

Master trusts and wrap accounts enable you to pool your resources with other investors to meet minimum investment amounts. You will need to consult a financial adviser to do this. Make sure that the financial adviser is knowledgeable about hedge funds. Note that using master trusts and wrap accounts is expensive. Although the applicable management expense ratios are wholesale ones, and therefore lower than retail funds, you pay fees at two levels. In recent years, however, costs have come down. Some commentators have said that master trusts and wrap accounts are designed with financial advisers in mind rather than investors. Remember that it is frequently difficult to get your money out because withdrawals have to be combined with other investors to meet minimum withdrawal and minimum balance requirements.

Hedge funds as a separate asset class

Traditionally investments are classified as shares (domestic and international), fixed interest (domestic and international), property and cash. Prudent portfolio management requires that you diversify across these asset classes so that if one performs badly you don't have 'all your eggs in one basket'. At times the promoters of other areas of investment have argued that new asset classes should be added, and hedge funds are one such category of investment.

Chief among the reasons put forward for treating hedge funds as a separate asset class is an argument that hedge fund performance is negatively correlated with the performance of the traditional asset classes. By this it is meant that if, say, the sharemarket goes down, returns from hedge funds can go up, and vice versa. Similarly hedge funds would be negatively correlated with international fixed interest if, when the returns from international bonds went up, the returns from hedge funds went down. If hedge funds were negatively correlated with traditional asset classes it would increase the attractiveness of hedge funds as an investment because benefits would flow from diversifying into hedge funds.

The fact is that an authoritative study of the correlation between hedge fund performance and the performance of the traditional asset classes such as shares and property has not been undertaken. Consequently, there is no evidence of the correlation, negative or otherwise, between hedge funds and the traditional asset classes. Therefore this cannot be used as an argument to support the inclusion of hedge funds as an asset class. In this context the most that can be said about hedge funds is that they have the potential to generate profits in both rising and falling markets, but you can still make losses in both.

Taxation and hedge funds

Hedge funds are managed funds (unit trusts) and do not pay tax on their income providing that all of their income is distributed to unitholders. Investors pay tax on income received and capital gains. A hedge fund cannot distribute losses but investors can offset losses they make when they redeem their units against capital gains. Because many Australian-based hedge funds are FOFs that invest in overseas hedge funds, you could be subject to Foreign Investment Funds (FIF) legislation, which means that you could be taxed on unrealised capital gains. Also, if you invest directly overseas in a foreign hedge fund, you will be subject to FIF legislation. However, you are exempted from FIF legislation if you have A$50 000 or less invested in foreign companies or foreign managed funds.

Normal CGT rules apply when redeeming units you have held for longer than 12 months—you can claim a 50 per cent discount. Also dividends may be partly or wholly franked or unfranked.

Key points

o There has been a huge increase in the amount invested in hedge funds in Australia since 1999. Much of this has come from everyday investors.

o Hedge funds have the potential to generate profits in falling markets, but there is no guarantee that they will.

- o The most common hedge fund strategy, and that adopted by the first hedge fund in 1949, is long/short equity. There are at least 14 other hedge fund strategies, including various forms of arbitrage.

- o Hedge funds can be broadly classified as equity-based funds, non-equity-based funds, single-strategy funds or fund of funds.

- o Hedge fund managers usually discuss 'risk' in terms of standard deviation. This measures volatility rather than risk.

- o Hedge fund performance varies significantly from one manager to another. Overall, single-strategy funds have performed better than FOFs, but generally returns have not been anywhere near those forecast by hedge fund managers.

- o After reading a hedge fund prospectus you will often have little idea of what a manager proposes doing with your money.

- o Hedge fund performance may possibly be negatively correlated with the performance of traditional asset classes, but this has not been confirmed by research.

15

Investing in bonds

One of the fall-outs from the global financial crisis was that investors began to turn their focus to lower risk investments such as interest-bearing securities. Ironically, one of the causes of the GFC was a collapse in the market for 'junk' bonds — which are a high-risk interest-bearing investment. Clearly, not all interest-bearing investments are low risk. Indeed these investments come in several forms, including government and semi-government bonds, debentures, corporate bonds and unsecured notes. At the outset it is important to distinguish between government bonds and fixed-interest securities issued by non-government organisations. As the word 'bond' carries connotations of being secure, many financial organisations use this to market their products; for example, there are managed investments called 'bond funds'. But not all bonds are risk-free and carry a government guarantee of payment of interest and repayment of the original investment. This chapter will concentrate on investing in government bonds, while chapter 16 will examine other interest-bearing investments.

For most of the 1990s, the main sources of bonds for individual investors were governments — both state and the Commonwealth. In March 2009 a bond issue aimed at individual investors by fund manager AMP signalled the re-emergence of a retail corporate bond market in Australia. Later in 2009 gaming company Tabcorp announced the issue of 'Tabcorp Bonds' to both wholesale and retail investors. These were the first retail corporate bonds in Australia since an issue in the 1990s by Telecom (which later became Telstra). In the intervening years companies found it cheaper to raise money through banks and other financial institutions and so the retail market was ignored.

However, as a result of the GFC, banks and other lending institutions reduced the amount they were willing to lend and increased interest rates on these loans. So companies have begun looking for other funding sources. In addition, many retail investors are seeking investments with less risk and more certain returns.

ASIC has also moved to provide retail investors with easier access to corporate bonds by issuing a consultation paper intended to assist with the development of a sustainable listed corporate bond market in Australia by providing relief from long-form prospectus requirements.

For most individual investors there are currently more opportunities to invest in government bonds in Australia, so this chapter will mostly concentrate on how to invest in these bonds. Nevertheless, most of the information in this chapter can be applied to investing in corporate bonds — the main difference being that you need to be more careful about the financial strength of the company issuing these bonds.

Bond terminology

There is basic terminology you need to understand before you become involved in investing in bonds:

- *Face value:* This is the amount the government promises to repay at maturity. Also called 'par' value.

- *Market value:* This is what another investor is prepared to pay you for your bond before it matures.

- *Coupon rate:* Another name for the interest rate.

- *Maturity date:* This is the date on which the government promises to repay the bond's face value.

For example, suppose a Commonwealth Government bond had a face value of $10 000, a coupon rate of 5 per cent and a maturity date of 31 December 2015. If you bought this bond at its face value this means that the government would guarantee to pay you interest of $500 each year — 5 per cent of $10 000. Usually interest is paid half-yearly so you would receive $250 every six months. The government also guarantees to repay you $10 000 on 31 December 2015. The coupon rate for this bond remains at 5 per cent for the life of the bond.

However, the coupon rate on government bonds issued in subsequent months or years can change. The coupon rate on bonds will vary according to the state of the economy, the rate of inflation, the general level of interest rates and the amount of money the government needs to borrow. So if interest rates went up after you bought this bond the government might now issue bonds with a coupon rate of 5.5 per cent. In this case, the market value of your bond would go down. Alternatively, if interest rates went down after your purchase, the government might start issuing bonds with a coupon rate of 4 per cent—in which case the market value of your bond would increase.

Investing in government bonds

By investing in government and semi-government bonds (such as a state electricity supplier), you are lending money to the Australian or state government. In return, you receive a fixed rate of interest until a specific date when the bonds mature. Then you receive the face value of the bonds back.

The main investing benefits that government and semi-government bonds offer you are:

- a steady income with interest paid every six months

- a fixed date of maturity

- a low-risk investment if you hold the bonds until they mature

- a degree of capital protection as both the interest payments and the return of capital are guaranteed by the government issuing the bonds.

More importantly, you are not locked into these investments. Most government issuers of bonds offer a 'buy-back' facility, enabling you to redeem the bond before its maturity date. If you redeem your bonds before their maturity date you could make a capital gain or capital loss, and this usually depends on:

- the time to maturity—the longer the time to maturity the greater will be either the capital gain or loss you will make

- market interest rates—if market interest rates have risen since you bought the bond you will suffer a capital loss; if market interest rates have fallen you will receive a capital gain.

Some conditions apply. For example, NSW Treasury Bonds will only be repurchased after the date of the first interest payment on a monthly basis. Requests for early repayment received on or before the 21st of the month are paid on the first business day of the following month with interest calculated to that day. The Reserve Bank of Australia operates a buy-back scheme whereby it will buy relatively small amounts of bonds, up to $100 000 per customer per day, at the market price.

Government bond issuers

Apart from the Commonwealth Government, the other major issuers of government bonds in Australia are shown in table 15.1.

Table 15.1: major issuers of government bonds

Government	Borrower	Contact details
NSW	NSW Treasury Corporation	<www.tcorp.nsw.gov.au>
Northern Territory	Northern Territory Treasury (NTT)	<www.nt.gov.au/ntt/tcorp>
Queensland	Queensland Treasury Corporation (QTC)	<www.qtc.qld.gov.au>
South Australia	SA Government Financing Authority (SAFA)	<www.safa.sa.gov.au>
Victoria	Treasury Corporation of Victoria	<www.tcv.vic.gov.au>
Western Australia	Western Australian Treasury Corp (WATC)	<www.watc.wa.gov.au>
Tasmania	TASCORP	Tel: (03) 6233 7880

Government bonds are part of the national debt and offer first-class security as to the payment of interest and repayment of principal. However, in other respects, as you will see, bonds are far from guaranteed.

All government bonds end their lives at their par or face value, which is the amount that appears on the bond certificate. Many start at a price lower than this. During their lifetime bonds will fluctuate either above or below their par or face value, depending on what is happening with interest rates. If bonds are trading above their face value it is referred to as trading at a 'premium'. If they are selling below their face value they are trading at a 'discount'. It is this potential for capital gains and losses that makes bonds interesting and attractive to many investors. In fact, turnover on the Australian bond market is much higher than in the Australian sharemarket.

Buying government bonds

You can buy government bonds directly from the authority which issues them. Application forms often appear in major daily newspapers or you can download them from the authority's website. Alternatively you can ring the authority directly or contact them by email. Also the Reserve Bank has application forms for some state government bonds. Many authorities do not borrow all year round, they only go to the marketplace when they need funds. Hence there will be times when particular authorities may not be issuing bonds.

Subject to availability, the Reserve Bank will sell selected series of Treasury Fixed Coupon Bonds and Treasury Capital Indexed Bonds through the Commonwealth Government Bond Facility for Small Investors. Treasury Fixed Coupon Bonds pay interest on a semi-annual basis at the prescribed coupon rate, applied to the face value. At maturity, the face value amount is repaid.

Treasury Capital Indexed Bonds pay interest on a quarterly basis at the prescribed coupon rate, applied to the face value. However, the face value is adjusted by indexing the principal to inflation. At maturity, investors receive the adjusted capital value of the security; that is, the face value as adjusted for inflation over the life of the bond. The minimum investment is $1000, and investments can be made in multiples of $1000 up to $250 000 per investor per day. Other state government authorities require a minimum investment of $5000. It is not compulsory for you to quote your tax file number but tax may be deducted from interest payments if no number or exemption has been recorded.

Bond yields

All bonds have two yields: the interest yield—also referred to as the 'flat' or 'running' yield—and the yield to redemption. The interest yield is the interest paid each year divided by the purchase price multiplied by 100. For example, if you bought a bond for $1000 which paid you $50 per year in interest, the interest yield would be 5 per cent. The bond market makes an allowance for accrued interest, and so your own yield calculation may differ slightly from the yield data published in the press.

The yield to redemption is the total return on the bond if held to maturity. This includes both the interest yield and the capital gain or loss when the bond is finally repaid at maturity. Redemption yields are either above or below interest yields depending on whether the trading price of the bond is above or below the par value of the bond—in this case

$1000. For example, if the trading price of the bond is below its par value the redemption yield will exceed the interest yield.

Selling government bonds

Selling bonds is also straightforward. Although newcomers to the bond market usually believe that if they buy a three-year or ten-year bond their money is locked away for this length of time, this is far from true. Nowadays government borrowing authorities offer 'buy-back' facilities which allow you to cash in your bonds at any time. You can also buy and sell bonds through many stockbrokers.

In general, the ability to 'cash in' bonds through buy-back arrangements makes them an extremely liquid investment which, in turn, is an important criterion in investment decision-making. You will always be able to sell a particular bond without difficulty, but whether you get back what you paid for it is another matter. The market value of bonds moves inversely to changes in interest rates. An example can best illustrate this.

Suppose you have a bond trading at $1000 and paying interest at 5 per cent. Then interest rates go up to 6 per cent. This makes your bond relatively unattractive because investors can get a higher interest rate elsewhere. So the market 'discounts' or marks down the market value of your bond so that it once again gives a competitive yield.

In the case of your bond, the market value might drop from $1000 to $950. For example, if it had only three years to run and was bought at $950, the interest yield would rise to over 5 per cent and there would be a compounded capital gain to redemption of 0.7 per cent per annum. This would raise the annual yield to redemption to around 6 per cent. If it had 10 years to run, the price might drop to around $910. At this point it would yield around 6 per cent, if held to maturity, making it once again competitive with prospective buyers.

Other factors may also affect the price of bonds so that yields are not all exactly the same. However, the basic principle is that the prices of all bonds are continuously adjusted so that their yields remain competitive in response to changes in interest rates. You should bear in mind that the longer the term of a bond, the more its market value will change in response to interest rate movements.

For example, on 30 September 2009 a Treasury Bond with a coupon rate of 6.50 per cent maturing on 15 May 2013 was selling for $107.078, which included accrued interest of $2.438 for every $100 of face value. This indicates the type of capital gains that are available with Treasury

Bonds. At the same date a Treasury Bond with a coupon rate of 4.50 per cent maturing on 15 April 2020 was selling for $94.522, including $2.066 of accrued interest for every $100 of face value. This shows that the market value of bonds can fall below their face value.

Gearing and bonds

Gearing, sometimes referred to as leverage, is where you borrow money to invest. Interest on the loan is a tax deduction so gearing can be a tax-effective strategy for investors on high marginal income tax rates.

With regard to bonds, because they are relatively safe, they can be used as security to borrow money. You can then effectively make a further bond investment with that money. Suppose you originally bought bonds with a par value of $10 000 for $91 per $100, for a total cost of $9100, and borrowed 50 per cent of that amount, or $4550. Say interest rates fell sharply and your bond price rose to $100. Your profit would be $9 per bond or $900. But since you only put up $4550 of your own money, your profit is nearly 20 per cent, less of course dealing costs and loan interest and charges.

However, gearing can also work in reverse. If interest rates rose it would multiply the losses you make.

The cost of investing in bonds

It is important, when considering investing in bonds, to appreciate that when you deal directly with the borrowing authority you do not pay upfront fees, entry fees, commissions or other hidden charges. The interest rate you are quoted for the amount and term you invest for is what you get. Even if you invest through an intermediary such as a stockbroker you usually do not pay a commission.

Some borrowing authorities charge fees on their buy-back facility. For example, the Reserve Bank has an administrative charge of 25¢ per $100 face value on its small sales facility. If you deal in the secondary market through a stockbroker you will have to pay a commission, which will vary from broker to broker and will also depend on the size of the transaction.

In general, dealing in bonds is cheaper than dealing in shares, but not all stockbrokers are involved in the bond market. You may have to ring the ASX to obtain a list of stockbrokers who are active in the bond market.

Security of government bonds

A question that may arise is: is it possible for a state government to be declared bankrupt? The answer is no, because if a government ever gets into financial difficulties it can always resort to raising additional revenue through taxes. Traditionally, Federal Government bonds have offered lower interest rates than state government bonds because the Federal Government is seen to be financially stronger.

Australian government bond issues are rated by independent rating agencies such as Standard & Poor's. The rating is a measure of a government's or a company's assessed ability to repay the principal on its debt as well as interest. The higher the rating the less likelihood of the issuer defaulting on repaying your capital. AAA is the highest rating awarded for long-term issuers, while BB and below is the lowest and is usually given to more risky or speculative investments. Information on the credit ratings of state governments in Australia is available on the Standard & Poor's website: <www.standardandpoors.com.au>.

For example, in February 2009 Standard & Poor's cited Queensland's 'projected deteriorating budgetary performance, which is a result of both declining revenues and structural operating expenditure' as a reason for downgrading its credit rating to AA+, the lowest of any state in Australia.

Types of bonds

Bonds are classified as follows:

- short-dated

- medium-dated

- long-dated.

Short-dated bonds have a term of up to two years. They are especially popular with banks and other financial institutions because of the certainty of repayment within a comparatively short space of time. For this reason redemption yields on these bonds have traditionally tended to be slightly lower than on longer dated issues.

Price fluctuations are less pronounced because these issues gravitate towards their par value the closer they get to their redemption date. But volatility has increased in recent years due to greater unpredictability in interest rates.

Medium-dated bonds have a term of between two and five years. Prices tend to be more volatile because of the length of the repayment period and the high incidence of high-coupon issues.

Long-dated bonds have a term of up to 10 years and longer. On average coupon values and redemption yields are slightly lower than medium-dated bonds. These bonds are highly exposed to trends in the economy and the factors affecting interest rates. Hence prices can be volatile, offering more scope for capital gains and losses than in shorter dated bonds.

Nowadays, most bonds are held in the form of 'inscribed stock', which means the owner's name is 'inscribed' on a central register. All subsequent transactions relating to the bond are also recorded in the register. This avoids the need for the borrowing authority to issue a security which has to be kept in a safe place. Instead a non-negotiable Certificate of Inscription, which confirms all relevant details, acknowledges your bonds.

As has been stated previously the word 'bond' is used by several organisations to describe securities or financing facilities offered by them. These types of bonds should not be confused with federal or state government bonds. For example, numerous insurance companies and friendly societies offer insurance bonds and friendly society bonds respectively. The security with these bonds is only as good as the organisations that offer them — they are not government guaranteed.

Monitoring your bonds

It is not as easy to monitor bond investments as sharemarket investments because not as much information is published on a regular basis. This is despite turnover in the bond market being higher than the sharemarket. Some information is given in major daily newspapers, but it is usually limited. More comprehensive information is contained in the *Australian Financial Review*. Bulletins are published monthly by the Reserve Bank. They are available within a few weeks after the end of the month, but they may be as much as two months out of date at the time of publication. Hence the April bulletin is available from early in May and may relate back to February data. A selection of bond prices is available on the Small Investor Bond Facility section of the Reserve Bank website.

Price swings in the bond market are less pronounced than in the sharemarket. Another difference is that nearly all bond prices will move in the same direction on the same day, whereas some shares will move up and some down, while others will not alter. The main influences on bond prices are a change in the level of interest rates or expectations of a change in the near future. So if you are going to invest in bonds you need to first consider what is likely to happen with interest rates in the near future. If you think interest rates will rise, you should be selling bonds or delaying the purchase of bonds. If you think that interest rates will fall you should be holding the bonds you already have and investing more in bonds, as a fall in interest rates increases the market value of bonds that are already issued.

The determinants of interest rates

A number of key economic indicators determine interest rates, including the:

- expected rate of inflation
- government's borrowing requirements and monetary policy
- balance of payments
- value of the Australian dollar
- level of interest rates among the major industrialised countries.

Different factors influence short-term rates as opposed to long-term rates. The chief factor influencing short-term rates is the government's monetary policy, as implemented by the Reserve Bank. The expected rate of inflation, the longer term balance of payments outlook and the government's borrowing requirements are more likely to influence long-term interest rates.

If all, or most, of these indicators are improving, interest rates are likely to fall, leading to an increase in the price of bonds. This is said to be a 'bullish' climate. If the opposite is true and market values decline, it is said to be a 'bearish' climate. A classic example of a bullish market existed in Australia in the 1990s when the interest rate on 10-year government bonds fell from 13.5 per cent to less than 6 per cent. Anyone who anticipated this development made handsome profits.

The yield curve

The yield curve maps the relationship between the yield and term to maturity of different bonds of the same type and is an important tool in assessing future bond valuations. Views on the yield curve also assist a portfolio manager's views on duration as expressed above. In Australia, anchored by the current cash rate set by the Reserve Bank, the shape of the yield curve represents where investors think interest rates are heading.

There are three main types of yield curves:

- *Normal:* When a yield curve is normally shaped, investors predict that short-term rates will be higher in the future. It is termed normal because long-term rates are higher than short-term rates. This is mainly because of the uncertainty and risk associated with longer term investments.

- *Inverse:* When a yield curve is inversely shaped, investors predict that short-term rates will be lower in the future.

- *Flat:* When a yield curve is relatively flat, investors are predicting that short-term rates will remain steady into the future.

The main source of information on the future direction of interest rates in Australia is from the Reserve Bank. The Reserve Bank sets the target 'cash rate', which is the market interest rate on overnight funds. It uses this to influence the cash rate through its financial market operations. Decisions to vary this interest rate are made by the Reserve Bank Board which meets every month except January. The Board's decision to either raise, lower or keep interest rates unchanged is explained in a media release after each Board meeting. These media releases are essential reading for serious investors in government bonds.

Volatility and bonds

As a general rule, the longer a bond has to run and the lower its coupon rate of interest, the more volatile it is. This is important, especially if you expect interest rates to fall. Short-dated bonds with less than two years to run are the least volatile because you know you can get back the face value of the bonds within a reasonably short period of time. Medium-dated bonds are riskier, but they are somewhat out of favour as they appeal to neither speculators nor seekers of long-term security of income. Long-dated bonds are the riskiest, with up to 10 years and more to run before repayment.

Much can happen to interest rates and bond prices during this time. Hence long-dated bonds are the most volatile of all.

Bonds compared with shares

The advantages of bonds are:

- Safety of capital; eventually the par value of the bonds will be repaid in full.

- Security of income, because the government will always pay the interest due.

- Fixed rate of interest; you know where you stand.

- Good liquidity because of buy-back facilities. This means that you can cash in your bonds at short notice.

- Good prospects for short-term capital gains if interest rates fall.

- Less monitoring is usually required with bonds than shares.

The disadvantages of bonds include:

- Interest from bonds is wholly taxable whereas dividends from shares may be franked and therefore not taxable in the hands of some shareholders.

- Bonds have a fixed rate of return, unlike shares which pay dividends that may increase.

- Bond prices fluctuate but they are unlikely to double or treble in value like shares can.

The question may be asked: is it better to invest in bonds or shares? The two are not mutually exclusive. As was seen in chapter 3, it is appropriate to diversify risk by including both shares and fixed-interest securities in your portfolio.

How risky are corporate bonds?

Corporate bonds are fixed-interest securities that are issued by a company, not the government. If you invest in corporate bonds you are lending money to the company. The main risk you take by investing in corporate bonds is that if the company issuing the bonds goes out of business you could lose all or part of your money. Corporate bonds are usually different from debentures, which are also fixed-interest securities issued by companies. Debentures are usually secured against property assets while corporate bonds may or may not be secured against property. A debenture is also always a fixed-rate investment, while corporate bonds may be fixed-interest or floating-rate investments. This means that the interest rate on the money you lend is either set in advance (fixed) or linked to a variable interest rate (floating).

You can buy (and sell) some corporate bonds on the ASX, just like you would shares after they have been issued in the primary market. If you buy bonds on the ASX, you will pay the market price, which may be higher or lower than the face value of the bond. You will also pay brokerage fees. It is essential that you find out whether there will be an active secondary market for the corporate bonds before you invest.

The risk level of a corporate bond depends on:

- The credit rating of the company issuing the bonds; that is, does the company have the financial capacity to pay you interest and return your principal at maturity?

- How each bond itself is ranked in the capital structure of the company; that is, where it would stand compared with other securities if the company was wound up.

ASIC has published a guide titled *Investing in Corporate Bonds?* which is available to download free from ASIC's website: <www.asic.gov.au>. This gives a detailed checklist of what factors you should consider before investing in corporate bonds.

Tax and bonds

Income from either a government or corporate bond is fully taxable at your marginal tax rate. You are not required to advise the bond issuer of your tax file number or Australian Business Number. However, if you do not provide a TFN or ABN and do not claim an exemption from providing a TFN or ABN, tax will be withheld equal to the top marginal rate of tax plus the Medicare levy. You may receive a refund of some of this tax when you lodge your income tax return if you have paid too much tax. In some cases you may be liable for capital gains tax on any gains on the sale of bonds.

Key points

- The buy-back facilities offered on some bonds ensure a lively secondary market. If you are interested in investing in bonds for possible capital gain, you should only invest in bonds that have this facility.

- Bond prices move inversely to changes in interest rates. If interest rates go up, bond prices fall, and vice versa.

- When investing in government bonds the payment of interest and the repayment of principal are guaranteed by the government, but the price of bonds fluctuates in secondary markets.

o   Investing in government bonds is safe because if a government ever got into financial difficulty it could raise additional revenue through taxation.

o   The longer the term to maturity of a bond the more its price will change in response to changes in interest rates.

o   When comparing the returns from shares with the returns from bonds you have to take into account the fact that some or all of the dividends may be tax-free due to dividend imputation. In contrast the interest income from bonds is fully taxable.

o   Retail corporate bonds are now becoming more common. Before investing in these bonds you should ensure that the company issuing the bonds has the financial strength to pay interest on the bonds and repay the principal at the maturity date.

16

Interest-bearing investments

A balanced portfolio includes investments in shares, property, fixed interest and cash; this chapter is concerned with that part of your portfolio allocated to fixed interest and cash. During the GFC, investors became nervous about financial markets in general, and this also applied to fixed-interest and cash investments. A number of finance companies went out of business in 2008 and there were concerns about investments as fundamental as term and 'at-call' deposits with banks. To alleviate this problem, the Australian Government guaranteed deposits with banks and similar institutions up to $1 million per depositor until October 2011. No fees are payable by depositors in return for the government taking this action.

Despite cash and fixed-interest investments often being regarded as boring, there are times when boring investments such as these give you the best return. While the return on these investments is usually much lower than from property and shares, their main attraction is that the risk of losing money is minimal. So 'cash becomes king' in times when the sharemarket and/or property markets are volatile or in a downtrend.

Chapter 15 focused on government-guaranteed bonds. After a government guarantee, the next best type of guarantee is one from a financially sound bank. Most investors are familiar with bank term deposits. They are safe investments (especially with the backing of the government guarantee until October 2011), but they do not offer the scope for trading in a secondary market and hence there is no prospect of making capital gains. Term deposits can usually be terminated prior to maturity providing you are willing to settle for a lower rate of interest than if you had held the deposit until maturity. Fewer investors understand how another bank-guaranteed investment — bank bills — work.

Bank bills

Bank bills, more properly called bank accepted bills (BABs), are fixed-interest investments guaranteed by the issuing bank. Until October 2011 they are also guaranteed by the Australian Government. They are classed as assets of the bank rather than deposits, and rank after depositors in the case of a bank defaulting. Bank bills have been traded in Australia for more than 90 years and during this time no bank has failed to honour its promise to repay the face value of a bill at maturity.

Bank bills are a form of short-term financing facility provided by banks. They can be used to provide finance to borrowers or as a form of short-term investment. They offer excellent security, high liquidity and incorporate ease of investment management.

There is a secondary market (or after-market) for bank bills and it is possible to make capital gains and losses through trading them. In this respect they are similar to government bonds. It is also a useful strategy to park money in bank bills in anticipation of a rise in fixed interest rates.

An important difference between bank bills and government bonds is that bank bills are issued for terms of 7 to 185 days. The usual terms are 30, 60, 90, 120, 150 and 180 days.

For many investors the trickiest aspect of bank bills is calculating interest. When you purchase a bank bill you buy it at a discount to its face value. For example, you might buy a bank bill with a face value of $50 000, which matures in 90 days, for $49 200. If you hold the bill for 90 days the bank will pay you the face value of $50 000. The difference between the purchase price and the face value, $800, is your interest. In this case you would have received $800 by investing $49 200 for three months. You therefore get a return of around 1.46 per cent for three months, or around 5.85 per cent on an annual basis. When you are investing in bank bills, you do not need to work this out for yourself because the bank will do it for you.

Table 16.1 shows the interest rates prevailing on bank bills since 2000.

The usual minimum for investing in a bank bill is $50 000 and there are no bank fees. A bank bill may be traded at any time. One way you can do this is to sell it back to the bank you bought it from, at the current market interest rate. If interest rates have declined since you bought the bill, the discounted price will have increased. Conversely, the price will have declined if interest rates have risen. Alternatively, you can sell a bill to another person at an agreed rate. As it is customary for a bank to keep possession of a bill for safe custody, you will first need to retrieve it to sell it to somebody else. Also, when the bill matures it will need to be presented by the new owner to the bank that accepted it.

Table 16.1: bank bill interest rates (Dec. 2000 to Dec. 2009)

Year	Cash rate % p.a.	30 days % p.a.	90 days % p.a.	180 days % p.a.
2000	6.25	6.26	6.07	5.87
2001	4.25	4.33	4.25	4.24
2002	4.75	4.84	4.82	4.79
2003	5.25	5.46	5.52	5.58
2004	5.25	5.41	5.43	5.47
2005	5.50	5.62	5.64	5.68
2006	6.25	6.37	6.44	6.53
2007	6.75	7.05	7.20	7.36
2008	4.25	4.31	4.08	3.70
2009	3.75	4.04	4.21	4.41

Source: Reserve Bank of Australia.

Arranging to buy a bank bill is not complicated and maintaining the facility is even simpler. To begin with you will need to lodge funds with a bank. You then select a bill on the basis quoted to you by the bank. The bank will then draw down the funds in your account. When it comes time for the bill to mature, the bank will usually forewarn you that it is maturing and quote you rates for buying another bill, or 'rolling' your investment over. You do not need to make a personal visit to roll over a bill; it can be done by telephone.

The financial pages of major daily newspapers contain information on the rates being paid on bank bills. They also contain information on 90-day bank bill futures where an index is usually quoted equivalent to 100 minus the yield per cent per annum.

One investment strategy is to lock yourself into bank bills when short-term rates are high and when long-term rates are expected to increase. They are also a good place to park your cash if you think that share prices are about to fall, as in the lead up to the GFC.

The government guarantee

The Australian Government guarantees deposits in authorised deposit-taking institutions (ADIs) until 12 October 2011. The ADI must be subject to prudential regulation by the Australian Prudential Regulation Authority (APRA). Basically, the guarantee covers Australian banks, approved Australian subsidiaries of foreign banks, credit unions, building societies and the foreign branches of ADIs. The guarantee applies to cash management accounts of banks, but not managed funds. On this basis, cash management trusts are excluded, but online savings accounts of ADIs — such as ING, AMP and UBank — are included. The guarantee is free up to $1 million per ADI, after which a fee applies to the amount above $1 million.

Cash management trusts

Until cash management trusts (CMTs) came along in the early 1980s, small investors were excluded from the benefits of investing in the short-term money market (STMM) where the interest rates generally are higher than those offered by banks to their ordinary depositors. The main reason small investors could not get a look in is that the minimum investment on the STMM is around $50000.

The success of CMTs is shown by the fact that in June 2009 they had assets of over $43 billion. This was up from around $31 billion in December 2002. The basic idea of a CMT is simple. Numerous small investors pool their resources to overcome the minimum investment barrier of $50000 for investing in the STMM. The minimum initial deposit with a CMT usually ranges between $500 and $1000, but some CMTs require a minimum deposit of $5000.

How safe are CMTs?

Most CMTs only invest in government-backed or bank-backed securities such as Commonwealth bonds and bank bills. This means that CMTs are relatively low risk. Some CMTs are allowed to invest in commercial loans; for example, they could lend money to BHP Billiton or other large corporations. But it is unlikely that any CMT would lend substantial amounts to companies with poor credit ratings. CMTs generally are only permitted to invest in short-term securities — that is, those with less than one year to maturity — which also reduces the risk of capital loss.

Capital guarantee

Some CMTs offer a capital guarantee. Of course, a guarantee is only as good as the financial strength of the guarantor, and most CMTs have no other assets apart from their depositors' money. In some cases the CMT is a subsidiary of a larger financial organisation which gives its guarantee to the fund.

In reality, the ultimate guarantee for depositors' money comes from where this money is invested. As the majority of CMT funds are invested in government-guaranteed and bank-guaranteed securities, there is little danger of suffering a capital loss by investing in a CMT.

Interest rates on CMTs

Interest rates on CMTs can move up and down significantly. They were around 17 per cent in late 1989 compared with around 3.5 per cent in February 2010. Rates are subject to daily change, usually by small amounts, and reflect movements in interest rates on the STMM. Movements in interest rates for CMTs (and other types of accounts) since 2000 are shown in table 16.2.

Table 16.2: interest rates for different account types

Date	Online savings accounts (% p.a.)	CMAs* at banks $10 000 (% p.a.)	CMTs (% p.a.)	3-month term deposit $10 000 (% p.a.)
Dec. 2000	NA**	3.30	5.75	4.10
Dec. 2001	NA	1.55	3.60	2.90
Dec. 2002	NA	1.90	4.05	3.10
Dec. 2003	NA	2.10	4.35	3.75
Dec. 2004	5.10	2.45	4.65	3.80
Dec. 2005	5.40	2.65	4.90	4.35
Dec. 2006	5.90	4.30	5.45	4.50
Dec. 2007	6.55	5.35	6.05	4.60
Dec. 2008	4.60	3.10	4.00	3.85
Dec. 2009	3.85	2.85	3.30***	3.65

* Cash management accounts.
** Not applicable.
*** Estimate.
Source: Reserve Bank of Australia.

You can expect the interest rate offered by most CMTs to be slightly below the rate on 90-day bank bills. Although CMT interest rates move in line with the 90-day bank bill rate, they do not follow this rate exactly. There is often a time lag between a rise in the bank bill rate and a rise in the CMT rate. Similarly, when bank bill rates fall, CMT rates frequently lag behind.

How long this time lag is depends on the skill of the CMT manager. If the manager thinks interest rates are going to fall, they can cushion this decline by investing in slightly longer term securities; for example, 180-day bank bills, instead of 90-day bank bills. By doing this the CMT can lock away some of its funds at relatively high rates of interest.

Choosing between CMTs

As there is sometimes a 1 per cent difference in the rate offered by various CMTs it is important not to put your money with one that consistently pays a lower rate than the rest.

Cheque facilities

The most attractive CMTs are those which allow you to withdraw by cheque. Unfortunately there is a catch. In some cases, the minimum cheque you can write is for $500 and you must also keep a minimum amount of around $2000 in your CMT account. With some CMTs this is higher.

Banks offer cash management accounts (CMAs) with the option of being able to write cheques. In these cases there is no lower limit on the amount of the cheque but you may earn no interest if your balance falls below $10 000.

A bonus of having a cheque withdrawal facility linked to a CMT or CMA is that your money continues to earn interest until the cheque is presented. Depending on the CMT/CMA, you may be charged other fees for cheques. For example, you may be charged for a cheque book and/or a fee per cheque.

Major banks' cash management accounts

Despite CMTs being one of the success stories of the 1980s, the major banks—ANZ, Commonwealth, National and Westpac—were slow to offer their customers similar accounts.

Until 1990 there were no CMT accounts offered by the four major banks. The Commonwealth Bank was the first off the mark to offer a CMT, and the ANZ, Westpac and National banks then followed. Some credit unions and building societies also have CMAs. As with all financial products, it pays to read the fine print and shop around before opening any of these accounts.

In contrast to other CMTs, the major banks require a relatively high opening deposit—usually $5000. This compares with an initial minimum deposit of between $1000 and $2000 for most non-bank CMTs. If your balance falls below $5000 with a CMA you either get a low rate of interest or none at all.

Unlike CMTs, CMAs have a tiered interest rate structure. The more you invest the higher the rate of interest you earn on your account. Make sure you earn the higher rate of interest on all your funds, not just on the excess.

CMAs are included in the government guarantee of $1 million per depositor, as are online savings accounts.

Online savings accounts

In recent years a number of organisations have established online savings accounts which often offer investors higher interest rates than CMTs and CMAs. The catch is that you can only access these accounts electronically, or in some cases by telephone, and they usually do not come with cheque books or access to ATMs. A typical online savings account is linked to an external bank account and withdrawals, which are generally available within 24 hours, are made through this account. Deposits can be made directly or through the external bank account. Providers include ING, AMP Banking and UBank. They argue that because they do not have branch structures their costs are lower and they can pass these savings on to customers in the form of higher interest rates.

Applying for units in a CMT

The interest rates on offer from CMTs are quoted daily in most major newspapers. Often the previous day's rate is given as well for comparison. As has been seen, there is more to investing in a CMT than picking one out of the financial pages without much to go on apart from an interest rate. The financial pages will not tell you what the minimum initial investment is, what the minimum additional investment is, what the minimum withdrawal is, whether it has a cheque book facility or not, the size of the fund, who the manager is, who the responsible entity is, who the directors are and so on. For this information you need a prospectus, which the manager of a CMT will happily send you. In fact, you can only apply for units in a CMT by filling out an application form which is attached to the prospectus. In turn, the prospectus will have been vetted by ASIC, although this does not mean, in any way, that ASIC guarantees it.

If you become a unitholder in a CMT you may have access to a cheque book facility. You will also usually be able to withdraw funds at 24 hours' notice by telephone. Once you open an account you do not need a prospectus to invest additional amounts.

You can enquire about an online savings account online, but you will have to fill out a form which requires that you send in your application by mail. Neither CMTs nor online savings accounts require that you produce 100 points of identification.

Debentures

Debt finance is attractive to many companies because it enables them to grow without giving up a stake in ownership with the consequent loss of a share of the profits. Corporate debt, in turn, takes a number of different forms. Cumulative preference shares, which were described in chapter 8, are, strictly speaking, part of a company's equity capital, but they take on the appearance of debt because preference dividends have to be paid before an ordinary dividend is paid. As has already been pointed out, if a cumulative preference dividend is 'missed' it accumulates. From the point of view of ordinary shareholders, therefore, cumulative preference shares are like debt.

In general, fixed long-term loans are not as common as they used to be. Borrowers and lenders have tended to negotiate variable-rate facilities. A debenture offers a fixed rate of interest payable ahead of dividends and is often secured by specific company assets, especially property. They are less risky than equities, but usually pay a lower rate of interest than other debt because they rank ahead of most other creditors in the event of winding up. They may be traded on the ASX, but nowadays few company debentures are listed. Debentures are sometimes referred to as 'bonds' but these are to be clearly differentiated from government bonds.

According to ASIC, you should ask yourself the following when investing in debentures:

- How does the yearly rate of return compare with other fixed-interest investments? If it is high, you are probably taking a risk.

- If the company is involved in property, what sector is it in? Would the company be especially vulnerable if the investment property market fell?

- Do you hold any security over real property? If not, the investment may be riskier.

- If debentures are issued by a company that offers finance to other companies, is lending done at arm's-length or are the loans generally offered to related companies?

- Are the financial statements of the company healthy? Financial strain may make it harder to pay interest and principal to debenture and note holders.

Table 16.3 shows a selection of debentures on issue in February 2010.

Table 16.3: selected debenture issues (February 2010)

Institution	Product name	Minimum $	Maximum $	1 year (% p.a.)	3 year (% p.a.)	S&P rating
Angus Securities	Angus Securities Limited Debentures	10 000	5 million	8.00	NA	B+
AuSec	First Ranking Note	5 000	None	8.30	9.50	Not rated
Bank of Queensland	Bonds	5 000	250 000	6.10	7.05	A2 BBB+
GR Finance	GR First Ranking Note	1 000	None	9.50	9.65	Not rated
National Australia Bank	Bonds	5 000	10 000	3.90	4.20	AA–
National Australia Bank	Bonds	10 000	20 000	4.50	4.25	AA–
Provident Capital	Debenture Stock	1 000	None	7.90	8.45	Not rated
Victorian Securities	Debenture Stock	25 000	None	–	–	Not rated

Source: © InfoChoice.

Remember that debentures are relatively illiquid investments. If you invest in a four-year debenture and want your money back early you may incur a penalty—usually in the form of a lower rate of interest.

Unsecured notes

An unsecured note is a security issued by a company to an investor which is referred to by the company as a 'note payable'. Although these notes are not secured, they are usually regarded as a stronger claim against a company than an open account because the terms of payment are usually specified in writing. Holders of unsecured notes rank ahead of shareholders but behind debenture holders in the event that a company is wound up.

In 2009 ASIC issued a specific warning to individual investors in fixed-interest securities. In particular, ASIC recommended that you take extra care with debentures, unsecured notes and other interest-bearing investments offering higher than usual returns. Higher returns means anything more than 1 or 2 per cent above the market rate for similar products. The main reason behind this warning was that a number of debentures and unsecured notes had been issued by property developers and financiers of property developers. Part of the fallout from the GFC was that many property developers ended up in financial trouble—the most notable of these being the Westpoint group of companies. Investors in Westpoint-related financial products had an outstanding total capital invested of $388 million as at January 2006 when the group collapsed. Liquidators and administrators of the various entities estimated total amounts available for distribution to investors in respect of a limited number of the entities was $57.2 million.

Income securities

In 1999 several companies issued perpetual income securities which at the time proved to be very popular with investors. Companies to issue these securities included National Australia Bank ($2 billion), Publishing and Broadcasting Limited ($300 million), AMP ($1.5 billion), Macquarie Bank ($400 million) and Woolworths ($600 million).

The name given to income securities varies from company to company. For example, Macquarie Bank call theirs income securities Perpetual Floating Rate Notes and Woolworths call theirs Woolworths Income Notes (WINs).

If you invest in income securities you receive quarterly interest payments where the interest rate is set in a fixed relationship to the 90-day bank bill rate. For example, the rate payable on Woolworths's income securities is two percentage points above the 90-day bank bill. So if the 90-day bank bill rate was 5.5 per cent, the rate of interest payable on the income securities would be 7.5 per cent (5.5% + 2.0%). As the interest rate payable on 90-day bank bills increases so too does the interest rate payable on income securities. Conversely, when the 90-day bank bill interest rate falls the interest rate payable on income securities falls. As can be seen, with this type of security you are not locked in to a lower interest rate for a short time if the general level of interest rates rises.

The principal amount of income securities is usually $100. They are issued in perpetuity—that is, they have no maturity date—and as such you continue to receive interest without having to roll over or reinvest your original investment. Income securities are listed on the ASX and you can buy or sell them in the same way as you do shares. In the event of the company winding up, the holders of income securities are paid after creditors and other liabilities, but before preference and ordinary shareholders.

The interest rate payable on income securities is set at the beginning of a quarter with the payment being made at the end of the quarter. For example, with Woolworths income securities the interest rate is set at 15 December (payable 15 March), 15 March (payable 15 June), 15 June (payable 15 September) and 15 September (payable 15 December). If any of these dates is not a business day, then the interest rate will be set or paid (as applicable) on the next business day.

To be entitled to receive an interest payment from a Woolworths income security you must be recorded in the register of holders on the record date, which is 11 business days before the date on which the interest payment becomes due. The Woolworths income securities trade on the ASX without an entitlement to the next interest payment—referred to as 'ex-interest'—four business days prior to the relevant record date. So if interest is payable on 15 June, the record date is 11 business days before this and the income securities trade ex-interest four business days prior to the record date. As the date on which the securities trade ex-interest approaches, the price at which they are traded on the ASX increases because you buy the securities with the next interest payment attached. Once the securities go ex-interest, however, the price will drop to reflect the fact that you have to wait approximately three months for the next interest payment.

Although income securities are issued in perpetuity, the issuing company usually reserves the right to redeem all or some of the securities after a specified date. For example, Woolworths has the right to redeem each income security for its face value of $100, plus any outstanding accrued interest, at any time on or after 15 December 2004.

Woolworths's income securities carry with them what is referred to as a 'dividend stopper'. If the company fails to make an interest payment, dividends cannot be paid on Woolworths's ordinary shares until four subsequent quarterly interest payments have been paid, or the missed interest payments are made up.

Income securities were first issued in May 1999 and they were extremely popular with investors. The first issuer, National Australia Bank, sought to raise $500 million and received applications for $5.8 billion. The bank subsequently raised the size of the issue to $2 billion. At the time of writing there are 14 issues of income securities listed on the ASX.

Income securities provide a return of between 1.25 per cent and 2.00 per cent above the 90-day bank bill rate. As such they return a higher yield than CMTs, CMAs and online savings accounts. CMTs, for example, traditionally return around 1 per cent less than the 90-day bank bill rate for about the same degree of risk. However, with CMTs the unit price is set at $1.00 whereas with income securities the price can fluctuate. Indeed, several income securities have traded below their issue price of $100. Not surprisingly, investors who suffered capital losses on income securities are not as keen on them as when they were initially launched. In addition, income securities have been superseded in the eyes of many investors by reset preference shares (see chapter 10), which generally offer franked dividends rather than interest income.

Disadvantages of interest-bearing investments

The main drawback for all types of interest-bearing investments is that they have limited appeal for taxpaying investors. For example, if you get 6 per cent on income securities and are paying 46.5¢ in the dollar tax, your effective return is around 3.2 per cent per annum—hardly anything to get excited about if inflation is running at 3 per cent.

How to invest in CMTs and debentures

To invest in debentures or to open a CMT not linked to a bank account you need to fill out a form contained in the company's prospectus. A prospectus is a legal document giving financial details of the company as well as basic information on interest rates, minimum deposits and withdrawals and how your money will be invested. Prospectuses can be obtained by telephoning the company and asking that one be sent to you, or in the case of debentures go to: <www.infochoice.com.au/investment/investment-broker/debentures.aspx>.

Selling debentures

Fixed-interest securities such as government bonds and debentures can be bought and sold in the secondary market through fixed-interest brokers. There are not as many fixed-interest brokers as there are stockbrokers. One reason why there are not a lot more retail fixed-interest brokers is that most investors do not realise they can trade their debentures or government bonds. There would not be many stockbrokers either if share investors only bought shares at the time a company issued a prospectus for a share issue.

Nevertheless, fixed-interest securities are an important component of any investment portfolio and in many respects the most secure and simplest investment you can make.

Selling your bonds or debentures is easy, provided you have details of your holding, such as maturity date, coupon rate, interest payment frequency and the amount initially invested. Your broker will offer you an interest rate (or indicative rate) to buy your bonds or debentures and give you an amount you stand to receive. This is known as the yield rate, not to be confused with the coupon rate, which is the interest paid on your original investment. Remember that the market value of debentures moves inversely to movements in interest rates. So if interest rates rise, the market value of your debenture falls. Not all brokers are active in the interest rate market. You can use the ASX website and the 'Find a broker' facility to get a list of brokers in your area who specialise in these investments.

Taxation and interest-bearing investments

Interest income is fully taxable in your hands at your marginal rate of income tax. If you sell a fixed-interest security, such as a debenture, for more than you paid for it you are liable for capital gains tax. If you have held the security for longer than 12 months, you can claim a 50 per cent discount. You are not obliged to provide a financial institution with your tax file number, but if you do not, tax will be taken out at the highest marginal rate of tax of 46.5 per cent (including the Medicare levy). If you are on a lower marginal rate of tax, you will receive a refund for the difference when you submit your income tax return.

Key points

o A well-diversified investment portfolio includes an allocation to fixed-interest securities and to cash, so make sure you are knowledgeable about the opportunities available.

o Investing in bank bills is appropriate if you expect long-term interest rates to rise, but the minimum investment is usually $50 000.

o Cash management trusts usually yield around 1 per cent less than 90-day bank bills, but the minimum investment may be as low as $500. Also they frequently have cheque book facilities.

o Online savings accounts usually offer higher interest rates than cash management trusts, but they generally do not have cheque book facilities.

o If you invest in debentures, stick to ones that have a good S&P rating, and it is generally wise to avoid debentures issued by property-related companies.

o It is possible to buy and sell debentures and bonds in the secondary market through fixed-interest brokers.

o Income securities are traded on the ASX and there is the possibility of capital gains or losses from these investments.

Options and futures

17

Options and futures are part of a broad range of financial products known as 'derivatives'. The term 'derivative' simply means that one financial product has been derived from another financial product. For example, an option over Telstra shares is derived from the shares themselves. Similarly, futures are derived from other financial products. Futures and options trading is one of the few investments where you can lose more than your initial investment. But this volatility, and the prospect of making huge gains in short periods of time, is also what some investors find attractive.

Institutional investors such as AMP Limited and professional fund managers account for about 60 to 80 per cent of trading in the Australian derivatives market. However, this still means that a sizeable number of private investors have realised the advantages that derivatives have to offer.

The most likely reasons why more private investors do not enter the options market are that they see options as being too risky or they are overwhelmed by all the jargon that accompanies options trading.

Exchange-traded options

Despite what at first may appear to be a mass of confusing jargon, the idea behind an exchange-traded option (ETO)—that is, an option traded on the stock exchange—is simple and easy to understand. When you buy an option, you are purchasing the right to buy or sell particular shares at a predetermined price on or before a specific date in the future. You can exercise this choice, or 'option', by buying or selling the shares at the agreed price. Or you can decline to do so. In that case, the option simply lapses or 'expires'.

Alternatively, you can simply trade the options themselves; for example, you can sell an option you have already bought. With traded options you can only deal in around 105 Australian shares, compared with over 2000 listed shares. You can also buy options based on the movement of the All Ordinaries index. You can find a list of companies and indices over which ETOs are traded on the ASX website: <www.asx.com.au>.

Common features of options contracts

All exchange-traded option contracts on the Australian derivatives market have the following standard features:

- *Contract size:* Usually option contracts are standardised, with each contract comprising 1000 shares—although there are some exceptions to this.

- *Expiry date:* Options have a limited life span and expire on standard expiry dates. An option ceases to exist after the expiry date.

- *Exercise or strike price:* The exercise price is the predetermined buying or selling price for the underlying shares if the option is exercised. There is usually a range of exercise prices available within the same expiry month.

- *Premium:* The premium is the price the buyer (also known as the taker) of the option pays the seller (also known as the writer) for the option contract itself. Premiums are quoted on a cents-per-share basis. To calculate the full premium of an option, multiply the quoted price by the number of shares per contract, usually 1000.

After you have bought an option contract you can sell it at any time before its expiry date. This is called 'closing your option position out'. Similarly, sellers of an option contract can buy back their position any time before the option's expiry date to close their position out.

Calls and puts

The two basic types of options are:

- A 'call' option gives the purchaser the right, but not the obligation, to buy the underlying share at a predetermined price before the expiry date. Essentially you can 'call' on another investor to sell these shares to you. If you sell a call option you are obliged to sell shares at a predetermined price if 'called upon' by the option buyer. As with all sharemarket transactions there must be a buyer and seller. So if you buy a call option, another investor must have sold it to you.

- A 'put' option gives the purchaser the right to sell the underlying share at a predetermined price before the expiry date. That is, you can 'put' your shares to another investor and this person must buy them. If you sell a put option you are obliged to buy the shares at a predetermined price if they are 'put upon' you by the option buyer.

Understanding price information

Let's now see how this information is published in the financial pages. Each option has four main characteristics:

- The type of option—whether it is a call or put.

- The name of the underlying share; for example, Telstra.

- The expiry date; for example, July.

- The strike or exercise price; for example, $3.50.

In the *Australian Financial Review*, options are listed under either call options or put options. Make sure you are looking in the right section as this makes a major difference to the interpretation of the figures.

Let's have a look at an example. A Telstra Nov09 3.12 call is a Telstra call option with a strike or exercise price of $3.12 that expires in November 2009. The strike price is the price you could buy Telstra shares at if you exercise your option; that is, you decide to actually buy the shares. Strike prices are usually fixed for the life of the option. But they may be altered if the company makes a bonus or rights issue.

Remember, you are not obliged to buy any shares under a call option contract—you simply have an option or choice about whether you should buy or not. For example, if Telstra shares were trading at $3.00 you would not exercise your option to buy these same shares for $3.12 under your options contract.

As options can be tricky, let's work through an example of a Telstra call option (as shown in table 17.1, overleaf).

Table 17.1 shows information on options on 5 November 2009 as presented in the *Australian Financial Review*. Telstra's share price on that day is shown as 'Last sale price'. In this case it was $3.17.

Table 17.1: Telstra options information

Telstra: Last sale price $3.17

Series	Ex price	Fair value	Last sale	Vol '000s	Open int.	Implied volatility	Delta	Annual return %
Jan 10	3.12	0.18	0.28	117	425	22.80	0.63	17.61
Feb 10	3.36	0.10	0.10	15	1568	21.70	0.39	9.68
Dec 10	3.00	0.40	0.40	60	253	29.20	0.70	6.26
Dec 10	3.50	0.18	0.18	45	1498	27.40	0.48	5.01

As you can see there are several Telstra call options—each one referred to as a 'series'. Indeed table 17.1 lists only a small sample of the Telstra call options available on that day—the main difference is their strike or exercise ('ex') prices, which range from $3.12 to $3.50, and their different expiry months.

Now look at the Feb10 3.36 call option. This is a call option over Telstra shares that expired in February 2010 and has a strike price of $3.36. A buyer paid 10¢ for this option as shown in the 'last sale' column in table 17.1.

Suppose you bought this option for 10¢. This is called the option premium or simply the price of the option itself. Effectively you would have bought the right to buy Telstra shares for $3.36 at any time between 5 November 2009 and when the options expired at the end of February 2010.

If you had bought Telstra shares in this way you would have paid $3.46 per share—10¢ for the option and $3.36 when you exercised the option. This compares with buying Telstra for $3.17 on 5 November 2009.

Why would you buy Telstra shares for $3.46 when you could buy the same shares for $3.17? For a start you have use of $3.07 until the end of February as you are only putting up 10¢ to buy the option—you could be earning interest on this amount. Alternatively, you may not have the money to pay the full price of Telstra in November 2009, but you have a bank fixed-term deposit maturing in February 2010. In the meantime you do not want to miss out if Telstra's share price takes off between November and February.

Time is money in traded options

The price of an option can be divided into two parts:

- its time value
- its intrinsic value.

A call option is said to have intrinsic value if the exercise price is below the current price of the underlying share. A put option has intrinsic value if its exercise price is higher than the current share price. This is a measure of the amount by which an option is 'in-the-money'. Time value is what is left over after taking away an option's intrinsic value from its price.

Thus intrinsic value equals the current price of the underlying share minus the exercise price for a call option, and the exercise price minus current price for a put option.

An example: on 5 November 2009, the last sale of Telstra Dec10 3.00 call options was 40¢ when the company's share price was $3.17.

So:

Intrinsic value = $3.17 – $3.00 = $0.17

Time value = Premium + Exercise price – Current share price

Time value = Premium – Intrinsic value

So for Telstra's Dec10 3.00 calls:

Time value = $0.40 + $3.00 – $3.17 = $3.40 – $3.17 = $0.23

An option's price is made up entirely of time value and intrinsic value. In the above example, the intrinsic value (17¢) plus the time value (23¢) equals 40¢, which is the option premium.

The time value of an option usually declines as the maturity date draws nearer since the potential for gain becomes more limited. So you would expect that this December 2010 option would have little time value in early November 2010 as there would only be two months before it expires.

If a call option is 'out-of-the-money'—that is, its exercise price is above the current share price—it has no intrinsic value and its price consists solely of time value. For example, the Telstra Dec10 3.50 call option in table 17.1 has no intrinsic value.

The decline in an option's time value increases as it approaches maturity, where an option's price is ultimately represented only by its intrinsic value. At maturity both an option's time value and intrinsic value could be zero.

Interpreting other option information

Option prices are quoted on a per-share basis. To get the cost of buying one contract—normally 1000 shares—you must multiply the price of the option by 1000. Hence, in table 17.1, the cost of one Telstra Jan10 3.12 contract (at its last sale price) would be: $0.28 × 1000 = $280. This does not include brokerage.

The 'fair value' column is generated by a computer model which aims to establish whether this particular option series is over- or under-priced. The computer model uses several assumptions in calculating this fair value figure, and if these assumptions are not correct then the 'fair value' determined by this model will also be incorrect. So take this fair value number as a guide only.

'Open interest' in each contract shows the number of contracts that are still 'live'—that is, which have not been 'closed out' or completed. Usually the higher the number of open interest contracts the more liquid the market and the greater chance you have of buying and selling the particular contract.

'Implied volatility' measures the expected changes in the share price that is implied by the price of the option. So an option with high volatility is expected to have greater price changes than a lower volatility option. Option traders use these figures to measure option prices against each other to indicate whether a particular option series appears to be under- or over-priced.

'Delta' indicates the theoretical movement in the option price for a given movement (usually a 10¢ change) in the price of the underlying shares. So, the figure of 0.39 for the Telstra Feb10 3.36 in table 17.1 in the delta column indicates that a 10¢ rise in Telstra shares could be expected to increase the option price by 3.9¢.

Call options have a positive delta between 0 and 1—indicating that if the price of the underlying shares rises so too will the price of the call option. Put options have negative deltas of between 0 and −1—indicating that if the share price rises, the price of the put option will fall.

The 'annual percentage return' figure relates to the return you could get if you bought shares in the company and sold call options at the same time. This is called a 'buy and write' strategy.

The formula used to calculate the annual percentage return is:

$$\frac{\text{Time premium}}{\text{Share price}} \times \frac{100 \times 365}{\text{No. of days to option expiry}}$$

Annualised percentage returns are not published for an option series during the month they expire because these figures change too rapidly to be meaningful.

Here is an example: suppose you bought 5000 shares for $5 and sold call options with an exercise price of $5.50 for 40¢ per share. During the time you held the shares, you received a dividend of $250. The shares rise to $5.50 and your options are exercised; that is, you are required to sell your shares for $5.50 each. The rate of return on this transaction would be as follows:

Buy 5000 shares @ $5.00	$25000
Plus Brokerage (@ 1%)	$250
Less Option premium received	$2000
Plus Brokerage on options	$80
Net investment	$23330
Sell 5000 shares @ $5.50	$27500
Less Brokerage (@ 1%)	$275
Plus Dividend received	$250
Less net investment	$23330
Net profit	$4145
Return if exercised	17.8%

This rate of return is then expressed as an annual rate. So if you received this return in a six-month period, you would double the rate to get the annual return. The annualised percentage return figures give you an indication of what option in a particular series offers the best value for a 'buy and write' strategy.

Generally, trading in a particular series of options finishes on the last Thursday of each month. Share options normally have a maximum life of 12 months and are attached to specific monthly cycles. Table 17.2 summarises the characteristics of call options.

Table 17.2: characteristics of call options

Call option taker	Call option writer
Pays premium	Receives premium
Right to exercise and buy the shares	Obligation to sell shares if exercised
Trades volatility	Trades time decay
Profits from market rising	Profits from market falling or remaining neutral
Risk is limited to the premium paid	Risk is unlimited if they don't own the underlying shares
Profit is potentially unlimited	Profit is limited to the premium received
Can write an equivalent option before expiry to close out	Can buy back before expiry or exercise to close out

Your option choices

Once you have bought an option contract you have four possible courses of action:

- *Hold the option until close to its expiry date.* But to hold an option too close to its expiry date can be risky. With an option time has value. Generally speaking, the longer the time to the option's expiry date the more time value there is in the option price.

- *Sell the option.* Because of time decay, if you hold an option approaching expiry you should treat your investment like a 100-metre dash—not a marathon. This is a major difference between holding an option and holding the shares. Options are a wasting asset, and they lose time value as their expiry date approaches.

- *Exercise the option.* By choosing to buy through a call option, you are buying 1000 shares at the option's exercise price plus what you paid for the option itself. If you want to buy fewer than 1000 shares, you could then sell part of your holding. Remember to factor in brokerage costs.

- *Sell the option and buy shares.* You can buy on the market whatever number of shares you wish to hold.

Another attraction of options: gearing

Let's start off by comparing the purchase of shares with the purchase of options. Say you feel that the price of a share (currently selling at $1.00) will rise. If you buy 1000 shares and the price rises to $1.05 then your outlay was $1000, your receipts on sale at $1.05 are $1050 and therefore your profit, before brokerage, is $50. Now consider how call options might have been used in these circumstances. We will look at two possibilities:

- Firstly, there is a small outlay on a call option. Remember that the unit you trade in—the contract—is 1000 shares. Let us say the option price is 4¢ at an exercise price of $1. You could therefore spend $40 (1000 × 4¢). This would give you the right to buy the shares (1000 of them) within a specified period at $1 each. If the shares rise (say to $1.05) before the option expiry date, you can exercise your right to buy. You buy the 1000 you are entitled to for $1000 and sell at $1050. You have therefore made, before expenses, $50 profit. This is the same as before. But this time the stake—all that you put at risk—was $40, leaving $10 profit. Your return on investment is 25 per cent as opposed to a much less attractive 5 per cent had you bought the shares at the outset.

- A second possibility would have been to spend the $1000 on 25 call option contracts. That would have given you the right to buy 25 000 shares (25 option contracts), and you would realise $1250 if the shares rose to $1.05 as before. After deducting your initial outlay of $1000, you are left with a $250 profit (before expenses). If the share had risen by 10 per cent to $1.10, the direct investment in the share would have yielded a profit of $100. But the option (again leaving expenses aside for the moment) would have yielded a profit of $1500 [$27 500 – ($25 000 + $1000)]. Likewise, a rise of 20 per cent in the share price to $1.20 would give the direct investor $200 profit. But the option buyer would do much better: $4000 [$30 000 – ($25 000 + $1000)]. The greater the rise in the price of the underlying share, the greater the appeal of the option as profits rise dramatically beyond a certain point. In this example, any rise from $1.00 to $1.04 would give a profit on direct investment. But there would be no profit if you bought call options. At a share price of $1.04, you would simply break even. If the share price rise is any smaller, the price of the options would fall—and you would make a loss on the transaction. But you might not lose all the money you have invested in the options as you could sell them for, say, 2¢ each, to recoup some of your money.

But what if the price of the share fell? You would lose everything. Say the price of the share fell to 95¢. The owners of shares would have lost $50. But they might hold on to them in the hope that they would subsequently rise. But the option (to buy) would not be worth exercising. The price you could sell the shares for is lower than what you would pay for them. So you would have lost your $1000, plus of course brokerage fees and GST.

Buying call options gives you greater potential profits if the share price rises. But you could lose all your investment if the share price falls and the option to buy at a much higher price becomes worthless. If you believe the market is going to fall, or if you believe one particular share will fall, then you may buy a put option. This gives you the right to sell shares at a pre-arranged price.

In the example above, if the share fell below 96¢ (the exercise price of $1 less the premium of 4¢) you would make a profit. Thus if you spent

$1000 on the put option and the price of the share fell to 90¢ you could purchase 25 000 shares at 90¢, costing $22 500. You could then sell them for $1 each by exercising the put option, and receive $25 000. Your profit would then be the share dealing profit of $25 000, less the purchase cost of $22 500, less the cost of the option, $1000, leaving a profit of $1500 excluding expenses. As we saw before, a greater move in the share price in the right direction yields even higher profits. A fall to 85¢ would give a profit of $2750. This example illustrates one of the major attractions of options — they give you the ability to profit from falls in the sharemarket as well as rises.

Share price index options

The introduction of an All Ordinaries index (AOX) option gives you the opportunity of getting a broad exposure to the sharemarket as a whole.

The All Ordinaries index is simply a number that measures the share price movement of the companies in the index. Suppose the share prices of all these companies each rose by 1 per cent on a particular day. This would be reflected in the index itself rising by 1 per cent, say from 4500 to 4545.

If the All Ordinaries index is simply a number, how do you buy it? Well, each index option contract is given a dollar value by using an 'index multiplier'. For AOX options this multiplier is $10. So if you buy the index when it is 4500 points you are buying a basket of shares valued at $45 000. If the index rose to 4600 points, the value of your contract would now be $46 000, giving you a profit of $1000.

Hedging

Hedging is an important use of options — to lock in gains you've already made. Strictly defined, hedging is the possibility of taking a contrary position in one market or contract relative to another in order to reduce your risk. The most common form of hedging in traded options is the purchase of a put option at the current price after a large rise in the price of the underlying share.

If, for example, you held shares and you had a feeling that the market was likely to fall, traded options enable you to buy protection. You could buy put options on the shares in your portfolio, providing your portfolio included companies on which traded options are available. Then if the shares did fall in price you would offset the loss by the profit on the puts.

Other option strategies

Using options to protect the value of your shares

Suppose you own 1000 shares in National Australia Bank (NAB) and the share price is $29, but you think that the price might be about to fall. Instead of selling the shares and perhaps becoming liable for capital gains tax, you could buy a NAB $29 put option. This option gives you (the buyer) the right but not the obligation to sell your 1000 NAB shares at $29 anytime up until the option expires. For this right you would have paid a premium of, say, 50¢ per share or $500 per contract (one contract covers 1000 shares).

If at expiry NAB is trading at $25, you could either exercise your put option and sell your NAB shares for $29 or keep your NAB shares and sell the put option on the market. This would give you a profit of the difference between the cost of the option (50¢) and the price you can sell it for (around $4 in this case), which is $3.50. Either way you have offset some of the fall in the value of your shares by buying a put option.

Alternatively, assume NAB shares rose to $32: you would let the option expire worthless. You have the right to exercise and sell at $29, but you don't have to. In this case the option would not have been any benefit to you so you would lose the amount of the premium: $500. However, the option has protected you against the price of NAB falling below $29.

So buying a put option locks in a selling price for your shares, and ensures that your maximum loss is limited to the price of the put option.

Using options income to offset declines in the value of a shareholding

Assume you own 1000 NAB shares with a current market value of $29 each. You decide to sell a NAB $30 call option. For this you would receive an option premium of, say, 40¢ per share. This transaction has given you 40¢ extra income—essentially it is like receiving an extra dividend, although this income is not franked.

By selling this option you have the obligation to sell your shares at $30 if the buyer of the option decides to exercise the option. Assume the value of the NAB shares had risen to $31 when the option expires. The option buyer would most likely exercise the option so you will be required to sell your shares at $30. You still keep the 40¢ option premium so you are selling your shares for $30.40 in total. The fact that you are selling shares for 60¢ below their current market value represents an opportunity cost to you.

If the shares had fallen to $25, then the sale of the option would have offset 40¢ of this fall, leaving you with a total loss on paper of 60¢

($1 less 40¢). Once the option has expired you can sell another call option to offset any further falls.

Low exercise price options

Low exercise price options, or LEPOs, are a leveraged security developed by ASX Derivatives (ASXD). LEPOs are extremely deep in-the-money call options. They have an exercise price usually of 1¢ and have a European expiry; that is, they can only be exercised on their last trading day. Because they are deep in-the-money options their price moves closely in line with movements in the underlying share price.

LEPOs are deliverable contracts. Each contract normally covers 1000 shares. If the buyer elects to exercise at expiry, he or she will take delivery of those 1000 shares from the writer at the exercise price.

LEPOs have a delta of near 1, so the buyers of these options will hold a position similar to buying the underlying shares. Sellers of LEPOs have a similar position to selling the underlying shares. LEPOs are not exact substitutes for owning the underlying shares because if you buy LEPOs you will not receive dividend income or have voting rights.

LEPOs allow you to get leveraged exposure to future share price movements without buying or selling shares. Accordingly, you save on the initial capital outlay as it is not necessary to fund the full price of the shares. To open a LEPO contract, buyers and sellers effectively pay an initial margin only, which acts as a 'performance bond'. With only a small initial commitment of capital, you can potentially enjoy highly leveraged returns on your money.

But there are significant risks. As each LEPO covers 1000 shares, for each $1 movement in the share price the value of each LEPO contract can be expected to move by an amount approximately equal to $1000. This means you have the potential to make profits and losses during the life of the LEPO on the same basis as trading the underlying shares.

If the underlying share price rises by $1, the LEPO buyer will have an unrealised profit of $1000, while the LEPO seller will have an unrealised loss of $1000. The reverse is true if the share price falls.

Accordingly, LEPOs are potentially high-risk, high-reward investments. Both buying and selling LEPOs involve risks that may not be suitable for all investors.

How are options traded?

Exchange-traded options are bought and sold on a computerised market called the Derivatives Trading Facility (DTF). When your broker receives your order it is entered into the DTF. The first order entered is the first to trade, in a similar way to the Stock Exchange Automated Trading System (SEATS) for share trading. If your order is not completed it remains on the DTF until it is modified or is removed by your broker. All orders lapse at the end of each day.

Margins

Margins are the cash or securities that you are required to deposit as collateral for your obligations to either buy or sell shares under the options contract or pay the cash amount in the case of index-based options. For example, you can sell a call option without owning the actual shares — but if you get 'called upon' to sell these shares you need to have enough money to settle the contract. You may also be required to put up an additional margin if markets move against you. Margin requirements are complex and may vary from broker to broker, and are different depending on the type of option strategy you are undertaking. You can get an estimate of the margins that apply to various option strategies on the ASX website: <www.asx.com.au/products/options/trading_information/margins.htm>.

Stop-loss orders

As the risk of loss when trading options and futures can be substantial you should consider placing 'stop-loss' orders with your broker each time you either buy or sell contracts. Stop-loss orders instruct your broker to close out your contract if the price of the contract rises or falls to a particular level. Such orders limit your losses while at the same time allow you to participate fully in the potentially unlimited profits that some strategies offer. However, you need to be aware that there are occasions where stop-loss orders are ineffective. For example, if there is a sudden and unexpected crash in the market there might not be buyers at your stop-loss level and the price of the contract might fall substantially below your stop-loss level before buyers appear. In this case your actual losses will be much greater than you initially expected when you placed your stop-loss limit.

How to find a broker to trade options for you

As interest in traded options grows, more and more brokers are trading for individual clients. For a list of brokers who trade in options for private clients contact the Australian Derivatives Market.

Australian Derivatives Market
PO Box H224
Australia Square
Sydney 2000
Email: info@asx.com.au

Alternatively you can contact the Australian Derivatives Market through the ASX website: <www.asx.com.au>. Brokers are obligated to send you the ASX's introductory booklet on traded options. They will require you to sign an OCH (Option Clearing House) Client Agreement Form which states, among other things, that you've read the booklet, that you understand the speculative nature of traded options and accept being bound by the OCH's requirements.

Why use the futures market?

The tremendous growth in futures trading worldwide has prompted an increase in the number of private traders using the futures market as part of their investment strategy. The main advantages of trading on futures markets include:

- the low transaction costs (up to one-tenth of investing directly in the sharemarket)

- the ability to leverage your position

- being able to 'short sell' (profit from falling prices)

- longer trading hours — 24 hours per day

- dealing with a registered futures broker who can also provide advice on foreign exchange, interest rates, commodities and global sharemarket movements.

Futures markets deal in futures contracts — agreements to buy or sell an item for delivery at a future date at a price determined today. This might be for a few months or up to three years from now.

These contracts may be for commodities such as gold or beef. They may be for financial instruments such as currencies, government bonds or bank bills. Or they may be for the stock exchange indices themselves.

Users of futures markets fall into two main groups:

- 'Hedgers' — usually people working in a particular industry, such as the beef or finance industry, who wish to transfer the risk associated with a commodity or financial asset. In most cases they are seeking to lock in today's prices to give them a guaranteed profit. Thus, futures markets can provide 'insurance' against the risk and uncertainty of the future.

• Speculators—who have taken a view on the likely direction of a price move and who are prepared to risk their money to make a profit.

Personal investors fall into the second category. They have no intention of actually supplying the particular commodity, or taking delivery of it. They are in the market purely to try to make a profit.

As with options, you can trade futures contracts. You are not locked into the contract until its maturity date. 'Closing out' is where you quit a futures strategy by taking the opposite position to the one you originally held. If you buy a futures contract, you close it out by selling a contract in the same commodity for the same month.

Australian futures markets

The Australian Securities Exchange, as it is now known, resulted from the merger of the Australian Stock Exchange and the Sydney Futures Exchange in December 2006, becoming the ninth largest stock exchange in the world. The ASX operates a diversified range of futures and options markets—including markets for equities and interest rates as well as agricultural, energy and environmental markets—that are rapidly evolving in response to market needs. On the ASX, futures contracts that are available over indices are: ASX SPI 200 Index Futures, S&P/ASX 50 Index Futures, S&P/ASX 200 Index Futures (also known as Mini 200 Futures) and S&P/ASX 200 A-REIT Index Futures.

Some futures contracts are non-deliverable; for example, you cannot physically deliver the Share Price Index to a buyer. These contracts are settled in cash; that is, any futures contracts still open at the termination of trading are automatically bought or sold back at the current price of the commodity, or current index level for futures based on an index. Only the 90-day bank bills contracts can be settled by delivering the actual bank bills involved.

Gearing

The major factor that makes futures markets so appealing to many personal investors is the high gearing. This makes it possible for you to control extremely large sums with relatively small amounts of money. Let's look at how this works in action using ASX SPI 200 Index Futures (SPI futures) as an example.

Using SPI futures you can either hedge your existing share portfolio or take a punt on the future direction of share prices. If you think the sharemarket is about to fall you would sell SPI futures. Alternatively, if you think the market is going to rise, you would buy SPI futures.

In practice, no delivery of shares can take place. All settlements take place in cash. The SPI contract is based on the S&P/ASX 200 index, which is a weighted index of the largest 200 listed companies on the sharemarket, representing over 90 per cent of the value of all shares traded on the Australian sharemarket.

The value of the SPI contract is the S&P/ASX 200 index multiplied by 25. So, if this index is 4000, the value of one SPI contract will be: 4000 × $25 = $100 000. To ensure that futures prices and the actual index come together at maturity of the contract, exchange rules provide that all futures contracts still open on the last day of trading are automatically closed out at the actual index value at that time.

Normally the SPI is above the actual S&P/ASX 200, but there are times when it is below it. When the SPI is below the S&P/ASX 200 it usually means that investors think that the sharemarket is more likely to fall than rise in the following weeks.

Individual traders account for about 30 per cent of all SPI business. The other 70 per cent comes from fund managers, insurance companies and institutional investors. Most of these large investors use the SPI to hedge their share portfolios and therefore have a different user outlook on the SPI from individual traders, who seek both long-term and short-term trading opportunities.

How this works and the effect of gearing

Let's look at a hypothetical example. Suppose that in March you decided that share prices were going to rise. You could have bought a SPI September contract for 4000, when the actual S&P/ASX 200 index was 3970. This is called 'going long'—buying in the expectation of a future rise in prices.

The value of your contract would be $100 000 (4000 × $25) but —and this is the key—you may only be required to pay a deposit of around $2850. This is called the initial margin. This margin varies between 2 and 10 per cent of the value of the futures contract and in part depends on your total exposure to the market and your broker's assessment of your financial position. You would, of course, also have to pay brokerage and clearing house fees.

This deposit should not be thought of as a down payment on the value of the shares being traded. In fact, it is a performance deposit and is made to ensure that you have funds with your broker. You must cover all potential losses in the form of margins or further payments. If you are unable to meet margin calls your broker may 'close you out'—liquidate your futures position—and the resulting loss will be deducted from your original deposit. In this way, unrealised profits of other market participants are protected.

Now let's look at what happens when you sell. Suppose that you picked the market correctly and the SPI September contract is closed out at 4200—the value of the S&P/ASX 200 index at the time. You calculate your profit as follows:

March 4, bought	1 SPI September contract @ 4000
Contract value	$100000
Deposit	$2850
Commission (negotiable, say)	$100
September 30, sold	1 SPI September contract @ 4200
Contract value	$105000
Commission	$100
Profit ($105000 – $100000 – $200)	= $4800
Profit in percentage terms	4800 × 100 ÷ 2850 = 168%

Brokerage rates are generally negotiable between client and broker, but as a guide, commission charged could be around $100, although this will vary depending on the volume and frequency of contracts traded.

Note that you achieved this dramatic profit of 168 per cent during a period when the S&P/ASX 200 index rose hypothetically about 5.8 per cent, from 3970 to 4200. Behind your power to make this significant return was, of course, the fact that you put up $2850 to control shares worth $100000.

Of course, gearing can magnify losses as well as profits. If the SPI September contract was closed out at 3600, you would have lost over $10000, nearly four times your original deposit.

The SPI often moves 30 points or more in a single day, which represents a profit or loss of $750 ($25 × 1 contract × 30 points) before brokerage, or a 30 per cent return or loss on original capital per contract. Also, your broker may call on you for additional 'margin' payments. After opening a position by either selling or buying a contract, you will be called upon to pay additional margins (variation margins) if the initial margin falls by more than 25 per cent. However, because client accounts are established with more than the minimum margin requirement (for example, $10 000), these additional margin payments (if any) are automatically debited from the account.

While this example illustrated the potential profit you can make trading futures, your potential losses can also be significant. In fact, unlike in the sharemarket, you can lose more than your original investment. Speculation in futures markets is a high-risk venture. Therefore, it is advisable to use only money you can afford to lose. Your minimum starting capital should be at least three times the minimum deposit for each contract you trade. For example, if you decided to trade one SPI futures contract when the deposit was $2850, your minimum risk capital should be around $8500.

One way of limiting your risk is to trade options over the SPI contract rather than the contract itself. Options over the SPI contract allow you to get access to the benefits of gearing and being able to profit when the market declines while limiting your downside risk to the initial price of the option.

Tax and options and futures

The tax treatment of options and futures trading can be complex and is beyond the scope of this chapter. A booklet entitled *The Tax Treatment of Exchange Traded Options* has been published by Deloitte and is available at <www.asx.com.au/products/pdf/taxation_of_exchange_traded_options_oct_2009.pdf>. Before you begin trading options or futures it is highly recommended that you read this booklet.

Key points

o Options are not suitable for all investors. There are numerous option strategies, ranging from ones that protect your share portfolio from sharemarket falls to those that are more akin to gambling. Before undertaking any option strategy you should understand the type of risks you are taking.

o As options have an expiry date—that is, they cease to exist after a particular time—you need to adopt a different investment philosophy. You cannot buy or sell options and then put them away in a bottom drawer until they come good. Options need to be watched daily.

o   If you decide to dabble in the options market you must adopt a more aggressive trading mentality. As all options have an expiry date you cannot use a 'buy and hold' strategy as you can with shares.

o   Before making your first options trade it is advisable to make a number of hypothetical trades so that you get some concrete idea of the level of risks you are taking. This will also illustrate how quickly options prices can move—both up and down.

o   It is essential that you understand your liability for margin calls if the market or the share price moves in the opposite direction to the one you were expecting.

o   Remember that you should only trade futures with investment funds earmarked for high-risk/high-reward strategies. While the potential for profit is high, there is also the risk of significant financial loss.

o   The leveraged exposure provided by futures can also lead to substantial losses.

o   At the time of your opening transaction, your outlay is limited to the initial margin. This means that the percentage return, either positive or negative, made on your initial investment is far greater than the movement in the underlying index. If the market moves against you, you may be required to put up variation margins or close out your position and crystallise a loss.

o   Unlike option contracts, where the buyer of the option can lose no more than the cost of the premium, both the buyer and the seller of a futures contract face potentially unlimited losses.

o   Consider using stop-loss positions to minimise your losses.

Property investing basics

18

Investing in property has been the foundation of many Australian fortunes.

Yet—despite what most real estate agents would have you believe—there are times when property prices are stagnant, and at other times they actually decline—such as in 2008 following the GFC. Moreover, prices in one suburb or in one state can be booming while at the same time property prices in other states or suburbs can be in the doldrums.

Just as the sharemarket can go through boom periods where the prices of many companies are bid to unrealistic levels, the same can occur in the property market. At such times it is wise not to become caught up in the exuberance of the crowds—particularly those bidding at auctions. As with all types of investments, you will be more successful if you can keep your head while others are losing theirs.

There are many traps for the naive and the unwary in the property market, with numerous instances of high-pressure salespeople talking investors into buying low-quality properties at over-inflated prices.

Different ways to invest in property

There are numerous ways of getting exposure to the property market, which all have advantages and disadvantages. Which one is best for you will depend on how much capital you have to invest, how much you can borrow, whether you want to take on the responsibilities of being a landlord and your tax position.

The main ways of investing in property are:

- *Home ownership:* You own the house or home unit in which you live. In most cases you will need to borrow over 80 per cent of the cost of the property from a financial organisation. Naturally, you would expect the value of your home to appreciate over time. However, this is not always the case. Apart from security of tenure—that is, you will not be asked to move because the landlord wants to sell—the main attraction of the family home is that any profit you make is exempt from capital gains tax.

- *Direct investment:* You are the sole owner of a property purchased for investment. For small investors this usually means restricting yourself to residential investment. Most people adopt a negative gearing strategy when buying investment property—this will be explained in chapter 20. You can either manage the property yourself or pay an agent to collect the rent and deal with tenants.

- *Property syndicates:* A group of investors pool their resources and buy property. The syndicate usually has a fixed life span of seven years and a minimum investment of around $10 000. Property syndicates generally invest in commercial and retail properties.

- *Unlisted property trusts:* A large number of investors pool their resources and have a professional fund manager select properties for them. The minimum investment is usually around $1000. These trusts are not listed on the ASX. To withdraw money from the trust you sell units back to the fund manager at a price determined by the trust's constitution.

- *Listed property trusts:* These are similar to unlisted property trusts except that they are quoted on the ASX. You can buy and sell these units through a stockbroker in the same way as you would with shares.

- *Property securities funds:* These are managed funds, usually unlisted, which invest in listed property trusts and property companies.

- *Diversified/balanced trusts:* These are unlisted managed funds that invest in a range of assets, including shares, interest-bearing securities and property.

- *Listed property companies:* These can be companies such as Lend Lease, Mirvac, Devine and Sunland Group. Shares in these companies are purchased on the stock market. The benefits of this approach are that you get a diversified portfolio of property interests and do not have the hassles of being a landlord.

Factors affecting property prices

As with most goods and services produced in a capitalist economy, the price of property is determined by demand and supply forces. On the demand side, the number of people who are looking to buy property is influenced by the level of interest rates and employment in the economy. If interest rates and unemployment rates are high there are fewer people who can afford to buy their own home. The level of interest rates determines how much people can afford to borrow to buy their home. Higher interest rates make other investments — interest-bearing deposits — more attractive and less risky than buying property.

Government policies, such as the First Home Owner Grant, can also influence the demand for housing, as can an increase in the number of migrants entering Australia. Internal migration — such as people retiring and moving to Queensland — can cause prices to rise in particular locations. On the other hand, if a major employer closes down — as was the case with BHP in Newcastle and Wollongong — this can have a depressing impact on house prices in the surrounding regions.

Supply of housing usually responds to trends in demand. As demand begins to rise it causes an increase in property prices, as the supply of housing is much slower to increase. This increase in price encourages builders and property developers to boost their activities.

In well-established areas it is often not possible to increase supply significantly, as there simply is not enough vacant land. In this case the only way for supply of housing to increase is for the area to be rezoned from single to multiple dwellings. In newer areas government policy can influence the rate of increase in housing supply through the speed at which vacant land is rezoned for residential use.

As prices begin to rise it results in fewer people being able to afford to buy. At the same time, the higher prices encourage more developers and speculators to enter the market in the hope of big profits. Ultimately, you have a situation where supply begins to outstrip demand, and developers have to lower their price expectations in order to sell their stock.

Direct investment

Buying an investment property is completely different from buying a home. The main difference is that buying a home is frequently an emotional issue whereas buying an investment property should be based on a logical and calculated process. Like any other investment, you need to consider how much you can invest, what the goal of the investment is and how long you want to hold the investment.

To make good returns on property it is likely you will need to hold it for the medium to long term; that is, five to ten years. However, there are occasions when the market is booming and you could make handsome profits in less than one year.

The first step to successful property investing is to do your homework and research the area in which you intend to buy. Start by reading the property sections of the major daily newspapers. They contain information on residential, commercial, industrial and rural properties.

The second step is to do a budget showing expected income from the property and expected costs such as council rates, interest and repairs. Do not overlook the costs that may be incurred when taking out a loan. These include establishment fees, security administration fees, property valuation fees, lender's mortgage insurance costs, life insurance premiums, building insurance, the costs of title searches and other enquiries, mortgage registration costs and legal fees. In addition, government stamp duty can run into tens of thousands of dollars. You should also check whether you will be liable for state government land tax.

The third step is to investigate the expected returns from specific properties, bearing in mind that you need a tool for analysis which will enable you to make meaningful comparisons between the different properties available.

Sources of information

Reading the property section of major daily newspapers is a start to understanding the property market. Major daily newspapers, and many local ones as well, publish mortgage rates for both residential and investment purposes on a regular basis. The Myrpdata website, <www.myrp.com.au>, has a property database with records on over 10 million properties. Another useful website is *Your Mortgage* magazine — <www.yourmortgage.com.au>.

Real estate agents can be a valuable source of information on properties, tenants and rents. Remember that they are agents — and are paid by the sellers, not the buyers. Consequently, they may be too optimistic about the prospects for a particular property, and the property market in general. One alternative is to get an independent valuation on a property that will give you an accurate idea of what the property is worth. The Real Estate Institutes in various states also publish data on median sales prices for property in most suburbs. Finally, there is considerable information on houses sold at auction that can give you an indication of prices for houses and home units in a particular area.

You will need to know what the future holds for the area you are investing in. Contact the local council and the relevant roads authority to see what they are planning. Your perfect investment may soon not be so perfect when you find an expressway is due to run through the backyard. Alternatively, a new highway that cuts down travelling time to the city can cause a rise in property prices.

A solicitor can provide you with a list of all the searches necessary for prudent purchase. While each search costs money, these outlays are minimal in comparison to possible future losses should you fail to become aware of something important affecting the property you are interested in buying. If you are investing in a home unit or townhouse, you should get a reputable search agent to obtain and appraise the body corporate records. This should include a comprehensive written report on the financial position of the body corporate and any major expenses, such as repainting, that are expected in the near future.

Types of property

Most investors start with residential property because they think that they know it better as they have bought their own home and/or been a tenant at some time. If you are a serious property investor you should at least consider the relative merits of other types of property within your price range, such as:

- commercial—blocks of units, shops, office space

- industrial—factories, warehouses

- other—such as car parking spaces in CBD buildings.

Clearly, if you consider that residential property prices are over-heated you could be better off investing in commercial or industrial property.

Before you decide what type of property you'd like to buy, you first need to determine what cash flow outcome you'd like to achieve. This is essential as all properties have different capital gains and cash flow features. For example, inner city properties are far more likely to generate capital gains than positive cash flow returns.

Commercial property has some advantages over residential property. Tenants with a commercial lease usually pay for most of the outgoings — such as insurance and rates — whereas landlords in residential property pay these expenses out of their own pocket.

On the other hand, trying to get finance on a commercial property can be more difficult since most lenders will generally only finance up to 70 per cent of the purchase price, whereas you can secure 100 per cent finance on residential property deals.

The benefits of investing in commercial property

Leases tend to be much longer with commercial property — anything from three to twenty years — and they are quite often secured by bank guarantees that make them a secure investment. Rent is reviewed annually and is usually increased either by the CPI or by 4 per cent, whichever is greater. Commercial tenants will also tend to maintain the property better as the look and condition of the property is important to their business and their staff. The return on invested capital on commercial properties ranges between 7 per cent and 10 per cent net (after all costs).

The benefits of investing in residential property

You need a smaller deposit for residential property; depending on your credit history and income, you can even borrow 100 per cent of the purchase price. Commercial mortgages require a deposit of at least 30 per cent. Interest rates on residential mortgages also tend to be lower.

The commercial property market can be less predictable than the residential market (where historically properties tend to double in value every seven to ten years). There are also different kinds of commercial property to consider, such as industrial and retail.

Although residential leases are shorter than commercial ones, residential properties are generally easier to let, meaning you will have less time when the property is vacant. It can take months to find a new commercial tenant. Whether you choose residential or commercial property, you still need to do considerable homework about the particular property and area before you buy. With proper research you should find that you are more comfortable making the decision about which type of property to invest in.

Some disadvantages of property investment

The stories you read in the newspapers and see on TV current affairs programs highlight the positive aspects of property investing—how a battler became a multi-millionaire through property investments. Usually these stories appear when the property market is booming. The other side of the story that is normally not told is what happens to property investors when interest rates begin to rise, vacancy rates increase and property prices decline.

Investing in property is unlike the sharemarket because houses, and property in general, are different products. For example, if you make a poor property investment, it is likely to have a much bigger impact on your portfolio than a poor share investment. This is mainly because you do not have the same level of diversification as you would if you invested an equivalent amount in the sharemarket. For example, you could invest $300 000 in one property or buy $30 000 worth of shares in 10 different companies. If one company in your share portfolio goes bad it could be offset by better results from the other nine companies.

Also property investments are illiquid and inflexible. If you invest in managed funds or shares and you need to access some of your cash, it is easy to sell part of your investments. For example, if you had a $100 000 share portfolio you could sell $25 000 worth of shares and have the money three days later.

In contrast, with a property it is an all or nothing deal. You cannot sell off 10 per cent of your property. When you do want to sell your property it will take several months before you get any money.

The costs of buying and selling property are much greater than buying and selling the same value of shares—and you need to take these costs into account when determining your real profit. In addition, there are ongoing costs such as council rates, repairs and maintenance, agent's fees and possibly land tax. If you own shares there are no ongoing costs—all you do is sit back and collect your dividends.

Sensible rules of property investing

Here are some property investing rules that should help you stay out of trouble.

Remember it's a business decision

When buying an investment property, do not look for the same things you would when buying a place to live in. You might like to live in quiet surroundings far from the maddening crowd. Yet if you try to rent out a property like that you might find that you have few takers. When buying an investment property, remember that you are making a business decision. So think about the features that potential buyers would find attractive when you come to sell it. Also think from a potential tenant's perspective—would you be prepared to rent out this property?

Carefully consider location

The old saying that the three principles of buying property are 'location, location, location' is still true today. Do not be talked into buying a property because it is cheap. What makes it cheap to buy today might also make it cheap when you try to sell it.

Reduce your risks by only buying properties that are unlikely to go out of fashion. Generally these can be defined as established suburbs up to 10 kilometres from the CBD of a major capital city. As your property will be tenanted, buy in areas of high rental demand close to transport and public amenities.

Many investors buy into rundown areas believing that eventually they will become popular. The risk with this is it may take several years, or even decades, for this to happen.

Consider the property features

The best aspect is a northeast-facing block that will receive the north sun in winter. Level blocks generally bring a higher price as occupants don't have to worry about stairs and the land is more useable. Building costs are usually higher with awkward blocks.

Desirable features include:

- views
- low-maintenance garden
- on-site parking
- storage
- good security
- low crime rate
- close to schools, shops and transport
- modernised bathroom and kitchen.

Do your budget

Make sure you do a detailed budget before you buy—not after. This is particularly the case if you are negatively gearing. Can you really afford to financially support this property for the next five years or more?

When calculating how much you can spend on an investment property you need to consider:

- your income
- the amount of surplus income that can support a negatively geared property
- the deposit
- your borrowing capacity.

Most investment properties in capital cities such as Melbourne, Sydney and Brisbane cost a minimum of between $350 000 and $500 000. As a rule of thumb, it is better to buy a quality two-bedroom apartment in a good suburb than a poor-quality house or semi in a not-so-great suburb.

Avoid borrowing more than you can afford to pay back in the hope that increasing rents will make up the difference. Do not forget to factor in all the purchase costs such as stamp duty and legal fees. Remember that some of these cannot be claimed as an immediate tax deduction. In addition, there are ongoing costs such as insurance, repairs and maintenance and council rates. Be sure not to overlook land tax as this can run into thousands of dollars per year—every year.

Shop around for the right loan

There are two ways to raise money to purchase an investment property:

- *Mortgage on the property:* Depending on your circumstances, most lenders will let you borrow up to 90 per cent of the purchase price, or even 100 per cent. You may be required to take out mortgage insurance.
- *Equity loan on your home:* If you already own or substantially own your home, you can borrow against the 'equity' you have accumulated. The danger here is that if things go wrong you could lose your home.

Once you have chosen a lender, you will need to decide between a principal-and-interest loan or an interest-only loan, and between fixed and variable rates. Lenders must give you information in line with amendments to the Uniform Consumer Credit Code (UCCC). This means that you should be told the Annualised Average Percentage Rate (AAPR) on your loan. In theory this should enable you to be able to more accurately compare loans provided by different mortgage lenders. In the past this was nearly impossible as some lenders had lower interest rates but a multitude of fees and charges while others had fewer charges but a higher interest rate. The AAPR is intended to show the total cost of a loan by estimating the total amount you will pay over the course of a loan when all fees, charges and interest payments are included.

Maintain your investment

It is important to protect the value of your investment through regular repairs and maintenance. Inspect the property at least once a year, and do not let minor problems become major repairs. Try to undertake repairs between tenants at times when the property is empty.

Choose the right tenants

Tenants can make or break your investment so it is important to choose them wisely. Paying an estate agent to interview prospective tenants and check their creditworthiness is usually money well spent. When it's time to raise the rent the agent is also in a more knowledgeable position and should know what it is realistic to ask for the property. However, if your agent does not do a competent job find another one that will.

Some suburbs have different occupancy rates from others and some blocks of units will also have different rates from others. Call agents in the area and get an idea of the availability and cost of renting in the area. If there are a large number of vacancies it might be better to choose another location. Good tenants on a long lease will help your cash flow. If the property you are considering has an unstable tenancy record find out why.

A common—but highly risky—strategy is to buy property in an upmarket area and target high-income tenants. Unfortunately, many property investors have discovered to their detriment that high-income tenants are often the most volatile segment of the rental market. When times are prosperous, they look for glamorous living in the newest kind of accommodation available with all the modern conveniences. When the economy contracts and they lose their jobs they move to cheaper accommodation, leaving investors owning expensive property competing for new tenants in a shrinking market.

In times of serious recession it's not unusual to expect vacancies of three months or more on premium property, which can make owning negatively geared property an investing cash flow disaster.

In contrast, there will always be demand for a house that the average family can afford to live in. It would be wise for you to focus your attention on purchasing a property that is less prone to market fluctuations, and then seeking to charge above market rates for a quality property to attract long-term tenants who want to treat your property like a home.

Consider what could go wrong

When doing your budget, consider what would be the financial implications of the interest rate on your loan increasing by one percentage point; for example, from 6 to 7 per cent. What would happen if your property was vacant for three or four weeks during the year? Carefully examine the property to determine what repairs are likely to be needed over the next five years. For example, how old is the hot water system? Is the property likely to require electrical rewiring?

Obtain professional advice

A good solicitor should be an integral part of your investment strategy. You can do conveyancing yourself. However, unless you have a lot of time on your hands to do all the necessary searches it is better to pay a solicitor to do this for you. There are now many flat-rate conveyancing companies in the market so it pays to shop around for the cheapest price.

Know your legal rights and responsibilities

While owning a home or unit for rent can make good sense, it is important that landlords are fully aware of their rights and obligations.

There are various responsibilities and legal obligations that you must observe in your role as a rental property owner. These are clearly set out by the various state Acts relating to residential tenancies.

The residential tenancies authorities in different states protect the rights of both tenants and landlords, and assist investors by offering advice on tenancies, as well as a rental bond custodial service and a mediation service to help in resolving disputes.

It is always desirable for landlords and tenants to enter into a written agreement so there can be no misunderstanding as to what each party's rights and duties are. For more information on tenancy agreements and such things as rental bonds, contact the relevant tenancy authority in your state; for example, in New South Wales it is the Department of Fair Trading.

Choose the right agent

ASIC does not license real estate agents who give advice only about property investments; they are licensed by state and territory agencies. So first check that your agent is actually licensed.

If a real estate agent gives you advice about financial products — such as insurance products or negatively geared investment packages — he or she must hold a licence from ASIC or be an employee or authorised representative of a licence holder.

You can check ASIC's databases, at <www.asic.gov.au>, to see if a real estate agent is licensed.

Obtain insurance

You need to insure your building for the full amount it would cost to replace it if it was destroyed, not what it cost to buy. Remember that there is no need to include the cost of your land, as this does not get damaged.

You will also need to consider contents insurance. With home units the building is insured by the body corporate, so you only need to consider contents insurance, not building as well. You will need contents insurance when you let a fully furnished property or holiday home. Other insurance you should consider includes public liability cover and fusion cover, which covers the burning-out of electric motors in such appliances as refrigerators and fans.

Be on your guard at property seminars

Property prices have not been the only things that have been booming in recent years. There has also been a boom in the number of people running seminars to explain how you can become rich by investing in property. The general advice given in these seminars could be summarised as 'borrow lots of money and buy lots of property'.

Now it is possible that in certain market conditions this strategy could work. But if the market falls or if interest rates rise, this could lead to financial ruin. Yet one thing is certain: the ones who are getting rich from these seminars are the people who are running them. Many of these seminars are run in an atmosphere of high excitement, where anyone who questions what is being said is viewed as a pessimist with a negative attitude to success.

If you do attend such seminars, here are some tips on how not to get talked into a poor investment:

- Never sign anything at the seminar.

- If the seminar is pushing a particular property investment it is essential to get independent advice on its real market value before you buy. Also check the prices of comparable properties in the same area.

- Always use your own solicitor—not one suggested by the seminar promoters.

- Higher returns inevitably mean higher risk.

- The promoters might offer to organise finance for you—always get quotes from other lenders as well.

- Be particularly suspicious if the offer is that everything will be organised for you—all you have to do is sign the cheque. You will usually be paying a high price for this service via excessive fees and charges.

- Ask to have all the fees, charges and commissions put in writing.

- Most promoters have figures that show enormous profits from any type of property investment. Ask yourself, what are the assumptions underlying these figures? What would happen if the property is vacant or interest rates rise?

- Never buy a property without inspecting it first.

- Negative gearing is often sold as a strategy that will make you rich in the future. When you buy a property from a seminar promoter you'll be making developers and sales agents rich today.

Key points

- Falling interest rates are a good sign for property investors —rising interest rates are a danger sign.

- Property investment is no more passive than any other form of investment. You need to regularly review and monitor your investments.

- Keep a formal record of your involvement in the property market by reviewing your position every quarter.

- Be extremely careful when buying property that a sales agent or a developer says has tax advantages—this is a red flag that the property is guaranteed to lose money.

- When it comes to real estate investing, the amount of money you'll make and the time it'll take you to earn it largely depends on what type of property you purchase in the first place.

- Some sales people can be extremely persuasive and persistent. They often use gimmicks such as offering you a 'once in a lifetime opportunity'. There are plenty of properties on the market, so do not fall for such tricks.

19

How to evaluate a property investment

When you invest in shares or interest-bearing securities, it is relatively easy to work out some of the investment return you are likely to receive. With shares you can calculate the current dividend yield — although you cannot be sure what capital gain or loss you will make. With interest-bearing securities you know when you invest the rate of interest you will receive. In contrast, if you buy an investment property for $500 000, you need to calculate the rate of return you are getting from your rental income minus your expenses. If you have negatively geared the property — where your rental income is less than your borrowing and other costs — you then need to determine what capital gain you need to make the investment worthwhile. You can then compare this rate of return with returns from other investments such as fixed-interest and shares.

This chapter outlines a technique called 'discounted cash flow', which enables you to calculate the rate of return you are getting on a property investment. In the second part of this chapter there are several tips on how to buy and sell property at auctions.

Discounted cash flow

The most widely used technique to evaluate a property investment is called discounted cash flow (DCF). Money has a time value. If you were offered the choice of receiving $1000 now or $1000 in one year's time, most people would opt to receive it now. Firstly, the person or organisation offering you the money might not be around in one year's time. Secondly, because of inflation, $1000 in one year's time would buy you less than $1000 today. Thirdly, if you received $1000 today, you could invest it and have more than $1000 in one year's time. For these reasons, money has a time value. DCF techniques explicitly recognise this time value in making investment decisions. This simply entails 'discounting' all future income and expenses from the property to a common date—the present day. After discounting future cash inflows and outflows to the present time you arrive at what is called the net present value (NPV). Let's look at an example of how to calculate NPV.

Compounding interest and discount rates

If the prevailing interest rate for investments was 10 per cent per annum and you had $1000 to invest, you would have $1100 in one year's time ($1000 × 1.10). In the terminology of DCF, it is said that the future value (FV) of the investment is $1100. At the end of two years the FV of the investment would be $1210 ($1100 × 1.10), and at the end of three years the FV would be $1331 ($1210 × 1.10). These calculations are similar to when you calculate compound interest.

DCF techniques look at the problem in reverse. A DCF approach asks: 'What is the present value (PV) today of receiving $1100 in one year's time if the interest rate is 10 per cent?' The answer is 1 ÷ 1.10 × $1100 = 0.9091 × $1100 = $1000. With DCF techniques the interest rate is referred to as the discount rate and the value 0.9091 (1 ÷ 1.10) as the PV factor. The factor is in effect the PV of receiving $1 in one year's time if the discount rate is 10 per cent. The PV factor can then be applied to any amount. So if $120 000 was to be received in one year's time and the discount rate was 10 per cent, the PV would be: $120 000 × 0.9091 = $109 092. Alternatively, if you had $109 092 today and invested it at 10 per cent, you would receive $120 000 in one year's time.

You can calculate PV factors for any number of years into the future and for any interest rate. For example, the PV of $1 receivable two years hence at 10 per cent is: 0.9091 × 1 ÷ 1.10 = 0.8264. For three years hence at 10 per cent it is: 0.8264 × 1 ÷ 1.10 = 0.7513. For four years hence at 10 per cent it is: 0.7513 × 1 ÷ 1.10 = 0.6830, and so on. You can calculate these factors long hand or by using a computer. Many finance books have PV factors for a range of discount rates included in them, and you can find PV tables on the web—such as at <www.studyfinance.com/common/table3.pdf>.

Using DCF to evaluate a property investment

Let's now look at how DCF can be used to calculate the rate of return you would get on a property investment. For example: suppose that you buy a property for $500000 and additional costs such as stamp duty and legal fees of $30000 are incurred as part of the purchase. Net rental income—rent minus running costs such as council rates—is expected to be $40000 per annum. At the end of four years you expect to sell the property for $590000—with costs associated with the sale being $11000. To avoid undue complications the impact of tax has been ignored. Taxes can be incorporated into this example using after-tax cash flow figures. It is also assumed that cash flows take place at the end of the relevant year. The NPV of these cash inflows and outflows using a discount rate of 10 per cent is shown in table 19.1.

NPV is the present value of net cash inflows minus the present value of net cash outflows. In this case it is –$7751.

Think of the discount rate as being a concept similar to inflation. Take the $590000 received from the sale of the property at the end of four years. If the inflation rate was 10 per cent, $402970 ($590000 × 0.6830) would buy you the same today as $590000 would in four years time. Using a discount rate to make calculations reflects the fact that money has a time value. You would prefer to receive money now rather than in the future. Inflation is one reason for this. Another reason is that if you receive money now, you are certain of getting it, whereas there is no guarantee you will receive it in the future. By using a discount rate you are explicitly taking these factors into account.

Table 19.1: discounted cash flows at a discount rate of 10 per cent

	Year 0 $	Year 1 $	Year 2 $	Year 3 $	Year 4 $
Price	–500000	–	–	–	–
Purchase costs	–30000	–	–	–	–
Rent	–	40000	40000	40000	40000
Sale price	–	–	–	–	590000
Sale costs	–	–	–	–	–11000
Net cash flow	–530000	40000	40000	40000	619000
PV of $1 at 10%	1.0000	0.9091	0.8264	0.7513	0.6830
PV of cash flow	–530000	36364	33056	30052	422777

NPV = –$530000 + $36364 + $33056 + $30052 + $422777 = –$7751

Because there is a negative NPV when using a discount rate of 10 per cent it indicates the rate of return on this property is less than 10 per cent per annum.

The actual discount rate you choose can depend on a number of factors. It may be the interest you have to pay on borrowed money. Or it may be the rate of return you can get on other investments. Essentially, 10 per cent is a target rate of return.

In the appendix is a detailed example of DCF analysis.

Internal rate of return

In the above example, the investment proposal has a negative NPV when using a discount rate of 10 per cent, so the return from the investment is less than 10 per cent. A question is: what rate of return are you deriving from this investment? To answer this you need to answer another question: what discount rate when used would result in an NPV of zero? The appropriate discount rate is known as the internal rate of return (IRR). You can calculate this by trial and error using tables found in most finance textbooks or you can use a computer or a fairly sophisticated calculator.

The IRR in this case is 9.55 per cent. You can compare this with the cost of borrowing money, and with the return from alternative investments.

Discounted cash flow techniques — NPV and IRR — can be used to evaluate any investment proposal, not just property. A basic and most essential requirement is that you first get accurate estimates of future cash inflows and outflows. You can then conduct sensitivity analysis. For example, you can ask 'what if' questions, such as what if rental income is 10 per cent less than forecast? What if the projected sale price is 20 per cent less than estimated?

The NPV and IRR methods are both used in practice to evaluate investment proposals. The NPV method is considered to be conceptually superior because with the IRR method it is possible to get two different rates for the same set of cash flows. Also the IRR method implicitly assumes that cash inflows can be reinvested at the IRR and this may be unrealistic. There are numerous calculators online which can calculate both the NPV and IRR, such as <www.datadynamica.com/IRR.asp>, but you need to have estimates of the buying and selling prices of the property plus annual cash flows you expect from the property.

Sensitivity analysis

It is possible to make changes in your assumptions about an investment and see what effect this has on the end result. Basically, you can ask a series of 'what if?' questions. This is especially easy when using Excel or a financial calculator. For example, in the above case, what if the sale price was $560 000 instead of $590 000? The answer is that the NPV would fall to –$28 231 and the IRR would decline to 8.4 per cent. You could also change your assumptions about net rental income and perhaps break this up into gross rent and outgoings. For example, you could ask what the effect would be if you had to make major repairs to the property part way through the investment.

Accounting for tax

It is necessary to incorporate income and capital gains tax into DCF calculations in order to get a true picture. On rental properties the Tax Office will allow the following expenditure as tax deductions: advertising for tenants, bank charges, body corporate fees, borrowing expenses, council rates, decline in value of depreciating assets, gardening and lawn mowing, insurance, land tax, pest control, property agent fees or commissions, repairs and maintenance, stationery, telephone, water charges and travel undertaken to inspect the property or to collect rent. If the property is negatively geared you can offset the loss against your other income and derive a tax benefit, which should be included in your DCF calculations as a cash inflow. For example, say you purchased a property and the outgoings including interest were $20 000 a year and rental income was $15 000. Say your marginal rate of tax was 39.5 per cent including the Medicare levy. A snapshot of your situation would be:

Annual rental income	$15 000
Allowable outgoings	$20 000
Taxable income	–$5 000
Tax benefit at 39.5%	$1 975

The above tax benefit should be included as a cash inflow in your DCF analysis.

Capital gains tax (CGT) is levied on the gain made on the sale of a property. Where the property has been held for longer than 12 months a 50 per cent discount is allowed. CGT is payable at your marginal rate of tax and should be included in DCF calculations in the year in which the property is sold.

Other considerations

When borrowing to invest, only that part of loan repayments which represents interest is allowable as a tax deduction. However, the part that represents repayment of principal still has to be taken into account as it is a cash outflow. So the two components have to be broken up. When the loan is paid off there will be a balloon repayment amounting to the balance of principal unpaid at that time.

The question of what rate of discount to use needs to be addressed. Factors which need to be considered include the cost of borrowing money, the return from alternative investments and the riskiness of the investment. Obviously if it costs you 8 per cent per annum to borrow money you will want a higher rate of return than this from your investment. If you can earn 10 per cent from an alternative investment, you will want to earn at least this from a property investment. And if you are faced with an investment where estimating cash flows is particularly difficult you will want to factor this in by using a higher discount rate than you otherwise would.

Negative gearing

Negative gearing is explained in detail in the following chapter. What it means is that the rental you receive from the property is less than the outgoings from the property—which includes the interest on borrowings used to buy the property. This is partly offset by being able to claim this loss against your other income. Even so, you usually end up with a negative annual cash flow from your property investment. Consequently, you need the price of the property to increase substantially in order to compensate you for these losses and also give you an adequate return on your investment.

In the earlier example, suppose that instead of receiving a positive net income of $40 000 you have a negative cash flow of $20 000, after taking into account the impact of your tax deductions. In this case you would need the property to sell for more than $850 000 at the end of four years in order to get a return of 10 per cent per annum on this investment. But this sale price does not take into account the amount of capital gains tax you would need to pay.

Many investors delude themselves about how well their property investments have performed because they do not take into account the time value of money in their calculations. Given that there are significant transaction costs when buying and selling property, it is essential that you do perform detailed calculations on your potential income and capital gains from a property investment before you put up your money.

Getting the best price when selling at auction

Buyers can really get carried away at property auctions. If you are selling a property by auction you need to maximise the chances of this happening. Just as inexperienced buyers at property auctions can end up paying too much, unwary sellers at auctions often receive less than their property is worth.

Unless you make a living out of buying and selling property you will probably only sell property at auction two or three times in your life, so it's essential to make the best of each of these occasions. Choosing the best real estate agent is critical to the auction's success. Start by interviewing at least three local agents. At the initial meeting, get the agent to outline fees, the type of auction campaign proposed and when the property will be open for inspection.

A minimum advertising campaign of four weeks is advisable, but six weeks is better. At this stage do not discuss your reserve price. Ask the agents for their opinion; don't give yours. Get the agents to discuss their version of the positive points of the property, outline their sales pitch to potential buyers and advise what price bracket they will quote them. Usually they quote the lower end of the price range to buyers in order to get more people in.

Before signing an agency agreement, ask to be shown their advertising campaigns for similar properties. Choose an agent on the basis of his or her proposed marketing plan, how clearly the agent identifies costs, whether the price estimates for the property are realistic and his or her ability and willingness to report regularly on enquiries.

Get it in writing

Get the agent to put all this in writing—an agent's written submission reveals much about his or her attention to detail and professional approach. Once you have selected the agent, you must provide a contract containing the minimum amount of information required by law. Also, get the agent to send you a copy of everything that is included in the advertising campaign, and insist he or she calls you at least once a week to keep you informed of progress. Make sure the ads highlight the attractiveness of the property—not the agent's name.

If your property goes to auction and doesn't sell, agents usually want sole licence to sell it for a month after the auction. It is best to keep agents on their toes by limiting this to one or two weeks. Make sure this is included in the original agreement.

Open for inspection

One decision you need to make is whether to have your property open for inspection or viewed by appointment only. Being open for inspection is usually preferable. You will get people just looking but you will get more people viewing your property. Also, 'by appointment' gives the impression the property is expensive and people deciding on whether or not to look probably won't be bothered.

Don't forget to ask where the auction will take place. The options are in the agent's rooms or on site. It is better to have the auction on site so buyers can feel the property's atmosphere.

Opening your property for inspection on a Saturday, early to late afternoon, is the best time. Opening on a Wednesday is not normally worthwhile. The agent should have an 'Open for inspection' sign on the property and/or a sandwich board on the street.

If someone makes an offer before the auction, don't look too excited. In particular, do not reveal your asking price unless, of course, the buyer is close to the price you want.

On the auction day make sure the house is clean and the lawns are cut. Normally buyers are allowed to inspect the property for half an hour before the auction. Just before the auction, give your reserve price to the agent in a sealed envelope.

Setting the reserve

Set a reserve price a little higher than you require. Remember, if the bidding reaches your reserve price you are committed to sell. You can reduce the reserve price during the auction if the bids are getting close. If the agent is encouraging you to drop your reserve price, ask the agent to lower his or her commission.

If you agree to sell your property, the settlement period is usually around six to eight weeks. You can ask for immediate release of the 10 per cent deposit put up by the buyer. It can be used to buy another property, or be put in the bank to earn interest.

Should you accept offers before auction? On the positive side, you may sell the property without the stress of an auction. It is possible that several buyers may engage in a bidding duel. The disadvantage is if the buyers make reasonable offers and feel they are close to your required price, they are less likely to go past that figure on auction day. Essentially you are revealing your hand to the agent and buyers.

If you are the seller, your responsibility does not end at the auction. On settlement of the property you must pay the agent the agreed commission. Generally, this is somewhere between 1 and 3 per cent of the sale price. The amount of commission often depends on your ability to negotiate, and how keen the agent is to have your listing.

Buying at auction

If you are thinking of investing in residential property you'll need to get used to bidding at auctions. Like it or not, the probability of having to buy your next property at auction is increasing. Indeed, if you are purchasing a property to live in you might also have to buy at auction.

Successful bidding at property auctions involves planning ahead —establishing what type of property you want, understanding the current market and, most importantly, knowing when to stop bidding.

If you are interested in a property, you need to get a copy of the property contract from the real estate agent and have it examined by your solicitor or conveyancer.

Pay particular attention to special conditions, such as penalty interest for late completion of the contract. Check the settlement period; that is, when you have to make final payment for the property. If the time frame doesn't suit you, try to arrange a change through the agent before the auction. Make sure it is put in writing. Changing the settlement period can be arranged on auction day, but you will be in a better bargaining position beforehand.

The auctioneer will outline the basics of the contract and then call for an opening bid. Agents are entitled to make one bid at the auction, but often the seller will arrange for a friend to make bogus bids even though this is not allowed by law. False bidding may take place at an auction without you knowing. The way an auction operates lends itself to such scenarios, so keep your wits about you.

Highest bidder

An auctioned property is sold to the highest bidder, provided the reserve price has been reached. The seller sets the reserve price, and often the exact figure is not known by the agent until just before the auction. If the bidding stops before the reserve price is reached the agent usually seeks advice from the seller. The agent will normally attempt to convince the seller to lower the reserve. There are three possible outcomes:

- The seller won't change the reserve price, the auction stops and the highest bidder has first right to negotiate on the property.

- The auctioneer announces the bids are close to the reserve and encourages further bidding.

- The auctioneer lets it be known the property is 'on the market'. This means the reserve price has been lowered to the current highest bid. If there are no further bids, the property will be sold to that bidder.

Tips for buying at auction

The first rule is don't let the agent know you are keen on the property —unless of course you are so keen you wish to make an offer before the auction. Some people like to bid from the start. Generally, this is not wise. It lets the agent and the auctioneer know you are a keen bidder. As the auction draws to a close, other bidders could believe you are running out of money, and will be more willing to bid against you.

A useful tactic is to wait for the bidding to near your price limit and then bid for the first time. But make the jump in the bid a big one. For example, suppose your limit is $300 000, the bidding reaches $280 000, and is going up in $2000 lots. Make a bid of $285 000 or $290 000. This often psyches out other buyers by giving the impression you have plenty to spend. If the bidding exceeds $300 000, you will lose the property anyway. Remember that if you are the highest bidder in an auction and the bid is above or equal to the reserve price, the property is yours.

If you are the successful bidder, you must sign the contract and pay 10 per cent of the auction price immediately—unless you have made other arrangements with the seller. This 10 per cent is non-refundable. There are no 'cooling-off' periods for property auctions. If you cannot come up with the remaining 90 per cent of the price, you can lose your 10 per cent deposit. Try to remember this if you are tempted to make a bid above your predetermined limit. Don't fall for the old trick when the auctioneer or agent says, 'It's only another $2000'. If you don't have it, don't bid it. Try to be as calm and clinical as possible. If you think you will get carried away and bid above your predetermined limit, ask someone else—a friend or a property adviser—to bid for you.

Key points

o   Before entering into a property transaction you need to estimate the cash flow you are likely to generate from the property and determine what price you would need to sell the property for in order to generate an acceptable rate of return.

o   It is better to be conservative when estimating future cash flows from your property investments—do not fall into the trap of believing that no one loses money from a property investment.

o   When estimating your likely return from property it is essential to take into account both income tax and capital gains tax.

o   When selling at auction there are many tricks to use and traps for the unwary. Be aware of what they are and you will have a better chance of selling your property at the best price.

o   When buying at auction, never get caught up in the excitement of the event and pay too much for the property—you will live to regret it.

20

Tax and property investments

One of the attractions of property investment is that there are considerable tax benefits associated with it. In particular, losses that you make if you 'negatively gear' your property investment can be offset against other income — such as your salary. But there are significant taxes that property investors pay — such as land tax, stamp duty and capital gains tax (CGT). Indeed, if you do not pay CGT you have made an overall loss on your property investment.

While there are numerous tax benefits with property investments you should not invest solely to obtain tax benefits. Moreover, tax benefits will not turn a poor investment into a good one. In addition, it is essential that you ensure you understand Australia's complex tax laws. This means claiming all the legitimate tax deductions to which you are entitled — and fully substantiating these claims. The Tax Office often targets property investors for tax audits, and the penalties for not declaring income or claiming deductions to which you are not entitled can be substantial.

Negative gearing

Negative gearing arises when the costs, such as interest, rates and maintenance relating to an income-producing investment, exceed the income from that investment. It can conceivably apply to any investment — it is not restricted to property. However, it is frequently used in the property market, especially the residential investment market. The loss made through negative gearing can be offset against your other income such as your salary, thereby reducing the amount of income tax you have to pay. This does not apply to your principal place of residence.

Although the concept of negative gearing may appeal to some investors, it is wise to take into account that you will need to make up the difference between the income from the property and its associated expenses from your existing income. Before you embark on making a negatively geared investment you should establish whether the investment will stand on its own before taking tax into account. As many investors have found out to their regret, tax benefits will not turn a poor investment into a good one.

Let's work through some numbers to illustrate how negative gearing operates. Jane earns $80000 per annum. She purchases a home unit for $250000 (including $7000 in buying costs). She obtains a loan for 90 per cent of the cost of the property ($225000) with a variable interest-only rate of 7 per cent per annum.

Rent is expected to be $250 per week. The rates and body corporate fees are $2000 per annum and there's also an 8 per cent rental management commission to be paid. To simplify this example we will not include any tax deductions from depreciation of either the home unit or its contents.

In the first year Jane's income and expenses from this investment are as follows:

Rental income: $250 × 52	$13000
Rental management: 8% × $13000	−$1040
Loan interest: 7% × $225000	−$15750
Rates, etc.	−$2000
Total	**−$5790**

Jane is then able to claim the loss of $5790 against her salary income and can reduce her overall tax bill as follows:

	Jane with no property	Jane with one property
Salary	$80000	$80000
Property tax loss	–	−$5790
Taxable income	*$80000*	*$74210*
Tax	−$17850	−$16113
Net income	**$62150**	**$58097**

Even though Jane has made a loss of $5790, the after-tax effect on her yearly income is only $4053 ($62150 − $58097). This means that Jane needs to find another $78 per week ($4053 divided by 52) to fund the negative cash flow from her home unit. This assumes that the interest rate on the loan does not increase and the home unit is fully rented for the entire year.

So negative gearing gives you the certainty of a loss each year. What Jane is hoping is that the capital gain she makes on the property—less any CGT that she needs to pay—will more than compensate her for these yearly losses.

Jane requires the value of the property to increase by $4768 per year, or 1.9 per cent ($4768 ÷ $250 000), to at least break even. For example, if Jane sold this property after one year for a net capital gain of $4768 and she paid CGT at a rate of 15 per cent, she would be left with $4053. This would offset the loss Jane is making on renting out the property. But this only breaks even on the property. Jane has $25 000 of her own money invested in the property and would be looking for some compensation for the risk she is taking. Plus there are costs involved when she buys and sells the property; for example, over $7000 in stamp duty in New South Wales when you purchase a property. In addition, there are agent's commissions and legal fees, which eat into the profits. This means Jane should not consider property as a short-term—less than three-year—investment. In order to recoup all the transaction costs of buying and selling, and to offset any negative gearing losses, she needs this property to appreciate by about 30 to 40 per cent over a three-year period.

Of course, if the price of the property fell she would make two losses —one on buying and selling the property and another because the rent did not cover her outgoings.

This calculation also does not take into account the time value of money. What Jane is essentially doing is incurring an actual loss today in the expectation of an offsetting capital gain at some time in the future. The loss is certain and the gain is uncertain. Even if the price of the property increases, you cannot get an actual lifestyle benefit from this appreciation until you sell the property.

In addition, there is the opportunity cost of the $25 000 deposit that Jane put into this property from her own resources. Let's suppose she could have invested this elsewhere for an after-tax return of 3 per cent per annum. That means there is another $750 after tax that this property should be returning each year.

Positive gearing

There is no law that says that you must negatively gear any property that you buy. It is possible to buy property that is positively geared; that is, where your rental income is greater than the expenses of running the property.

For example, imagine Jane purchased a property that had the following annual outcome:

Property income	$13 000
Property expenses	–$11 000
Subtotal	$2 000
Tax payable @ 31.5%	–$630
After-tax profit	**$1 370**

Unlike the previous negatively geared example, if Jane purchased this type of property then her yearly after-tax income would increase. That is, she'd have more money from investing in property from day one (before any capital gains), not less.

Income tax deductions

As a general rule, you can only declare the income you earn from property and claim related expenses if your name is on the property's title deed. Importantly, there are some expenses that can be claimed as a tax deduction in the financial year in which they are incurred. Some expenses cannot be claimed immediately but are included in the CGT cost base when you sell the property. For CGT purposes, the date you enter into the contract is your date of purchase, not the settlement date.

As indicated in the example above, it is possible to make considerable tax savings through investing in residential property. Allowable deductions include:

- *Interest:* If you borrow money to buy an investment property, you can claim the interest as a tax deduction. Similarly, you may be entitled to claim the interest on any loans used to buy items for use in the rental property, such as a refrigerator, furnishings or carpet. Basically you can claim a deduction for interest that is incurred in order to earn income from the rental property.

- *Building allowance:* Where residential income-producing property has been built after 16 September 1987 and it is used for assessable income-producing purposes, a building allowance of 2.5 per cent of the original qualifying construction cost may be deducted every year for 40 years, regardless of the resale price. The allowance is 4 per cent (25 years) if construction commenced on or after 18 July 1985 and before 16 September 1987.

- *Depreciation:* Assets such as electrical appliances, furniture and fittings, carpets and curtains can be depreciated over their effective lives.

- *Outgoings:* These include costs incurred in the managing or the running of an investment property, including agent's commission, the cost of professional services such as accountant's and solicitor's fees, insurance, rates, repairs and maintenance, cleaning and gardening. Also the cost of your travel and car expenses incurred when inspecting the property are allowable deductions.

If the property is not available for rent for the full year, some of these expenses may need to be apportioned on a time basis. This is particularly important to remember if the property is a holiday home or unit and is reserved from time to time for your own, or your family's, use.

If you have a negatively geared investment property and are a PAYG (pay as you go) taxpayer, you can apply to the Tax Office for a reduction in your PAYG instalments, instead of waiting to recoup some of these expenses via your income tax return.

The expenses incurred in buying and selling your investment property, such as the purchase cost of the property, conveyancing costs and advertising expenses, cannot be claimed as a deduction against the rental income from the property. However, such costs may be taken into account when you sell the property, to calculate any capital gain or loss on the sale.

If the property is not your primary residence you will then pay tax on any capital gain when you sell it. A capital gain is the difference between the 'cost base' and the net sale price—after selling expenses. The cost base is the price you paid for the property along with any expenses when buying and capital improvements made during ownership (but it does not include deductible expenses).

Land tax and property investment

Land tax is an annual state government tax that needs to be paid by property owners based on the land value of their combined investment properties. Land tax applies in all states and territories except the Northern Territory. In most states the house in which you live, or your principal place of residence, is exempt from land tax. However, in some states, such as New South Wales, if you rent out your principal place of residence for six months or more of the year, this property is then also included for land tax purposes.

Each state has its own land tax laws. For more information on land tax you can visit the relevant State Treasury website:

- New South Wales: <www.osr.nsw.gov.au>

- Queensland: <www.osr.qld.gov.au>

- Victoria: <www.sro.vic.gov.au>

- Western Australia: <www.dtf.wa.gov.au>

- South Australia: <www.revenuesa.sa.gov.au>

- ACT: <www.revenue.act.gov.au>

- Tasmania: <www.treasury.tas.gov.au>.

Land tax can be included as an expense for your property investment or included as part of your cost base for CGT.

Common tax mistakes

The Tax Office has identified the following areas where mistakes are commonly made in income tax returns submitted by rental property owners. Every year the Tax Office publishes a guide to rental properties explaining how to treat rental income and expenses and this is essential reading for all rental property investors. This is available free from the Tax Office's website: <www.ato.gov.au>.

Construction costs

Certain types of construction—including extensions, alterations and structural improvements—can be claimed as capital works deductions. The land on which a rental property is constructed cannot be claimed. Instead, the land forms part of the cost for CGT purposes.

Deductions can be claimed for the decline in value of some types of depreciating assets in residential rental properties (for example, curtains, blinds, dishwashers, refrigerators, stoves, television sets and hot water systems). But construction costs cannot be claimed as depreciating assets.

Initial repairs and capital improvements

Initial repairs to rectify damage, defects or deterioration that existed at the time of purchasing a property are capital expenditure and may be claimed as capital works deductions over either 25 or 40 years, depending on when the repairs were carried out.

Capital improvements (such as remodelling a bathroom, or adding a pergola) should also be claimed as capital works deductions.

Apportionment of interest

Sometimes loans are used for both investing and private purposes; for example, to both purchase or renovate a rental property, and to buy a boat. The interest expense on the private portion of the loan (the boat) is not deductible.

Legal expenses

Conveyancing expenses incurred on the purchase and sale of your property are not deductible. Instead, these form part of the cost for CGT purposes.

Some legal expenses incurred in producing your rental income are deductible; for example, the cost of evicting a non-paying tenant. Most legal expenses are of a capital nature and are therefore not deductible. These include the costs of:

- purchasing or selling your property

- defending your title to the property.

Travel expenses

Where travel related to your rental property is combined with a holiday or other private activities, you may need to apportion the expenses. You may be able to claim local expenses that are directly related to the property inspection and a proportion of accommodation expenses.

Apportionment of rental expenses

If your holiday home is used by you, your friends or your relatives free of charge for part of the year, you are not entitled to a deduction for costs incurred during those periods.

It is also important that you have a clear intention to rent out the property. If you made no attempt to advertise the property or set the rent so high it is unlikely a tenant could be found, the Tax Office could find that there was no intention of renting your property and your rental claims would not be allowed.

Deductible borrowing expenses

The correct way to claim expenses of more than $100 incurred in arranging an investment loan is to spread the deduction over five years or over the term of the loan, whichever is less. If your borrowing expenses are $100 or less, you can claim the full amount in the financial year they are incurred. A common mistake is to claim all deductible borrowing expenses in the first year they are incurred.

Ownership interests

If you purchase a rental property as a co-owner and are not carrying on a rental property business, you must divide the income and expenses for the rental property in line with your legal interest in the property. This is despite any written or oral agreement between co-owners stating otherwise. A common mistake occurs when a property is purchased by a husband and wife (as co-owners) and the income and expenses are not split in line with their legal interest in the property.

Prepaid expenses

If you prepay a rental property expense—such as insurance or interest on money borrowed—that covers a period of 12 months or less and the period ends on or before 30 June, you can claim an immediate deduction. A prepayment that does not meet these criteria and is $1000 or more may have to be spread over two or more years.

Body corporate fees and charges

You may be able to claim a deduction for body corporate fees and charges you incur for your rental property. Payments you make to body corporate administration funds and general purpose sinking funds are considered to be payments for the provision of services by the body corporate and you can claim a deduction for these levies at the time you incur them. If the body corporate requires you to make payments to a special purpose fund to pay for particular capital expenditure, these levies are not deductible. Similarly, if the body corporate levies a special contribution for major capital expenses to be paid out of the general purpose sinking fund, you will not be entitled to a deduction for this special contribution amount.

You may be able to claim a capital works deduction for the cost of capital improvements or repairs of a capital nature once the cost has been charged to either the special purpose fund or, if a special contribution has been levied, the general purpose sinking fund.

If the body corporate fees and charges you incur are for things such as the maintenance of gardens, deductible repairs and building insurance, you cannot also claim deductions for these as part of other expenses. For example, you cannot claim a separate deduction for garden maintenance if that expense is already included in body corporate fees and charges.

Expenses you cannot claim

Expenses for which you are not able to claim deductions include:

- acquisition and disposal costs of the property

- expenses not actually incurred by you, such as water or electricity charges borne by your tenants

- expenses that are not related to the rental of a property, such as expenses connected to your own use of a holiday home that you rent out for part of the year.

What records do you need to keep?

You need to keep proper records in order to make a claim, regardless of whether you use a tax agent to prepare your tax return or you do it yourself. You must keep records of:

- the rental income you receive and the deductible expenses you pay—keep these records for five years from 31 October or, if you lodge later, for five years from the date your tax return is lodged

- your ownership of the property and all the costs of purchasing/ acquiring it and selling/disposing of it—keep these records for five years from the date you sell/dispose of your rental property.

Read and keep all documents you receive about your property investment. In particular you must keep documentary evidence of any expenses incurred to be able to claim them as tax deductions. It is wise to get specific advice on what you can and cannot claim as deductions—otherwise you might find yourself with problems if audited by the Tax Office. In general you need to keep tax records for five years. However, if you make a capital gain on the property you need to keep these records for five years from the time you sell the property. This could mean keeping these records for 10 years or longer.

If someone else is managing your property, make sure they keep you informed of what is happening:

- Insist that they give you written records and reports. Chase them up if they don't arrive.

- Ask questions if you're not sure. Reputable investment managers will be happy to answer your questions and will expect you to take an interest in your investments.

- Make sure you give all your instructions to your estate agent in writing. Also tell them what limits they have to act on your behalf.

Key points

o To maximise your tax deductions you must keep complete and accurate records of all expenses relating to your property.

o Negative gearing is a successful investment strategy only if the asset you have purchased goes up in price. This strategy will multiply your losses if the price of the property falls.

o Some tax deductions can be claimed in the financial year in which they are incurred while others reduce any capital gains liability you have when selling the property.

o Even though you receive considerable tax benefits from investing in property this does not guarantee that it will be a successful investment.

o You need to find out whether your property investment will be liable for land tax; this can adversely affect your overall investment return.

21

Listed and unlisted property trusts

The GFC had an impact on the market for property as much as other areas of investing. The property sector was hard hit by the GFC with asset values tumbling and investing activity being hampered by frozen credit markets. The crisis exposed some fundamental flaws in the structure of property trusts—both listed and unlisted. Firstly, these unlisted trusts invest in property that is a longer term investment but offer investors virtually an 'at-call' withdrawal facility. When a considerable number of investors try to withdraw their money at the same time this is a major problem for the trust. Secondly, many listed and unlisted trusts borrowed heavily to take advantage of the booming market in 2006 and 2007. But when the property market turned down this high level of debt magnified the problems faced by these trusts.

While interest rates were reduced to historically low levels, many property managers found it difficult, or sometimes impossible, to refinance loans when they became due. Some property companies, such as Westpoint, collapsed, while the share prices of those listed on the ASX plummeted by around 40 per cent or more. A fundamental problem was that loan-to-valuation ratios had become extraordinarily high in the property industry in the lead up to the GFC, and when credit dried up managers were forced to sell properties at reduced prices to pay off some of their debts.

As has been seen in previous chapters, investing in property is unlike the sharemarket because property has significantly different investment characteristics. For example, if you make a poor property investment, it is likely to have a much bigger impact on your portfolio than a poor share investment. Also property investments are illiquid and inflexible. If you invest in managed funds or shares and you need to access some of your cash, it is easy to sell some of your investments. But it may take months to sell a property. For these reasons you need to take a longer term view when allocating that part of your investment portfolio earmarked for property.

Property investment structures

When most first-time property investors buy property they generally buy it in their own name or jointly with their spouse. But there are other structures you can use to invest in the property market. Choosing the best structure to purchase property is one of the most important decisions you will make as it will influence the amount of income tax and CGT you will pay. It also affects the extent to which your property is secure in the event that legal action is taken against you for, say, the recovery of damages. This is referred to as 'asset protection'.

The main structures you can use to buy property are:

- *Individual:* Individual ownership is the most common and simplest form of ownership, especially for the family home or investment properties. The main drawback of this type of ownership is that it does not provide any flexibility in minimising income tax or CGT. It also offers little in the way of asset protection because any legal action taken against you may impact on the property.

- *Company:* Companies offer limited liability and a flat tax rate of 30 per cent. However, companies cannot claim a CGT discount.

- *Trust:* Basically a trust is where one person or persons, the trustee(s), manages income and/or capital on behalf of another person or persons, called the beneficiary or beneficiaries. The legal owner of the trust's assets is the trustee(s). There are two basic types of trusts:

  - *Discretionary trust:* This is a flexible structure because income and capital gains can be distributed to various beneficiaries at the trustee's discretion. The other advantage is that the trustee has until 30 June each year to decide who is to receive the income and/or capital gain so this gives the greatest scope for tax planning.

  - *Unit trust (managed fund):* Unlike discretionary trusts, unit trusts have unitholders who have an equitable interest in the trust assets. Distributions of income and capital are made to unitholders in proportion to their holdings of units.

- *Superannuation fund:* Self-managed superannuation funds have become popular because superannuation is a compulsory form of investment. Superannuation funds may own property. But they are not allowed to borrow to invest. Superannuation funds previously were able to get around this restriction by using a unit trust to borrow to buy the property and have the super fund own units in the trust. But this loophole has been closed for what are referred to as 'closely held' trusts.

- *Joint venture:* This is where two or more, usually large, investors get together to pursue a joint interest for profit. The joint venture may be incorporated as a company or else it is governed by a joint venture agreement. A joint venture can include property investment domestically or internationally.

At an individual level, discretionary trusts are often the best structures for owning appreciating assets such as investment property and shares because income can be distributed between beneficiaries at the trustee's discretion. So the trustee can make best use of each beneficiary's tax position. Capital gains can also be distributed between beneficiaries at the trustee's discretion. The assets of the trust are protected from legal action against beneficiaries. New beneficiaries can be added and usually there are no implications for CGT.

In this chapter we will examine the following types of property investment structures, all of which are companies or unit trusts (managed funds):

- property syndicates

- unlisted property trusts

- listed property trusts

- property securities funds

- diversified/balanced trusts.

Each of the above has different features, including different degrees of risk, different tax implications, different potential returns, different liquidity issues and different diversification benefits. You therefore need to be conversant with each type of structure.

Property syndicates

A property syndicate may be either made up of a small group of large investors or a large number of everyday investors. In the case of the former, a small group of investors pool their resources and buy property in a joint venture or company arrangement. The syndicate may be managed by one of the investors for a fee or the group may engage an outside manager. The syndicate may have an unlimited life or run for a fixed term after which all properties are sold and the proceeds distributed. Minimum investment is high and the constitution of the syndicate is laid down by way of incorporation as a company or in a joint venture agreement. If a company is formed, the syndicate pays tax at the company rate of 30 per cent. This is a structure that is best suited to large investors who are knowledgeable about the property market.

A syndicate may also consist of a large group of everyday investors. Here there is a minimum investment of around $10000 to $25000, which makes the syndicate much more within the reach of small investors. Depending on the particular syndicate, it may own just one property or a portfolio of properties. The syndicate is managed by a professional property manager who, for a fee, arranges leases, collects rent and maintains the property or properties. Investors in the syndicate may receive distributions monthly, quarterly, semi-annually or annually. The time frame of the syndicate is usually fixed—for example, for seven years—after which the syndicate's portfolio is sold and the proceeds are distributed to investors, or the syndicate could be rolled over for another seven-year period. This type of property syndicate is usually set up using a trust structure, and as such does not pay tax providing that all of its earnings are distributed to investors.

Distributions from a property syndicate usually contain a tax-deferred component, which is generally 15 to 100 per cent of the distribution. Tax-deferred distributions effectively represent the excess of the income distributed by the syndicate over the taxable component of those distributions. The excess is sheltered from tax because of deductions such as capital works, depreciation on plant and equipment and other tax timing differences. Investors do not pay tax on the tax-deferred component until the syndicate is wound up, and then at the concessional rate for CGT. However, if during the life of the syndicate tax-deferred distributions reduce the cost base to zero, then all future distributions are taxed in full and the tax-deferred component does not apply.

Here is how it works. Assume the following:

- You invest $10 000 in a property syndicate with a life of seven years.

- $800 is received in distributions each year (8% p.a. × $10 000).

- The tax-deferred component is 40 per cent or $320 per year. This is the amount by which the original cost base of your investment is reduced.

- The taxable component is 60 per cent or $480 per year.

- After seven years you receive $12 000 when the syndicate is wound up.

In your income tax return you should include a distribution of $480 each year. The original cost base of your investment reduces by $320 per year so by the end of the seventh year the original cost base is reduced by $2240 to $7760. The sale price of $12 000 less the new cost base of $7760 results in a capital gain of $4240. After applying the 50 per cent CGT discount, you will pay tax on $2120 at your marginal rate. (This example has been simplified because in reality distributions and their tax-deferred component will vary during the lifetime of the syndicate. The syndicate manager discloses the tax-deferred component each time it makes a distribution.)

One of the drawbacks of investing in property syndicates is that they are illiquid investments. It is generally difficult to get your money back before the end of the syndicate. Also property syndicates are 'closed ended', which means that they are closed to new investors during the life of the syndicate. There are other property investment structures that overcome both of these drawbacks.

Unlisted property trusts

Unlisted property trusts are property syndicates for everyday investors that are open ended; that is, new investors can enter at any time and existing investors can redeem their units on the terms laid down in the product disclosure statement (PDS). A large number of investors pool their resources in a retail managed fund (unit trust) and have a professional fund manager select properties for them. The minimum investment is usually around $1000 and the trusts may be geared, which means that they borrow to invest, or ungeared, which means that they do not borrow. These trusts are not listed on the ASX. They are called 'open ended' because investors can buy new units from the manager, or sell units back to the fund manager at the redemption price. While this introduces more liquidity to a property investment structure, a fund manager may have difficulty at times satisfying redemption requests because property is not a liquid asset. Consequently, the manager may have to dispose of properties at forced sale prices. For this reason a manager will attempt to meet redemptions in a short space of time — for example, five days — but it reserves the right to extend this to six months if the property market turns down.

An unlisted property trust manager may have the right to borrow funds and thereby increase the total amount invested in property. This strategy, referred to as 'gearing', is a riskier strategy because in times of a property market downturn the manager will nevertheless be required to pay interest on these loans. It also has the potential to magnify gains if the interest rate payable is less than the return from property investments. A measure of the extent of gearing is the loan-to-valuation ratio, which is the ratio of borrowed finance to the total current valuation of all properties held by the trust. A useful rule of thumb is that the loan-to-valuation ratio should not exceed 1:2, which means that borrowed funds do not exceed 50 per cent of valuation.

Where an unlisted property trust has borrowed to invest, you need to be aware of the extent to which it is able to service loan interest payments. The best tool for assessing this is the interest cover ratio, which measures the extent to which interest payments are covered by earnings before interest. A useful rule of thumb is that the interest cover ratio should not be less than 2:1, which means that interest payments are at least twice covered by earnings before interest.

Property held by unlisted property trusts may include commercial (for example, office), retail (for example, shopping centres), industrial (for example, warehouses) and healthcare (for example, hospitals and medical centres). To reduce risk it is preferable that a property portfolio be diversified with regard to the above categories and also geographic locations. Unlisted property trusts may invest in direct property, other unlisted property trusts and listed property trusts (see below).

Unlisted property trusts are suitable if you seek regular income payments from property and want to invest in a diversified property port-folio. They are also attractive if you want some direct property exposure but may need to access all or part of your investment at relatively short notice — with the understanding that this might not always be the case. Unlisted property trusts are best suited to investors with a five-year investment outlook. They attempt to maintain good liquidity through investing in a range of property assets and cash, generally enabling you to request withdrawals when you choose. However, as has been seen, this liquidity may be compromised during difficult times.

Listed property trusts (REITs)

Listed property trusts, also referred to as real estate investment trusts (REITs) or Australian real estate investment trusts (A-REITs), are similar to unlisted property trusts except that they are quoted on the ASX. Whereas you would need to contact the fund manager of an unlisted property trust to find out what the redemption price is on any particular day, you can follow the progress of REITs in the sharemarket tables. The fact that REITs are listed on the ASX enhances liquidity because you can normally expect to be able to buy and sell these units easily, although not necessarily at the price you would like. REITs do not keep reserves of cash and do not need to dispose of properties at forced sale prices to meet redemptions. The share price of REITs is still affected by movements in property markets, but these movements do not translate into a REIT having to sell properties.

The S&P/ASX 200 A-REIT Index (formerly the S&P/ASX Listed Property Trust Index) tracks the movement of the share prices of most REITs. At February 2010 REITs in this index had a market value of $64.8 billion, which is around 6.2 per cent of the total Australian share-market capitalisation. During the GFC, the value of this index fell by over 40 per cent, which was more than the fall in the S&P/ASX 300 index. Highly geared REITs got into difficulty when liquidity evaporated and they could not roll over their existing loans. It seemed that many investors had confused REITs with the type of property they would invest in when buying the family home.

There are also S&P/ASX 200 A-REIT Index Futures, also known as Mini Property Futures or XPJ Index Futures. These began in 2002 and they are now actively traded by fund managers. Volumes in these futures have grown steadily since their inception, with particularly high volume in December 2008 and June 2009.

Advantages of REITs

By buying REITs you gain exposure to both the value of property that the trust owns and the potential for rental income generated from the properties. The trust's manager takes responsibility for selecting properties, maintenance, administration, property rentals, property improvements and disposing of properties. You need not be an expert on property yourself. Although it varies from case to case, a REIT manager can diversify investments across property markets, geographic regions, lease terms and types of tenant. Types of property invested in include:

- industrial, including investment in factories, warehouses and industrial parks

- office, including investment in medium to large office buildings in and around major cities

- hotel and leisure, including investment in hotels, resorts, cinemas and theme parks

- retail, including investment in shopping centres

- diversified, consisting of a combination of industrial, office, hotel and retail.

REIT dividends are paid either quarterly or semi-annually, which enables you to regulate your cash flow. There may also be the opportunity for capital growth. It is possible that an increase in dividend yields across the sharemarket in general may prompt an increase in REIT dividend yields. Management costs tend to be lower than for unlisted property trusts and transaction costs on buying or selling shares are lower than for unlisted property trusts. The tax-deferred component on REIT income is passed through to investors.

Disadvantages of REITs

Many REITs gear to make property investments and the level of gearing may be difficult to establish because of the underlying investments of REITs. For example, a REIT may invest in other REITs which also gear their investments. Gearing has the effect of magnifying gains and losses so it is essential that you know what the real level of gearing is, and this may be difficult to determine. In February 2010, accounting firm PKF reported that well below 50 per cent of REITs disclosed their actual level of gearing having regard to debt maturity, the type of debt and the type and structure of underlying investments. The problem is accentuated because a REIT may embark on property investing with a joint venture partner that does not disclose its level of gearing.

REITs are subject to market risk in that if the property market in general declines, the value of REIT share prices will similarly decline. This risk can be mitigated by diversifying out of property. However, a problem arose in that for a long while REITs were considered to be almost 'blue-chip' investments and no one foresaw that this image would be shattered. REITs are subject to fluctuations in market sentiment and a downturn can be caused by such things as asset devaluations across the board.

Past performance is no guarantee of future performance and this applies to REITs as much as any other investment. Past dividends may not be maintained and may vary over time. Just because a REIT has a history of paying a specified dividend does not mean that this will continue.

Interest rates may rise, making the cost of borrowing more expensive. This can lead to reduced dividends. The more highly geared a REIT is, the greater the impact will be on profits. Similarly, a REIT may have difficulty rolling over its debt finance, as happened during the GFC.

Stapled securities

REITs may be either standalone REITs, which means that they operate in the manner described above and provide exposure to an underlying portfolio of property assets, or alternatively they may have stapled securities. Stapled securities provide investors with exposure to a professional manager and/or to a property development company, in addition to a real estate portfolio. A stapled security is one where an investor owns two or more securities that are usually related and bound together through one company. Typically, a stapled security consists of one REIT share and one share in the related funds management company that cannot be traded separately. The REIT holds a portfolio of property assets while the related company carries out the funds management and/or development activities. When you trade a share in a REIT structured this way you also trade the stapled security. However, the returns from each are different.

Property securities funds

Property securities funds can be listed — for example, a REIT — or unlisted. They invest in the securities of other listed and/or unlisted property trusts and property companies, rather than in direct property itself. For property securities funds liquidity is not the same issue as for unlisted property trusts, because it can sell off securities to meet redemptions. If its underlying investments are in unlisted property trusts that invest in direct property, the problem that property assets may need to be disposed of at forced sale prices still arises. In this situation, redemptions may be delayed. Also the investment portfolio of unlisted property securities funds may need to be disposed of at forced sale prices if redemption requests are greater than the available cash on hand to pay out redemptions. Unlisted property securities funds are more common than unlisted property trusts that invest in direct property. During the GFC the prices of units and shares in listed and unlisted property securities funds fell dramatically.

Diversified/balanced trusts

Diversified/balanced trusts are unlisted managed funds which invest in a range of assets, including shares, interest-bearing securities, property securities and cash. Because their portfolios are diversified, investors in diversified and balanced trusts are cushioned to some extent against a downturn in one sector. Investors were not cushioned during the GFC when the price of shares and property securities fell simultaneously and credit dried up. During this time, trusts that had a high proportion of their assets in cash fared the best.

Property cycles

Property moves in cycles like any other form of investment. Unlike shares where price movements are uniform across the country, property may be booming in Perth and be in the doldrums in Adelaide. Also the market may vary within cities as well. Obviously you need to be attuned to the factors that affect real estate prices.

An effective strategy in making real estate investments is to switch from the industrial market to the office and retail markets by way of listed and unlisted property trusts. But whatever strategy you adopt, it is imperative that you keep abreast of developments in the property market and factors that affect the market such as inflation and interest rates.

Once you have acquired an interest in property, your investment and the market conditions affecting it must be monitored and re-evaluated regularly. As with other investments it may be advisable to cut your losses and move into other areas if the property does not perform up to your expectations.

Mortgage trusts

Mortgage trusts are an investment in mortgages rather than an investment in property, but the ultimate security for a mortgage is property. Most mortgage trusts will only invest in first mortgages, but a few will invest in riskier second mortgages as well. A second mortgagor cannot, in the case of default by the borrower, be paid until the first mortgagor has been paid in full. Investing in mortgage trusts can be risky. The prime example of this was the collapse of the Estate Mortgage Group in the early 1990s. During the GFC a number of mortgage trusts were subjected to heavy demand for redemptions and managers had to initiate a freeze. This proved to be difficult for many self-funded retirees who relied on their earnings from mortgage trusts to fund living expenses.

Information on mortgage trusts is not regularly found in the financial pages, but there are several organisations sponsoring them. You should consult a stockbroker or bank for further information.

Syndicates and property trusts

Syndicates and property trusts have opened the door to many investors who would otherwise not have the ability to invest in property. You can now buy units in a trust or syndicate which may invest in a variety of properties, on a large scale, which a small investor would not have the opportunity to invest in.

As was highlighted at the beginning of this chapter, property trusts may be of two types: unlisted or listed. The chief advantage of investing in a listed property trust is that, like shares, they are more liquid because selling your investment is as easy as selling your units through a stockbroker.

With an unlisted property trust you have to apply to the manager of the trust to redeem all or some of your units and you buy back at the trust's net asset backing. In the event that the manager of an unlisted trust was inundated with applications to redeem units at the same time, it may have to sell off property to finance redemptions. This can never happen with a listed property trust because unitholders sell through the sharemarket. If a listed trust was the focal point of heavy selling, the trust's share price would fall, but the manager would not be required to sell off any properties in order to satisfy the demand. The unit price of a REIT can trade above or below its asset backing.

Property trusts, whether they are listed or unlisted, can be structured to offer different types of returns:

- high capital growth and low income

- high income and modest capital growth

- balanced returns of income and capital growth.

The appropriate property trust for you to invest in will depend upon your attitude to risk, your need for regular income and your tax position.

Split trusts

With a split trust you can elect to own growth units, income units or a combination of the two. As the holder of growth units you would get most of the capital growth, while as the owner of income units you would get most of the income. Split trusts distribute more income, and do not use borrowings to finance additional purchases or get involved in property development to the extent that a property growth trust does.

Product disclosure statements

If you are interested in investing in a property trust that is unlisted you will need to obtain a product disclosure statement (PDS). An investment adviser would be able to advise you on how to get one. But be aware that an investment adviser may have more than a casual interest in what you do because he or she may get a commission.

When you obtain a PDS it is essential that you study its contents carefully and make your own evaluation, even if you ask an investment adviser for his or her opinion. In particular you should make an assessment of the quality of the trust's portfolio. Ensure that the property it holds is not overly specialised. For example, property trusts that are spread over different sectors — retail, commercial, industrial, hotel, healthcare — and over different locations are generally less risky than ones that concentrate on only one or two sectors and/or locations. Another important consideration is what percentage of the portfolio is currently leased and when these leases expire.

Key points

o   The GFC impacted heavily on the property market. For example, share prices of listed property trusts (REITs) fell by more than the sharemarket as a whole. Managers of unlisted property trusts that invested in direct property were forced to sell off property assets at low prices.

o   A decision on which structure to use for making property investments has repercussions which need to be considered before you enter the property market.

---

o   Property investment is no more passive than any other form of investment. You need to regularly review and monitor your investments.

o   Keep a formal record of your involvement in the property market by reviewing your position every quarter.

o   REITs can no longer be considered 'blue-chip' investments.

22

Investing in collectables

Successful investing in collectables, such as art, antiques, coins, stamps and wine, generally involves collecting for love, passion and money. You would never fall in love with investment property, shares, bonds or your cash, but with collectables it is important that they appeal to you as well as provide an opportunity for profit. This chapter is for those of you who wish to invest in the markets for collectables.

The first rule of collecting is to be genuinely interested in your chosen specialisation. Collecting solely with an eye to making money is unlikely to pay off because you will lack the appreciative eye and patience of the true collector.

The market for collectables was unpredictable during the GFC. On the one hand collectables were not subjected to the same volatility that affected more conventional investments such as shares. Except in unusual circumstances the value of a collectable does not jump markedly one day and fall the next. During the GFC there appeared to be more likelihood of a steady increase over time, although the market for collectables is also subject to market sentiment, fashion and emotion. However, overriding this was the fact that economic recession usually has a detrimental effect on collectable prices because consumers consider spending on them to be discretionary expenditure—plus they do not generate any income. During the GFC people were short of money and feared that worse was to come so they cut back their outlays on collectables. Now that the GFC is over, however, the markets for collectables are more buoyant.

It is important to appreciate with collectables that, unlike investments in property, shares, fixed interest and cash, there is no income stream associated with your investments. You do not receive dividends, interest or rental income. However, as you will see, there is an exception to this in terms of the art rental market.

Types of collectors

A collector buys particular pieces that in the future may be worth far more than present prices. It is essential to appreciate that fashions change, and what may be in demand at one time may be out of favour at another. For example, with antique furniture, Victoriana was once in high demand but then high-quality 20th century retro became the fashion. A similar thing happened with rugs, where tribal rugs not made for the commercial market became more collectable than Oriental rugs.

There are five types of investment collectors, namely:

- traditional collectors

- speculators

- expert collectors

- collectors of sets

- collectors of objects you can use.

Traditional collectors stick to what is tried and true, such as 'blue-chip' items that have been appreciated by collectors for many decades or even centuries. This includes all works of museum quality, Old Masters, Impressionists, early editions of great writers, pre-revolutionary French furniture, Georgian silver and ancient Greek and Roman coins. This is an expensive approach and you may have to save long and hard to buy just one small item, but over time it is about as risk-free as you can get.

Speculators buy inexpensive items in the hope that in time they will become more valuable. Examples of speculative collectors' items that have handsomely paid off include early Pop Art, Tiffany lamps (originally created around 1895 but which really took off in the 1950s) or, in the 1890s, the work of a group of scruffy Paris painters who later became known as the Impressionists. However, these are the success stories. What you do not hear about are the countless collections of items consigned to people's attics when it becomes apparent that no one is going to beat a path to their doorstep. Basically, the speculative approach is a high-risk strategy with the odds stacked against you.

Expert collectors undertake a lifetime of serious study of their chosen field of specialisation. This enables them to gain an edge in finding undervalued items and enables them to beat dealers at their own game. Becoming an expert requires considerable dedication, time, love and study of your subject area. The 'expert' route to successful collecting is one of the best and least dangerous, always assuming that you do indeed qualify for the title.

A collector of sets makes up complete collections or sets in the hope that the sum will be more valuable than the total of the parts individually. On a simple level, two matching candlesticks will be more valuable together than singly. Likewise a complete set of an artist's prints will be worth more than the prints singly.

A collector of objects which can be used concentrates on things that can be employed for a purpose—furniture is the most obvious example. Instead of buying contemporary furniture with little or no resale value, a collector buys antiques that with any luck will one day be worth more than he or she paid for them. China also qualifies, along of course with paintings. Wine is another example because if you do not sell the wine you can drink it. Also some people collect motor vehicles, which they use. This is a sound approach where you can win doubly by getting enjoyable day-to-day use of your investments.

Areas of collectables

The range of collectables in which you can invest is vast and the popularity of each changes over time. Depending on what is in favour, they include:

- Australian Colonial furniture
- English and European furniture
- English and European pottery and porcelain
- Chinese ceramics and works of art
- Art Nouveau and Art Deco ceramics, glass, furniture and works of art
- Indigenous art
- Japanese art
- silver
- music memorabilia
- books
- original prints
- Australian jewels
- Australian Impressionists
- 19th century Australian Colonial and Traditional paintings
- coins and medals
- Islamic works of art including rugs and pottery
- antiquities

- Australian glass
- English, German and Italian glass
- British paintings
- modern Australian paintings
- contemporary Australian Art

- cars/automobilia
- stamps
- wine
- sporting memorabilia.

The first step is to establish your chosen area(s) of specialisation and the second step is to assess the market(s).

How to assess the markets for your investments

The investment criteria that help you to assess the market for any specific type of collectable include:

- risk
- ease of management
- your potential return
- liquidity.

When assessing risk, the first thing you will need to be concerned with is the length of time the market has been established. New markets, such as that for Contemporary Art, may fluctuate widely according to availability and whether the particular painter is in or out of fashion. When trying to minimise risk, consider whether or not there is a substantial body of background information. An area of collectables that is well covered by easily obtainable reference work including books and specialist magazines will be more assessable because the collector has knowledgeable references to consult. An example of a magazine that is an aid in research is *Australian Art Collector*: <www.artcollector.net.au>.

When assessing ease of management, consider whether you will need to spend money to keep the collectable in special conditions. Nowadays, generally apartments and houses are drier, creating problems with many natural materials such as wood or ivory. On the other hand, dryness is good for paper and metals. The cost of special conservation measures—referred to in the industry as preventative conservation—such as humidifiers and wine cabinets may affect the popularity and market strength of the collectables needing them. Additional security systems can also add to the expense of a collection. Broad markets with many collectors make it easier for thieves to sell stolen goods. For example, stamps are easier to sell than a Picasso painting, although Picassos get stolen too. Check the Stolen Paintings Record before you purchase an expensive European painting.

Generally speaking, the more valuable a collection, the greater is the need for security. Also the greater is the need for adequate insurance, which can add substantially to the costs of maintaining a collection.

When assessing your potential return, consider the stability of the market and the degree to which prices fluctuate. While the prices of some items, such as furniture, remain relatively stable, others, such as tribal art, move erratically in and out of favour. Note whether there are buyers in many countries because that makes for stable markets and it compensates for currency fluctuations. For example, if foreign currencies are strong against the Australian dollar, expatriate buyers will fill a gap left by Australians at home. In Australia there will always be a high demand for Australian art. Beware of investing in overseas art unless you are prepared to sell overseas.

In terms of liquidity, consider how easily you can sell your collectables without being forced to make a distressed sale for less than what you paid for them. Many markets, especially those for more obscure collectables, are illiquid and you may have trouble getting your money back when you want to. Also there are often wide movements in fashion. For example, these days discreet types of collecting, such as stamps and coins, have given way to more decorative elements used for outward display. A final factor is that each sector has different levels of difficulty for the would-be investor/collector and some can be extremely difficult to master. Much will depend on your own interests and tastes.

Buying collectables

To succeed in investing in collectables you will need to both buy astutely and sell when prices are on the boil. The first rule of buying is to purchase the best items you can afford. You may have to wait longer to save the necessary money, or you may have to settle for a smaller item, but always buy quality over quantity. The main reason is that you will find it easier to sell, both in good markets and bad. Also, as well as retaining their value better in bad markets, good-quality collectables tend to appreciate in value faster than lesser-quality items.

When buying collectables, the chances are that you will attend galleries and auctions and get a feel for the market. But before you buy it is essential that you develop as much knowledge of your specialist area as possible. Museums, galleries and exhibitions provide you with an opportunity to view items while books and magazines give you background and history. Also seminars and antique fairs enable you to learn about attribution and pricing. However, the best way to learn is to visit antique shops, local markets, auction sales and everywhere your collectables are for sale.

Unless placed by dealers, 'for sale' advertisements in newspapers can signify a bargain. The reason is that the selling prices do not reflect a dealer's mark-up, which varies but is usually between 33 per cent and 50 per cent. You can also visit junk shops and local markets. Stall holders pay lower overheads than dealers with an established business in a gallery or shop, therefore you may find a bargain at a market. However, there is a higher likelihood of fakes and frauds, so you need to be on your guard.

Member associations will often help you build a collection for better prices than if you purchase on the open market. For example, stamps, comic books, car parts and coins may all be purchased through regional clubs or associations at lower prices than on the open market and with an accurate assessment of the item on offer. Because of their mutual interest, association members may be open to barter and trade, and a serious collector would benefit by joining such an association.

Trade fairs, for example antique and record fairs, are becoming increasingly popular and a knowledgeable buyer can do well. The vendors know the value of what they are selling, however, and their prices will reflect this. For safety, be sure that you are buying from members of the trade association and that you receive the same guarantee as if you were making your purchase at a regular retail outlet.

When buying from a dealer, the price is generally fixed. There may be a small discount for cash or for some other reason, but do not suppose that you can wheel and deal or treat his or her shop like a bazaar. A dealer's price is a considered price, partly based on market demand and partly determined by what the dealer paid for an item. No prices are ever pulled out of the air.

If you are concentrating on one particular area, finding a major dealer and then getting to know and trust him or her is similar to relying on a good financial adviser. It will cost you money, but it is worth it. This person may let you know when he or she encounters a collectable of the sort you are interested in and, for a small fee, bid for you at auctions. Also, for furniture and paintings, where the item will be making an impact on your surroundings, a dealer may lend you a piece to see how it 'fits' before you buy it.

You may have an opportunity to buy from a catalogue without viewing an item. However, it is essential if at all possible to view any items before you buy or to consult with an authority who can assess damage and condition. This is where a conservator can be productively employed to give an estimated cost for associated repairs that are required. In Australia the conservators' professional body is the Australian Institute for the Conservation of Cultural Materials (AICCM): <www.aiccm.org.au>. Catalogue sales usually carry the same guarantee as retail purchases.

Buying at auction

When considering auctions as a means of buying collectables, you should first ideally obtain a copy of the catalogue. The best way to buy catalogues is to subscribe to an auction house directly. You will usually be able to get a substantial discount over the single-copy price if you sign up for a series. Successful dealers and collectors file and cross-reference catalogues and keep them indefinitely so you should always keep catalogues, however minor the auction. In order to save space, most catalogues use a form of shorthand which is usually explained in a glossary of terms. You should make sure you read and understand this. At major auctions, for example those conducted by Christies or Sotheby's, catalogues will contain price range estimates and it is useful to compare these estimates with what the items actually bring. If you are a serious collector you should subscribe to online reference material. For example, the *Australian Art Sales Digest* gives all auction results in Australia by artists: <www.aasd.com.au>.

In catalogues, the key points to watch out for include:

- dates

- measurements

- condition

- attribution

- type of work

- provenance.

When considering dates, note that few paintings are dated by the artist, so the dating is probably done by the auctioneer and it may not be precise. The absence of a date in an otherwise dated catalogue may suggest that a piece is modern. The word 'circa' followed by a date indicates that a work was done at roundabout that time.

Prints and drawings are measured in millimetres but other objects may or may not be described in metric terms. Paintings are usually measured in centimetres.

The condition of an item is a highly subjective area: one person's tiny chip may be another's total disaster. The absence of a condition report in a catalogue may mean that an item is in perfect condition or it may mean that it is a total write-off. The only viable solution is to ask questions of the auctioneer or, better still, make your own inspection. For example, if you are interested in a painting, have the back taken off and hold it up to the light. If the vendor will not take the back off, it may be because the paint is flaking off the canvas and if you held it up to the light you would see this.

Attribution is also tricky because experts often disagree and an attribution by one expert may be hotly contested by another. The words 'attributed to' in a catalogue should always sound a warning signal.

The technique and material used to produce an artwork can affect its value. Types of work include gouache, water colour, monotype, print, drawing and lithograph. The type of work will affect the value. For example, a print would generally be worth less than an oil by the same artist. Also, the lower the print number the higher the value, other things being equal. Works on paper are worth less than works on canvas or board because of the fragile nature of paper.

Provenance is the concept of establishing a chain of ownership and authenticity. This is important in preventing fraud and may be of historical interest as well.

Something to watch out for at auctions is 'A' lots. These are items that arrive after a catalogue has been published and they are then printed on an additional sheet that is distributed at the auction. A problem with 'A' lots is that there is no time for expert opinion and therefore the risk that an item is a forgery is increased. If you have bought a forgery, you might not find out until you try to sell it.

Having thoroughly researched collectables you are interested in, there are certain strategies you can follow at auctions which will give you the best chance of obtaining a collectable at a good price. For a start, do not get carried away by the moment. Set upper limits on your chosen items and stick to them. If you are not confident you can do this, get someone else to bid for you. Arrive at the auction venue early, especially if you want a seat. Then follow early lots and note down the prices in your catalogue. This will give you a useful feel for the performance of the market against the price estimates. When the auctioneer calls the lot number(s) you are interested in, do not jump in immediately; let someone else make the initial running.

When you want to bid, attract the auctioneer's attention by raising your hand, your catalogue or a paddle which is provided by the auction house. If the bidding is lively, the auctioneer may ignore you because he or she can only take bids from two places at a time. Do not worry; if you still want to bid, keep your hand, catalogue or paddle in the air and the auctioneer will get around to you. When the auctioneer does take a bid from you, any subsequent nod, wink or twitched finger is enough to indicate you are still in the running. When you have reached your limit, shake your head and the auctioneer will sell to someone else, providing that the item has reached its reserve.

If you are the highest bidder, and your bid is equal to the reserve or higher, the hammer comes down and you are the new owner. There is no cooling-off period. You cannot take the item home, find that it does not fit with your surroundings and take it back. Once your name and the price are recorded, a legally binding contract has been entered into between you and the previous owner. The auctioneer is an agent only and there is no contract with this person, but it is he or she who will pursue you through the courts if you default on your purchase.

It is important that you have an idea of who else is bidding for the lot you are interested in. For example, if a well-known dealer or collector is bidding for the same item this should give you confidence that the collectable is a good one. Also, the practice of telephone bidding has become more popular in recent years. Auctioneers have a love–hate relationship with telephone bidding. They hate it because it slows down an auction thereby reducing momentum, but they love it because it adds mystique and facilitates overseas buyers.

If you feel the need to question auction room procedures, contact the Auctioneers and Valuers Association of Australia (AVAA): <www.avaa.com. au>, telephone (02) 8765 1573, email aucval@atu.com.au. The AVAA is governed by a constitution ratified by the Australian Securities & Investments Commission and all members are bound by a code of ethics. Any member who breaches the AVAA's code of ethics is liable to disciplinary action.

Selling collectables

In selling collectables, as with buying them, you have two main avenues to choose from: dealers and auctions. If you have built up your collection with purchases from one main dealer, you might make him or her your first port of call. Sometimes a dealer will offer to buy your total collection back from you. If that is the case you have to work out a price. The dealer will probably ask: how much do you want for it? However, it is far better if the dealer makes an offer so get him or her to do this. If the amount sounds in the vicinity of what you are looking for, add 10 per cent in your mind and negotiate from there. For example, the dealer might offer you $50 000. You could then say that you had $55 000 in mind but that you would settle for $53 000. Then see what the dealer says.

If the dealer does not offer you anywhere near what you think your collection is worth, there could be good reasons, including:

- Most collectors start in a small way and build up their collections as funds and confidence increase. Hence the bulk of the value usually lies in the most recent purchases which show the lowest return.

- The dealer has been over-charging you. This would be unfortunate, but you are supposed to know about your collection and presumably you would have had contact with other dealers. So it is a case of caveat emptor (let the buyer beware).

- Your feeling for the state of the market is too optimistic.

- You have overestimated the quality or condition of your collection.

- The dealer is trying to get your collection cheaply. In this case go to other dealers.

If the dealer offers you an appropriate price and you accept it, one of the main advantages is that you receive your money in a few days. The proceeds from auctions take weeks or months to arrive, especially if your collectables are passed in at one or more auctions because the items do not reach the reserve price. Also you are spared the wait, correspondence, catalogues and the tension of the auction process. One minute you have a collection and the next you do not, eliminating further uncertainty. However, this is also a disadvantage because your years of hard work, excitement and skill have disappeared without leaving a trace. Also, because you bypassed an auction, only one or two people have quoted on your collection and the chance of an auction room bidding war has been eliminated.

Selling at auction

Depending on the make-up of your holding of collectables, you should have an idea of which auction houses specialise in your area. When selling at auction, you should contact two or three of them by telephone and ask to speak to the head of the department personally. This is your first contact with an auction house that will potentially be selling your collectables and you should commence evaluating them right from the start. If the person you have rung is doing a good job, and depending on the value and type of your collectables, he or she will make an appointment to view them (or if not the head of the department personally, then some other qualified person belonging to the auction house).

If you ask two or three auction houses to report on your collectables, it is a good idea to not tell each of them that you have also asked others. The reason is that they may be tempted to value your collectables at a higher price in the hope that they will get your business when what is best is that you get a realistic estimate. You may be given some idea of value on the spot, but more often the auction house representative will take notes and photographs and return to the office to research past prices, and you will be contacted later with prices. Many auction houses, for example Christies, will store your collectables at no cost if you commit to auction with them.

The auctioneer's commission is generally payable by the seller and it varies from house to house and time to time, but 17.5 per cent of the hammer price may be taken as a guide. Sometimes there is a buyer's premium which may be 10 per cent of the hammer price, in which case the seller pays 7.5 per cent. The auctioneer is paid the same no matter what Australian state or territory you are in, although major auction houses such as Sotheby's and Christies conduct most of their big auctions in Melbourne and Sydney.

The price estimate range of each lot is either printed in the catalogue or handed out on a separate sheet and is a guide for prospective purchasers. It implies neither an upper nor a lower limit. Clearly, no owner would wish for an upper limit on price, but to protect a lot from going too cheaply a reserve is set. The relationship of the reserve to the price estimates is governed by the auction house, expert opinion (if any), state of the market and the owner. Sotheby's and Christies will not charge a commission on unsold lots if the reserves are agreed at their suggested levels. When it comes time for an auction, the auctioneer may agree with the owner that he or she be able to exercise discretion with regard to the reserve.

Illustrations in catalogues are arranged by the auction house and range from shared black and white photographs to single-item colour pages. You are less likely to be able to negotiate photographic charges than commission. With some auction houses, for example Christies, signing the contract gives them a free hand to illustrate your lots up to a certain figure. Others, such as Sotheby's, agree on the figure at the time of signing.

It is your responsibility to get your collectables to the auction house or its nearest office, unless they provide a free collection service. If not, they can recommend a good local carrier—it is better to use a good one rather than a cheap one. If the expert who visits you comes by car, you can make up your mind on the spot and, if it is feasible, he or she may be able to take the property immediately. Insurance is set at reserve price or half way between the upper and lower price estimates.

Make sure that you clearly understand all terms before signing the contract. The contract is usually in the form of a letter or form which sets out the commission structure, price estimates, suggested reserves, illustration charges and any other costs or relevant information. You can expect to receive a copy of the catalogue before the auction. With some auction houses your agreed reserves will be confirmed or, if not yet fixed, they will be when you receive the contract.

Investing in art

More so than with many collectables, art is a matter of personal taste. However, the markets treat art as they do any other commodity and the business of investing in art is based on the principle that you buy a painting or print and it increases in value. Success in the art marketplace is not easy. There are many artists and many different art forms, and the sheer quantity of works, media, periods and styles can make for an intimidating task. Also values can rise and fall alarmingly. Nevertheless, if you are prepared to do your homework, investing in art can be lucrative.

In Australia today art is recognised as a strong emerging market in which there is international as well as domestic interest. From 1997 to 2007 art sold at auctions in Australia increased steadily, and in 2007 it fetched $175 million, up from $105 million the previous year, representing an increase of 66.7 per cent. This market fell back to $108 million in 2008 and to $88.2 million in 2009, sparking suggestions that the 2007 figure might be regarded as an aberration in future years. The total art market in 2008, including primary sales through galleries, art consultants and private treaty sales, none of which are formally recorded, was considered by Art Equity Pty Ltd to be closer to $500 million.

Art as an asset class

As you have seen in this book, there are four prime asset classes: shares (domestic and international), fixed-interest securities, property and cash. From time to time, promoters of investments will attempt to enhance the credibility of their investments by encouraging the investing public to consider them as an asset class in their own right. In 2001 it was hedge funds, while more recently it has been 'alternative' investments which were described as asset classes in their own right. The truth is that none of them are separate asset classes. Nevertheless, the *Australian Financial Review* in October 2008 described art as an 'asset class for all kinds of weather'.

Categories of artists

Artists are generally grouped into three broad categories:

- emerging artists
- mid-career artists
- established artists.

Emerging artists have talent but they are at the beginning of their careers. They do not have significant auction records, so seek works that are keenly collected and well-represented in respected commercial galleries and have won significant art prizes. The opinion of respected art consultants is important. You may hold their artwork for a long time so buy work that you like. Emerging artists are relatively unknown to the market and the prices of good work start at around a few thousand dollars.

Mid-career artists have established a solid career and they have been working for many years. In most cases they have a history of selling at auctions and prices for their work are increasing. These artists are also displayed in national and regional galleries and they have been published in the art press. They have an established genre or style for which they have become well known. Artworks by these artists can represent outstanding investments because if they make the step to the next grade, prices take off.

Established artists have a long secondary market history and you can track the prices paid for their work. These artists hold national or international significance and are in most major private and public collections. Many artists in this category are no longer alive. Their works may be valued in the hundreds of thousands of dollars, or even millions, although not all of their works may be costly. The works of established artists provide better liquidity but returns are not necessarily going to be as great in percentage terms compared with other categories of artists.

Art rental market

Providing you have a suitable painting, there is an opportunity to derive rental income from it while you remain the owner. However, you will need to be careful with what you buy and consult with an organisation that offers this facility before you make a purchase. The two largest in Australia are Art Equity Pty Ltd, <www.artequity.com.au>, telephone (02) 9262 6660; and Artbank, <www.artbank.gov.au>, telephone 1800 251 651. Artbank is a government-funded initiative that specialises in contemporary art. It has showrooms in Melbourne, Sydney and Perth. Art Equity has a gallery in Sydney.

In Australia the government and corporate sectors have displayed works of art in commercial buildings such as offices and hotels for many years, and the recent trend is for organisations to rent rather than buy. The reason is that it involves less outlay and it enables businesses to change displays more often. The corporate rental market has opened up excellent opportunities for investors to buy portfolios of artwork that appeal to the corporate sector on a rental basis. Typical contracts run for two or three years and you can expect underwritten returns of 5 to 7 per cent per annum. In most circumstances, a rental portfolio can be bought with self managed super funds but you should talk to your financial adviser first.

Rental opportunities start at approximately $10 000 to approximately $50 000. You will have to seek advice on what artwork is suitable for renting because not all works sold are appropriate. If you buy an artwork for rental, you will be obliged to pay additional costs over and above the purchase price as follows:

- A portfolio management fee to cover storage, transportation and insurance. This is about $50 per work per year.

- An independent valuation fee, which is a third-party valuation for provenance and insurance. This is about $150 per work.

- A framing/stretching fee necessary for the work to be hung in a rental scenario. This is about $250 per work.

Rental income is paid monthly and it is guaranteed by the company arranging the rental. At the end of the contract the work is returned to you, but you could renegotiate another rental.

Resale royalty legislation

At the end of 2009, the Federal Government passed the *Resale Royalty Right for Visual Artists Act 2009*. The legislation was introduced in order to ensure that Australia's visual artists receive a portion of the proceeds from the resale of their works sold in the commercial art market. The scheme covers original works of art such as a painting, a drawing, a print, a collage, a sculpture, a ceramic, an item of glassware or a photograph. Under the scheme, artists receive 5 per cent of the sale price when original works are resold through the art market for $1000 or more. The scheme applies to living artists and for 70 years after their death. The resale royalty right only applies where the seller acquires a work after the legislation takes effect. This will be some time in 2010. In its 2008–09 budget the government had announced funding of $1.5 million to support the scheme's establishment. For further information go to: <www.arts.gov.au/artists/resale_royalty>.

The 5 per cent royalty payment is an additional cost you will have to pay when you sell art through the art market for $1000 or more. However, it does not apply to personal sales where you are not classed as an art market dealer. For example, if you sell a painting to a friend or colleague privately, the legislation does not normally apply. The legislation represents an increased administrative cost for dealers and auction houses, which they will simply pass on to buyers and sellers.

Art and do-it-yourself superannuation funds

Art is a potentially viable investment for DIY superannuation funds providing that it is formally incorporated into the fund's investment strategy. Also transactions need to be at arm's-length and you cannot display a work of art except as part of a rental agreement. Consequently, you will need to have adequate storage arrangements yourself or pay someone else to store it for you. Capital gains tax legislation applies but the fund is entitled to a 33.3 per cent discount on works of art held for longer than 12 months. There is more about superannuation in chapter 23. If you intend having your do-it-yourself superannuation fund invest in art, seek independent advice first.

Investing in wine

Investing in wine makes for a solid protective asset in times of uncertainty and market turmoil. The law of supply and demand is in your favour and good wine offers a first-rate opportunity for making a profit. You can also drink some of it along the way.

A major problem with investing in wine is storage, because wine must be kept in a cool, humid and preferably dark location where daily temperature fluctuations are minimal. If you do not already have a wine cellar, you can have one built, invest in a wine cabinet or use commercial storage. The cheapest approach will depend on how many bottles you propose buying. Say the price of investment-quality wine in Australia was around $100 per bottle on average. If you had $50 000 to invest, you could purchase 500 bottles. Also, say that your investment time horizon is 10 years. In this case the purchase of a wine cabinet at around $7000 would yield the lowest cost to store per bottle.

One good thing about investing in wine this way is that after you have bought the wine and the cabinet you can put everything away for 10 years and not have to worry about it, unless of course there is an electricity failure or you have to move house. A disadvantage is that the cabinet takes up a lot of space. Also, transaction costs are high when dealing in wine compared with shares or bonds, and insurance may not cover refrigeration storage.

What sort of return can you expect? In 2007 a study was done for the American Association of Wine Economists on investing in wine in Australia and the UK (see <www.wine-economics.org/workingpapers/ AAWE_WP06.pdf>. The study found that the after-tax return from investing in good-quality wine in Australia over the long term was 5 to 6 per cent per annum. This is not high because inflation has to be taken into account as well, but if you enjoy taking an interest in wine, it is a hobby that can pay off.

Investing in coins

Coins can also be considered a form of investment. Their value will depend on an array of factors, including the age and availability of the coin, its condition (for example, whether it is dented, scratched or stained) and fluctuations in the markets for precious metals. There are also bullion coins, such as the Krugerrand, which consist mainly of precious metals and which have little value beyond that of the metal itself. The Krugerrand is a series of 22-karat gold South African coins first minted in 1867.

Investing in coins has always been attractive because of their rarity and portability, and the fact that there are few storage problems. Security risk is low if stored properly; the best bet is a safety deposit box at a bank or at home. However, there are well-established dealers who control the market and who have a key role in determining the value of coins.

Collectables and taxation

Collectors of stamps, coins, art, wine, china, porcelain or other collectables are generally engaged in a hobby or private recreational pursuit and are not subject to income tax. However, if you conduct a business of dealing in collectables, you will be subject to income tax. As to what constitutes a business and what a hobby, the Tax Office will have regard to turnover, the need to keep elaborate records, the frequency with which management decisions need to be made and so on. For example, if you buy and sell a few paintings during a year, you will not be deemed to be in business. But if you buy and sell 100 paintings during a year you probably will be and hence be required to pay income tax. If you are in doubt, it is best to consult a tax accountant.

Specific sections of the Tax Act apply to collectables and CGT. If you acquire a collectable for more than $500, you will be required to pay CGT when you sell it. If you have held the collectable for more than 12 months, you can claim a 50 per cent discount. Capital losses from collectables (acquired for more than $500) can only be offset against capital gains from collectables. If a capital loss from a collectable exceeds capital gains from collectables in an income year, the excess is carried forward to be applied against future capital gains. Capital losses from other assets, for example shares, can be offset against any 'net' capital gains from collectables.

Key points

o   There are many markets for collectables that represent good investments.

o   The first and most important rule is to only invest in collectables that appeal to you and in which you have an interest. You may own them for many years and it is important that you like them.

o   Thoroughly do your homework and research your area of interest, and then specialise in a specific area, region or time period.

o   Become comfortable in your relationships with dealers and attend auctions of items in your specialty.

o   Consider seeking professional advice before you take the plunge.

o   Collectables do not provide you with regular income, unlike shares, bonds and property investments. However, you can offer artwork for rental to the corporate market providing that it is in demand. Investigate this before you buy.

o   Consider joining associations or clubs as you will probably get better deals as you avoid the mark up of dealers and the commissions of auction houses.

o   Remember the first and most important rule: only enter a specialty area if you have a genuine interest in the subject and will get real satisfaction from the process of collecting, buying and selling.

23

Superannuation

When you talk to most people about superannuation, their eyes generally glaze over. They usually say retirement is too far away and they will think about it more carefully a couple of years before they retire. But by then it could be too late as they could find that their retirement savings are inadequate to support a reasonable standard of living when they retire.

Think about it this way. The average person's life can be divided into three distinct segments: the first 20 years or so are spent growing up and being educated and are normally funded by parents; the next 40 years are spent working; the third phase is, on average, around 20 years of retirement. During your working years, you need to generate sufficient income to buy a home, raise and educate a family, provide for day-to-day living costs and set money aside for retirement.

Average life expectancy of Australians is now around 80 years for both males and females. So if you retire at 60 your retirement savings have to last you for at least 20 years. Indeed many people live into their late 80s and early 90s. That's why it's essential to get used to the idea of investing in super today. When you retire that's what you will be living on — the income from your retirement nestegg. What's more, the government has made it clear that you must be more financially responsible for your retirement because it simply does not have enough money to give more generous aged pensions.

Although superannuation is not as tax-effective as it used to be for some people, it still provides an efficient and focused path for achieving your retirement goals.

Superannuation is efficient because of the generous tax concessions that allow your money to work harder and accumulate faster than it does outside the superannuation system. For example, the maximum rate of tax payable on investment earnings by a super fund is 15 per cent. In contrast, the top personal tax rate is 46.5 per cent. Accumulating wealth through a super scheme is focused because, in general, once your money is in super you cannot withdraw it until you retire.

What is superannuation?

Stripped of all the jargon, superannuation is simply a way of putting aside money during your working life to support you and your family when you retire. Superannuation is like a bank account which accepts deposits at any time, subject to certain limits, but does not allow you to make any withdrawals until you retire.

You then have the option of taking out all your money in a lump sum or converting your money into a pension and making periodic withdrawals to meet your spending needs. Naturally, there are taxes you must pay. But, for many people, these are at a lower rate than those applying to most other investments. For this reason, superannuation is often referred to as being 'concessionally taxed'. As superannuation is concessionally taxed the government does not allow you to put all your savings into superannuation.

Currently the federal government forces most workers to contribute to superannuation through the Superannuation Guarantee system, whereby superannuation contributions are automatically made by their employers. It is compulsory for employers to pay super contributions into your super account of at least 9 per cent of your wages. These contributions are not taken from your wages, but are benefits paid on top of your wages. You can also 'salary sacrifice', which means that you can elect to contribute more than the compulsory 9 per cent of your salary into superannuation.

Types of super funds

There are two main types of super funds:

*   *Accumulation or defined contribution funds:* The amount paid out depends on the investment performance of the fund and the amount of your contributions. If the fund sustains considerable investment losses, there is a possibility that what you are paid out is less than the amount you contributed.

- *Defined benefit funds:* This is where the amount you are paid out is defined; usually it is calculated as a percentage of your final salary before you retire and the number of years you are a member of the fund. This means you have much more certainty about the amount you will receive when you retire.

How super is taxed

There are three ways that super is taxed:

- on contributions to your super fund

- on investment earnings of the super fund

- when you withdraw money from the super fund.

There were significant changes to superannuation implemented from July 2007, and more changes were made in the 2009 Federal Budget. As a result of these changes there are now two types of contributions that you can make into super and they are taxed differently:

- Before-tax or concessional contributions include Superannuation Guarantee, salary sacrifice, extra employer and self-employed contributions (for which a tax deduction can be claimed). Before-tax contributions into super, such as employer and salary sacrifice amounts, are taxed at a rate of 15 per cent. An annual limit of $25 000 per person applies to all before-tax contributions made to super. People aged 50 or over in the period from 1 July 2007 to 30 June 2012 are allowed to contribute up to $50 000 a year until 1 July 2012, when the $25 000 limit will apply to everyone. Contributions exceeding these limits are taxed at 46.5 per cent.

- After-tax or non-concessional contributions are contributions made from your salary, after tax has already been paid at your marginal tax rate. They include spouse contributions and personal after-tax contributions. These contributions are not taxed when they are paid into your super fund because income tax has already been deducted from your wages. Individuals under 65 years of age can make after-tax contributions of up to $150 000 per year (or $450 000 over three years). Contributions in excess of these amounts will be taxed at 46.5 per cent. If you're 65 or older you can contribute up to $150 000 in after-tax contributions per year as long as you meet a work test—you have to have worked at least 40 hours during a consecutive 30-day period in the year. Low-income earners who make after-tax contributions to super may be eligible for a government co-contribution of up to $1000. People over 75 years of age cannot contribute to super.

Tax deductions

Some people are eligible to claim a tax deduction on contributions to super, subject to the same age-based limits as for employees, if they have already paid tax on these amounts. This includes:

- employed people, where their employer is not providing, and has no obligation to provide, superannuation contributions

- entirely self-employed people

- substantially self-employed people where assessable (and any exempt) income, plus reportable fringe benefits received, on which employer superannuation contributions are based, is less than 10 per cent of their total assessable income.

Tax file numbers

The tax rates above apply if you have provided your super fund with your tax file number (TFN). If you have not supplied your TFN, your contributions may be taxed at 46.5 per cent. Super funds cannot accept after-tax contributions if you have not supplied your TFN.

Tax on investment earnings

Investment earnings in a super fund are taxed at a maximum rate of 15 per cent. Capital gains are taxed at 10 per cent and there is a CGT discount of 33.3 per cent for investments held for more than 12 months.

Tax on withdrawals

From 1 July 2007, super payouts are made up of two components — a tax-free and a taxable component. The tax-free component does not count towards your assessable (or taxable) income. The taxable component may include two parts — one where tax has been paid and one where tax has not yet been paid. These are called taxed and untaxed elements respectively.

To work out how your super payout is taxed, you only need to understand how the taxed and untaxed elements of the taxable component are taxed. The tax-free component is not taxable. The taxed element has already had tax paid on it in the super fund. It may or may not need to have additional tax paid on it once it is paid out. You may still need to include the taxed element in your tax return. The untaxed element is the part of your payout that has not had any tax paid on it in the super fund, but which is still taxable. It needs to be included in your tax return as assessable income.

The tax-free component comprises:

- Non-concessional contributions (equivalent to undeducted contributions) from 1 July 2007. No tax deductions had been claimed on these contributions and they were not included in the fund's assessable income. These are mainly personal, after-tax contributions.

- A 'crystallised segment' fixed at 30 June 2007. This covers benefits relating to pre–July 1983 service and undeducted contributions before July 2007.

The remaining amount of a superannuation payout is known as the taxable component.

Super benefits paid in cash from taxed super funds will generally be tax-free for people aged 60 years and over. This includes both lump-sum and pension payments. For people under 60 years of age who are eligible to receive their benefit, the tax treatment of lump-sum withdrawals has been simplified. One component of the benefit will remain tax-free while the taxable component will be taxed at the rates shown in table 23.1.

Table 23.1: super benefit tax rates

Components	Tax treatment
Tax-free	Nil
Taxable	• If aged under 55, taxed at 21.5 per cent. • If aged between preservation age and 59 years, the first $150 000 will be tax-free and the remainder will be taxed at 16.5 per cent.

How much super do you need?

If you only contribute to super through the Superannuation Guarantee charge it is unlikely that you will accumulate enough money to retire comfortably. How much money do you need to retire and therefore how much money should you be putting into superannuation today? There is no simple answer to this as everyone's needs are different.

The main factors you need to consider are your target age for retirement and the level of income you will require to maintain your lifestyle when you retire. As a rough rule of thumb many people aim to achieve 60 to 70 per cent of their current pre-tax income when they retire—but this could be higher or lower depending on individual circumstances. To get some idea of whether you are on track for a comfortable retirement you can use MLC's Superannuation Calculator, available on MLC's website: <www.mlc.com.au/SuperannuationCalculator>. You simply fill in:

- your age today

- the age at which you would like to retire

- whether you are male or female

- your current savings in superannuation

- your annual contributions to superannuation from you and your employer

- the income you want to achieve per annum after you retire in today's dollars

- the assumed rate of return for your retirement savings.

The model can help you:

- estimate how long your assets at retirement will last

- see whether you have enough money to cover living and other expenses each year

- see how different decisions may affect your retirement income.

Let's have a look at a couple of examples.

Robert is 50 years old and wants to retire at 65. He has $100 000 currently in superannuation and has a taxable income of $70 000. The income he wants to achieve in retirement is $40 000 per annum and he assumes he will get 7 per cent on his retirement earnings. Given these assumptions, Robert is in for a rude shock as on these assumptions he will outlive his retirement savings by about eight years.

Sarah is 35 years old and wants to retire at 60. She has $50 000 currently in superannuation and her taxable income is $50 000. The income she wants to achieve in retirement is $40 000 per annum and she also assumes that her retirement earnings will return 7 per cent per annum. Sarah is likely to outlive her super savings by about nine years.

What these examples illustrate is that many people underestimate the amount of money they will need when they retire if they are to maintain a comfortable standard of living. In addition, many people retire early without calculating how long their retirement savings will last. The greatest danger in retirement is that you outlive your capital and have to revert to living on the aged pension. Current government policy is that the aged pension will be pegged to around 25 per cent of average weekly earnings in Australia—and this is unlikely to become more generous in the future.

Consequently, it is essential that you continually review both the amount you have accumulated in super and whether your current level of superannuation contributions are adequate to fund your desired standard of living when you retire.

Choice of fund

Most employees are able to choose the fund into which their employer's Superannuation Guarantee contributions are deposited. However, there are some employees covered by industrial agreements and members of defined benefit funds who do not have the option of choosing their super fund. If you do not nominate a super fund for your employer's contributions, your employer will pay your contributions into a 'default' fund they choose, or which is specified in an industrial award covering your employment.

So at the very least it is important that you take time to understand the structure and investment philosophy of your employer's default fund. It is sensible to compare the default fund with at least two other funds, preferably one industry fund and one retail fund. In general, industry funds have lower cost structures than retail funds.

You are able to choose a fund at any time, but you cannot make your employer change your fund more than once a year. You must also give your employer written confirmation from your chosen fund that it will accept your employer's contributions.

Questions to ask

There are five questions that you should ask before investing in any super-annuation fund.

1 How much is it going to cost?
Funds have a variety of different charges, many of which may seem small, but they can add up to a substantial amount.

Some of the charges to look out for include:

- contributions fees — anything up to 5 per cent of all contributions received may be lost in fees

- asset fees — where a percentage of your account balance is used to cover costs; although it may sound like a small percentage, remember that as your account grows so does the fee

- trustee fees — a small percentage fee charged to cover trustee expenses

- rollover fees — some funds charge a percentage of all funds rolled in from another fund

- establishment fees — in some cases there is a one-off charge for starting a policy with a fund

- investment management fees

- entry or exit fees.

Are you charged a low flat administration fee per week or a percentage of your account balance? Are you charged for switching between investment options?

2 What life and disability insurance arrangements are available, and how much will they cost?

An important aspect of superannuation is the insurance to cover death or disability. It is important to examine the detail of the cover offered and how much it will cost you. Because of their size and bargaining position, industry funds are often able to offer their members cover at rates that are substantially cheaper than what is offered by other funds.

3 What commissions or agents' fees are paid?

Large industry funds do not pay any agents' fees or commissions, which is one reason why they are so much cheaper than many other funds. You should always try to find out how much is being paid by the fund in fees and commissions.

4 What sort of returns to members has the fund achieved?

In the long term, the most significant factor affecting your retirement benefit will be the investment return of the fund after costs and tax. You should look to see whether your fund has been providing satisfactory returns over the past few years. You should also carefully examine the investment objectives of your fund, both to see if they are suitable for you and to establish whether they have been meeting their goals.

Before deciding to join a particular super fund, examine a recent breakdown of where the fund invests its money. Is it predominantly in shares or in less risky fixed-interest investments? You may be prepared to go into a relatively high risk fund when aged in your 30s or 40s, but as you reach retirement age it may be sensible to switch to a lower risk fund where the capital you have accumulated will be safer.

5 Do you understand the reports this fund sends to its members?

All funds are required to provide annual reports and statements to members. Read some recent annual reports and other communications sent to members. Are you able to understand these reports? If you cannot understand these reports it may be wise to investigate another super fund.

Setting up your own super fund

If you want to maximise superannuation's tax advantages and retain control of your investments, you should consider setting up your own self managed superannuation fund. Provided your fund has fewer than five members it will be exempt from the more onerous regulations that apply to larger funds. While many experts advise against setting up your own fund, with the help of your accountant or financial adviser you should find a fund is fairly simple to run.

A self managed super fund is a private superannuation fund into which either you or your employer makes contributions. To be classified as an 'excluded' fund, there must be fewer than five members and usually the members of the fund also act as the trustees. Being a trustee of your own fund means that you have absolute control over where the fund invests its money—so long as these investments are in accordance with the fund's trust deed and superannuation regulations.

If you are in a traditional superannuation fund you are constrained to invest within the limits set down by the trust deeds of these funds. The range of possible investments might not be as expansive as you might like. One of the advantages of a DIY fund is that you have access to a broader range of investments.

Most traditional super funds only offer you a choice of the following three basic investment options:

- shares—all your money is invested in local and overseas shares

- balanced—your money is spread over investments in shares, property and fixed-interest securities

- secure—funds are mainly invested in interest-bearing securities.

The actual portfolio allocations within these categories are determined by the investment manager of the super fund—not by you. For example, the 'shares' option might mean that the fund can invest up to 20 per cent in overseas shares and the remainder in local shares. In contrast, if you run your own fund you could decide to put 10 per cent into overseas shares and 90 per cent into local shares.

In addition, large public super funds usually are conservative in the types of companies in which they invest. They are more likely to restrict their share investments to the largest 50 to 100 listed companies. If you are running your own fund you could devote a small proportion of the fund to smaller listed companies and/or some speculative mining and oil companies that offer the possibility of significant returns but are too small for large super funds to invest in.

As you are a trustee of the self managed fund you have the ability to decide to manage some of the fund's portfolio yourself and use managed funds in areas where you do not feel competent. So you could decide to invest directly in Australian shares while using a managed fund to invest in overseas sharemarkets.

As the trustee of the fund you have the authority to delegate virtually all of the tasks associated with running the fund to service providers of your choice. What's more, you can change those service providers without winding up the fund or selling your investments. The fund is your property and is not owned by the service providers you engage. In contrast, if you are a small investor in a large public super fund, it is you who has to leave the fund if you are dissatisfied with the service or investment performance. In the process you could incur unnecessary fees and taxes.

Whether a DIY super fund is an appropriate and cost-effective option for you partly depends on how much money is likely to be in the fund. Generally you need at least $120 000 to make it cost-effective—otherwise the annual costs involved in running the fund will severely impact on your investment return.

Costs of self managed super

Annual costs of running a DIY fund vary according to its size and complexity and whether your fund is an active or passive share investor.

Costs of running a DIY fund include accounting fees in preparing a tax return and complying with government legislation. Many costs are either fixed irrespective of the size of the fund or do not increase at the same rate as the fund's assets increase. So if the size of the fund doubled some of these costs might only increase by 10 or 20 per cent.

As a rough guide you could expect administration costs to be between $1000 and $1500 per year. Depending on the amount of assistance you may require, the establishment fees for a small self managed super-annuation fund may range from $500 up to $2000—depending on whether you set up a company to act as trustee. If you only have $10 000 in the fund, annual costs could erode 7 to 10 per cent of your asset base. On the other hand, if your fund has $200 000 invested the annual fees would only represent around 0.5 per cent of your asset base—much less than you would pay in a traditional super fund. Consequently, if you have relatively small amounts in super you are probably better off in a large public super fund or in a master trust structure.

Even if you do not have around $120 000 in super at the moment it still could be worthwhile setting up a self managed fund if you think that you and the other members of the fund would accumulate this amount in one or two years' time.

A self managed fund may become a more cost-effective method of managing your superannuation than a large public super fund. The distribution and allocation of expenses within a large public fund can be very complicated and result in some members subsidising the costs of other members. In a self managed fund there is more transparency and there may also be greater opportunities to realise cost savings both in expenses and in the management of tax liabilities.

Tax planning

Another important advantage of self managed super funds is that they open up more tax planning opportunities. These are in addition to the fact that income earned by super funds is taxed at a maximum rate of 15 per cent. For instance, when you start paying yourself a pension from a self managed fund you can do this without first selling your superannuation assets and transferring them to a pension fund. This avoids the need to take capital gains—and therefore become liable for capital gains tax—plus you avoid brokerage and commissions on the sale of the investments.

You are also more in control of when capital gains and capital losses are taken by the fund. As capital losses can only be offset against capital gains you can time when you sell assets in order to minimise your liability for capital gains tax in a particular year. With the assistance of a tax professional you will discover you can manage your tax liabilities within the fund more efficiently. For instance, the imputation credits generated from share investments can be targeted more effectively to offset taxes on your contributions, golden handshakes or the investment income of the fund.

Small business owners

Many DIY funds are formed by small business owners because the fund is able to invest in assets owned by the business — such as a factory or office space. This again highlights that self managed funds have more investment flexibility as the more traditional super funds would never allow you to transfer your personal assets into their fund. There are some restrictions on the amount of non–arm's-length assets that a DIY fund can purchase. If you invest in wine it must remain in your cellar and not find its way to your dinner table, and if you invest in jewellery you are not allowed to wear it. Basically the assets of the super fund cannot be used by you or anybody else for personal benefit.

More importantly, as a trustee of the fund you would need to be convinced that you will receive a satisfactory rate of return from such assets. Also, consolidating a family group's superannuation into a self managed fund can eliminate the duplication of superannuation accounts and expenses.

You do not need to be self-employed to get the benefits of a self managed fund. If you are an employee you still might find it worthwhile to set up your own fund. If you change jobs frequently during your career — and this is an increasing trend in the job market today — having your own super fund could save you many thousands of dollars over your working life. Whenever you change jobs you simply get your new employer to make contributions to your self managed fund, which is the same fund your previous employer contributed to. By doing this a DIY fund can minimise transaction costs and expenses associated with transferring from one super fund to another.

It is the ability of self managed funds to change with the changes in your life that makes them so attractive. As they also form part of your estate they can ensure a seamless transfer of superannuation benefits between generations in your family.

Starting and running the fund

A self managed super fund is exactly what is says: it is self managed. So there are several significant decisions you need to make to both set up and run your own fund. For instance, you need to decide what investment strategy the fund will follow and whether you will make most of the investment decisions yourself or delegate this to outside fund managers. As the fund is a separate legal entity you will need to open up a bank account, as well as ensuring that you maintain adequate accounting records of investments of the fund and income received. You might also need to arrange for your existing super to be rolled into your new fund and determine the level of contributions from different fund members. The trustees should also apply to the Tax Office for a tax file number—otherwise any investment income will initially be taxed at 46.5 per cent.

The key to getting the best investment return while minimising the costs of running your own super fund is to set up sound record keeping and adopt a systematic long-term approach to your investments. If you do not monitor your investment portfolio carefully and adapt your investment strategy to suit changing investment conditions you could find that your fund's investment performance is substandard. Remember the wealth you accumulate through your super fund will probably be your principal source of income when you retire. So it is essential that you put adequate time and effort into maximising your super payout.

The main disadvantage of a DIY fund is that it will take up more of your time. How much more depends on whether you take an active or passive role as a trustee of the fund. Remember, you could delegate all the day-to-day investment responsibilities of the fund by investing most of the money in unit trusts. If you are directly investing in the sharemarket you need to be constantly monitoring the fund's share investments. Spending more time devising and implementing your fund's investment strategy could be a problem if you are self-employed and work long hours. It could also be a problem if you spend a lot of time travelling overseas as part of your employment.

A real danger with a DIY fund is that if you do not spend enough time monitoring investment markets and implementing a long-term investment strategy the fund's investment performance will suffer. As a result there is often a tendency to play it safe and leave too much of the fund's money in short-term interest-bearing deposits. While this is a sensible strategy if sharemarkets are in a decline, over the longer term having too much money in cash will reduce the fund's investment performance.

Managing your own super fund is not a suitable option for everyone. You must have sufficient funds in super to make self-management a cost-effective strategy and you must be prepared to set aside some time to develop and implement a sound investment strategy. The main benefits of taking this step are that you will have a wider range of investments in which to invest and have far more tax planning opportunities.

To set up a self managed super fund you need to address the following issues:

- Get a suitable trust deed which sets out the rules and conditions under which your fund operates.

- Choose a trustee—this can be either a family company or an individual.

- Establish an investment strategy.

- Determine the contribution levels for the fund and consider the benefits of salary sacrificing; that is, instead of having a salary of $80 000, consider having a salary of $65 000 and have $15 000 paid into your own super fund.

- Decide what type of benefits the fund will pay—lump sum or pension.

- Decide how the fund will be wound up.

Other benefits of self managed funds

Self managed funds can, in certain circumstances, acquire business assets such as property or equipment. For example, your super fund could purchase a factory unit which could be rented to your business in an arm's-length rental arrangement.

Care needs to be taken to ensure that the sole purpose test is not breached; that is, the fund's objective is to provide retirement benefits, not to prop up your business.

A self managed fund may be able to acquire shares which you own in your own name. Let's say you have $50 000 in your employer's fund and you own a portfolio of listed shares with a market value of $50 000. You could establish a self managed fund, roll over the balance in your employer's fund into it, and then purchase your shares at market value, free of brokerage. Of course, you will need to assess your own tax position resulting from these transactions, but this is the only way you can realise the cash value of your shares while retaining your investments.

There is no doubt that a self managed superannuation fund is ideal for many people. Such an arrangement can be extremely cost-effective, but it is essential that appropriate expert advice is obtained, otherwise the financial advantages of a self managed fund may fizzle away.

Key points

o   There are many tax benefits of saving for your retirement via superannuation—but the downside is that your money is tied up, normally until you reach the age of 55.

o   For most employees it is now compulsory that 9 per cent of their salary is placed into superannuation. But most experts agree that this will not be enough for most people to live on comfortably when they retire.

o   It is essential that you become actively involved in choosing your superannuation fund, otherwise you will become a member of your employer's default fund.

o   As superannuation for most people is a 30- to 40-year investment, fees and charges by super funds over this period can significantly erode your superannuation payout.

o   Setting up your own superannuation fund is an option for many people, but you need to educate yourself about investment markets and be prepared to spend time devising your fund's investment strategy.

o   Do not put off thinking about superannuation until a few years before you retire—if you are unprepared you face the possibility of outliving your savings. This will have a severe impact on your retirement lifestyle.

o   Remember that most Australians will need to accumulate enough money to support themselves for 20 years after they retire, and the government is unlikely to make living on the aged pension a desirable option.

Appendix:
Detailed DCF analysis

What follows is a more detailed example illustrating how to use DCF analysis and taking into account the impact of tax on cash flows.

Melanie Walker (not her real name) had been successful in accumulating wealth through residential property investment in the Sydney metropolitan area over a period of 15 years. She would look for apartments in areas where there was a strong demand from renters, often overseas families whose breadwinner was engaged in business. In today's market Melanie's strategy was to aim for a 10 per cent per annum return knowing that because of the uncertainties of forecasting rents and property prices into the future she needed a buffer in case her projections were astray.

Melanie was assessing the merits of investing in an apartment in an upmarket part of Sydney's eastern suburbs. Details of the property were:

- three bedrooms, two bathrooms, tandem lock-up garage with adjoining workspace area

- favourable northerly aspect with views

- close to park

- built in the 1920s and renovated in 2006

- size 105 sqm

- strata levy $700 a quarter

- last traded in 2005 for $425 000

- Melanie would borrow 80 per cent or $616 000 at 6.25 per cent

- purchase price $770 000

- currently let for $800 pw

- cost price including stamp duties and solicitor's costs is $805 225

- settlement December 2009.

Melanie had a five-year time horizon for investment. She was unsure how to estimate the sale price in five years' time but she thought there was a good chance that there would be a threefold increase in capital value. She also thought that rental income would increase at a significantly greater rate than strata levies and other outgoings. Melanie was also experienced with DCF techniques and she knew she could test how sensitive her assumptions were to changes in the variables once she had input the data. Melanie's marginal rate of tax is 46.5 per cent (including the Medicare levy).

			Cash flow			
	2009 ($)	2010 ($)	2011 ($)	2012 ($)	2013 ($)	2014 ($)
Rental income		41600	47840	55016	63268	72758
Less: Bank fees		−1500	−	−	−	−
Strata levies		−2800	−3000	−3200	−3400	−3600
Outgoings		−2500	−2600	−2700	−2800	−3000
Interest		−38201	−37521	−36798	−36028	−35208
Taxable income		−3401	4719	12318	21040	30950
Tax at 46.5%		1581*	−2194	−5728	−9784	−14392
Capital gains tax (see opposite)		−	−	−	−	−394035
Less: Principal repayment		−10567	−11247	−11970	−12740	−13560
Balloon loan repayment		−	−	−	−	−555915
Net sale price						2500000
Outlay	−805225					
Net cash flow	−805225	−12387	−8722	−5380	−1484	1553048
PV of $1 at 10%	1.0000	0.9091	0.8264	0.7513	0.6830	0.6209
PV of net cash flow	−805225	−11261	−7208	−4042	−1014	964288

* Income tax benefit.

Capital gains tax

Net sale price	$2500000
Less Outlay	$805225
Capital gain	$1694775
Less Discount (50%)	$847388
Net capital gain	$847387
Tax at 46.5%	$394035

NPV = $964288 − $805225 − $11261 − $7208 − $4042 − $1014 =
    $135538

IRR = 13.42%

Melanie calculated that if the net sale price was 10 per cent less than forecast—that is, $2250000—CGT would be $335910 and the NPV would be $16402 when using a 10 per cent discount rate. The IRR would be 10.44 per cent.

Index